KINGDOM
MANNA

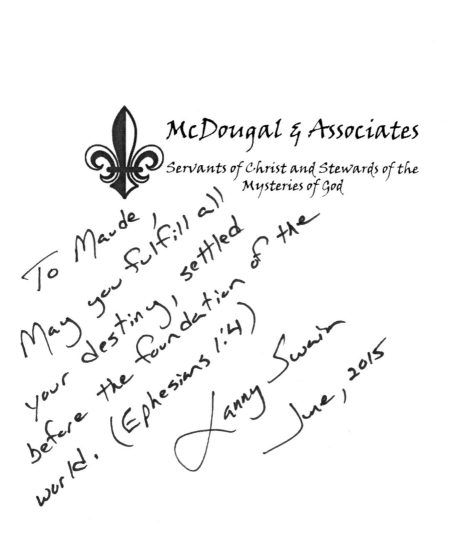

McDougal & Associates

*Servants of Christ and Stewards of the
Mysteries of God*

To Maude,
May you fulfill all
your destiny, settled
before the foundation of the
world. (Ephesians 1:4)

Lanny Swaim
June, 2015

KINGDOM MANNA

Volume I

150 Short Readings for the Bride of Christ

by

Lanny Swaim

Published by:

McDougal & Associates
18896 Greenwell Springs Road
Greenwell Springs, Louisiana 70739
www.ThePublishedWord.com

McDougal & Associates is an organization dedicated to the spreading of the Gospel of Jesus Christ to as many people as possible in the shortest time possible.

ISBN 978-1-940461-27-4

Printed on demand in the US, the UK, and Australia
For Worldwide Distribution

DEDICATION

I dedicate this book to:

My Daddy, Donald Swaim, who had the wisdom as a young father to place me in God's hands when I was three years old because I was asking questions about spiritual matters that he couldn't answer.

My Mama, Fonda Hedrick Swaim, who read Bible stories to my brother, sister and me when we were young.

My wife, Cathy, whose love completed me and healed me when I was a broken man, whose friendship has comforted me through troubled times, and whose trust has encouraged and supported me for many years. The marriage covenant we share has taught me more about my covenant with the Lord and who we are as the Body of Christ and the Bride of Christ than anything else I have ever experienced.

Scott Ross, who introduced Jesus to me in the spring of 1970.

Tom Watson, who introduced the baptism with the Holy Spirit to me in the summer of 1970.

Doug Fortune, who, in 2008, confirmed to me revelation I had been receiving that I had heard no one else teach, the confirmation of that revelation giving reason and purpose to the experiences of my life since September 11, 2001.

The Remnant Bride of Christ that encourages me and confirms the eternal purpose and destiny we share.

My Lord Jesus, in whom I live, move and have my being (Acts 17:28).

ACKNOWLEDGMENTS

Thanks to Pam Carmichael, for introducing me to Diane McDougal through a mutual friend of theirs. Pam is a long-time friend and precious covenant sister. Her encouragement, advice and prophetic words to me have greatly impacted my life and ministry.

Thanks to Diane McDougal for her advice and encouragement and for recommending me to Harold McDougal of McDougal and Associates.

Thanks to Harold McDougal for his editing expertise and advice concerning the publishing of this book and especially for the way in which he conducts business for the Kingdom.

The 150 Readings in KINGDOM MANNA, Volume I began as daily and then weekly emails sent to those in my address books. Thanks to those who have consistently read them and especially to those who have responded with comments and encouragement.

Contents

INTRODUCTION

The 16th chapter of Exodus tells how God fed the Israelites in the wilderness with bread from Heaven. Each morning it fell like dew and remained until the sun melted it. Each family gathered enough for that day, except on the sixth day of the week, when they gathered enough for two days, so they would not have to gather on the Sabbath. On each day (except the sixth day), if they tried to keep any of this bread until the next day, it spoiled, and worms hatched out of it.

When the Israelites first saw this bread, they called it *manna*. Manna literally means, "*it is a portion*" or "*what is this?*"

In John 6:32-35, Jesus said, "*Verily, verily, I say unto you, Moses gave you not that bread from heaven; but my Father giveth you the true bread from heaven. For the bread of God is he which cometh down from heaven, and giveth life unto the world. I am the bread of life: he that cometh to me shall never hunger; and he that believeth on me shall never thirst.*"

Like many things in the Old Testament, the manna from Heaven was a type and shadow fulfilled in the New Testament. John 1:1 tells us: "*In the beginning was the Word, and the Word was with God, and the Word was God.*" Then, in verse 14, we read: "*And the Word was made flesh, and dwelt among us, (and we beheld his glory, the glory as of the only begotten of the Father,) full of grace and truth.*" Jesus is the living Word of God, and the Bible is the written Word of God.

In order to mature and be sustained spiritually, we must continually feed on the living Word of God and on the written Word of God. I have found it extremely important in my own life to continually feed on God's Word. In addition to reading and studying the Bible, I read and listen to numerous other teachers/preachers/prophets, etc. I thank

God for CD's and even newer technology. Much of the time when I am driving or doing manual labor, I am listening to someone teach or preach the Word.

These short KINGDOM MANNA writings will provide another source for you to feed on God's Word. It is my desire that they encourage and build you up mentally, emotionally and spiritually, equipping you for success in your life and ministry.

It is my prayer that as you read these and study the scripture references you, too, will receive revelation from the Holy Spirit.

These teachings are short and, in no way, intended to be a thorough study of any of the subjects addressed. I suspect that as you seek the Lord and receive what He has for you in these readings, you will probably have more you could teach me than I have taught you. If that, in fact, becomes the case, I will consider my work a success.

In addition to teaching, these short writings include prophetic words and personal testimony.

Preface: The Remnant Bride

And it shall come to pass afterward, that I will pour out my spirit upon all flesh; and your sons and your daughters shall prophesy, your old men shall dream dreams, your young men shall see visions: and also upon the servants and upon the handmaids in those days will I pour out my spirit, and I will shew wonders in the heavens and in the earth, blood, and fire, and pillars of smoke. And it shall come to pass, that whosoever shall call on the name of the Lord shall be delivered; for in mount Zion and in Jerusalem shall be deliverance, as the Lord hath said, and in **the remnant whom the Lord shall call.**

Joel 2:28-30 and 32, Emphasis added

Many be called, but few chosen.　　　　Jesus in Matthew 20:16

These shall make war with the Lamb, and the Lamb shall overcome them: for he is Lord of lords, and King of kings: and they that are with him are called, and chosen, and faithful.　　　　Revelation 17:14

There is a group of people on earth today chosen by God to manifest the Kingdom of God in earth as it is in Heaven. In order for these people to manifest the Kingdom of God on earth, that Kingdom must first manifest in them. While it must manifest in each of them individually, it will only come to completion or fullness as it manifests in them corporately.

Within the Christian church, the true Body of Christ exists. This true Body of Christ is perhaps much smaller than the Christian church at large, identifying it as a remnant. Just as Eve was taken out of Adam (see Genesis 2:21-23), completing him, there is a remnant within the remnant, which God is calling out of the Body of Christ to be the Bride of Christ. This much smaller remnant, the Bride of Christ, has been experiencing an intense and severe process of tests and trials as she is being prepared for betrothal to the Lord. She will then complete the Body of Christ, being the firstfruits of many that will literally bring the Kingdom of God on earth as it is in Heaven.

Some of those who are called to be part of the Bride are in local churches, while some of them can't seem to fit in anywhere. Some have an understanding of the process they have been going through, while others have no idea what is going on. There are even those not yet born again (born from above) who will become part of this group.

The Old Testament prophet Joel wrote about this group in Joel 2:32, speaking of the day in which we live: *"And it shall come to pass, that whosoever shall call upon the name of the Lord shall be delivered: for in mount Zion and in Jerusalem shall be deliverance, as the Lord hath said, and in the* **remnant** *whom the Lord shall call"* (Emphasis added).

Webster defines a *remnant* as: "a remaining, usually small part; a leftover; a fragment or scrap." God has always had a remnant, a chosen people through whom He could manifest His presence in the earth. Among others, He had Noah and his family, Abraham and his family, then the Israelites, then the Jews, then the first-century Christians (initially a remnant of the Jews).

Remnants are people whom God has chosen to represent Him and to manifest Himself in and through. God has to have someone to manifest His presence in the earth. He gave the earth to man and gave man authority over the earth. So, in order to have a presence in the earth He needs a person or a people.

In Matthew 20:16 Jesus tells us that many are called but few are chosen. If you are chosen, you did not do the choosing. If God waited on us to choose Him, I don't think anyone ever would. The sin nature we are born with desires darkness rather than light. By nature, we are all very selfish and self-centered individuals. Perhaps this is why so many people substitute religion for a genuine spiritual experience and relationship with Jesus. Religion deceives people into believing they are okay with God, when, in reality, they are far from Him.

Throughout the first two thousand years of Church history there have been numerous remnants. These were groups that embraced a little deeper revelation and that had a more intense hunger for the things of God than the *status quo*, groups like the Lutherans, the Methodists, the Anabaptists, the Pentecostals, the Charismatics and others.

Today there is a new remnant. While all of the past remnants have manifested the Kingdom of God in part, I believe this new remnant is going to manifest the Kingdom of God in its fullness.

Jesus is building His glorious Church without spot, wrinkle or any such thing, holy and blameless, that the gates of Hades (Hell) will not prevail against (see Ephesians 5:26-27 and Matthew 16:18). He is building it on the foundation of apostles and prophets (see Ephesians 2:19-22). He is establishing a true five-fold ministry to serve the Body of Christ, encouraging and equipping believers for success in life and ministry, until we all come into the unity of the faith and the knowledge of the Son of God, becoming conformed to the measure of the stature of the fullness of the Anointed One (Jesus) and His anointing (see Ephesians 4:11-13).

I believe we are entering the time when this glorious Church is emerging on the world stage. God not only wants to re-establish the apostolic Church that began in the first century; He wants to take that Church to completion or fullness, bringing about the restitution of all things. The time just ahead is going to be the most exciting and the most glorious time in all of history until now.

As you read these short writings, I believe those of you who have been experiencing this process of preparation will be greatly encouraged. Those of you who realize you are of the Remnant Bride of Christ realize you need continual encouragement and understanding of the things you have been and are even now experiencing. I believe many more of you will discern that you are a part of this Remnant, bringing purpose to your life experiences of late.

I also believe that reading these writings will spark hunger in many more who are not yet seeing the Kingdom, which is emerging in this seventh millennium since creation as the glorious Church is being built. Even if you are not yet a believer, I pray this book will be your guide into, not only the most exciting part of your life, but also into the most exciting time in history since Creation.

Surely we were born for such a time as this!

All glory to God!

FOREWORD

Near the end of 2007 the Lord began to speak to me about sending out a daily email that would include teaching, prophecy and testimony. Realizing it would be a major undertaking and commitment, of course I said yes, I will do it. Then I asked for His help.

On December 31ˢᵗ of that year I sent out an introduction and on January 1ˢᵗ of 2008 I sent out the first KINGDOM MANNA (a title which the Lord had given me).

The first KINGDOM MANNA teachings were on subjects that have been taught to me and have become revelation to me since I was first born again (born from above) in the spring of 1970. The more I wrote, which required reading and studying the Scriptures on my part, the more I began to see things in the Scriptures I had not seen before. Much of what I was seeing added clarity to and built upon what I already considered to be Truth, but some of what I was seeing contradicted what I thought to be Truth. My first response was to say to the Lord, "I can't teach this. I've never heard anyone else teach this."

All that changed one Friday night as I was holding a meeting in a hotel in High Point, North Carolina, when Doug Fortune walked into the room. After the meeting, Doug and I talked, and I discovered that he had written books on some of this new (new to me) revelation I was getting from the Scriptures.

The first of Doug's books I read was *Dawning of the Third Day*. I read it in two sittings and then re-read it. It not only confirmed things I was seeing, but also introduced me to much more that has become revelation to me and opened the door for even more revelation.

As I continued to write the KINGDOM MANNA emails I became aware that the Lord wanted me to format the writings into book form and publish them. Today, as I continue to write and send out new emails, there is the potential for several volumes of KINGDOM MANNA books. The one you are now reading is Volume I. I am working on Volume II, with several, if not many more, to follow.

These short readings are intended to inform, edify and encourage you. You may want to read one each day. You may want to read several each day or you may read them all in one sitting. However you read them, I suggest and encourage you to read them over and over. Each reading will not only refresh your memory, but I suspect you will see new things (revelation) with every new reading.

I also suggest you read and re-read the scripture references, reading the scripture verses before and after the references and looking up and reading related scriptures. My hope and purpose is that you will receive revelation of your own directly from the Holy Spirit as these writings become revelation to you.

My prayer is for this book to challenge you as you continue on your journey into the things of God. It may challenge mindsets you have held for a long time. If that be the case, please don't become offended, but, rather, remain open to the Spirit and allow Him to lead you into all Truth.

One thing is certain: We can only walk in the revelation we have, but it is imperative that we do so if we are to continue on with the Lord. As we do, He will bring clarity and/or correction where necessary, until we all come into the unity of the faith and of the knowledge of the Son of God unto a perfect (corporate) man, measured by the fullness of Christ (see Ephesians 4:13). Glory to God!

Lanny Swaim

Winnabow, North Carolina

THE
READINGS

Prophetic Word 1

I am hovering over the earth. My eyes are searching to and fro, seeking those whom I can trust, seeking those who will obey me, those who will simply hear and obey. For the thing I am about to do is different from that which you have been accustomed to. It is different from that which you are used to. It is a new thing. Not new for me, because I know the end from the beginning, but new for you. So don't try to make the old pattern fit the new, for new wine must be poured into new wineskins.

I am releasing new revelation into the earth. It has been in the earth since before the beginning, but it is now being released to those who can receive it. They are My trusted ones, My chosen ones, whom I have known since before the foundation of the earth, and they will spearhead the greatest move of God the world has ever known.

Never before has there been a time like this time. Never before has there been a day like this day. You cannot be bound by tradition. You cannot be bound by religious ideas, doctrine and theology that did not originate with Me. Much that you consider to be necessary is not of Me. Much that you think is important is not important at all.

There is a shaking that has begun, a sifting, separating the wheat from the tares. Only that which is of Me will remain. All else will fall by the wayside.

Those of you who are chosen by Me will do great exploits, for I am manifesting Myself in you. I am manifesting My Kingdom within you, and you will walk as I walked in the earth. You will walk in greater power and authority than I walked in because of the time in which I lived and the time in which you live. For you see, I walked under the Old Covenant, as a prophet, as the Son of Man. You walk under the New Covenant, as prophets unto Me, as prophets unto My people, as prophets unto the nations. And you are the Sons of God.

You will speak to entire nations, and they will change. You will speak to entire groups of people, and they will come into My Kingdom. Everything I did and everything I said led to the cross. Everything you do and everything you say is leading to the King of kings and Lord of lords ruling and reigning on the earth.

I have said it. I have proclaimed it. Never before has there been a time like this time.

Stop praying for Me to change the nations. Stop praying for Me to change your situation. You prophesy to the nations. You prophesy to your situation. You speak it out in the power and authority of My name and of My Word, and it will come to pass ... if you waver not. It must come to pass. ⚜

KINGDOM MANNA: Reading 2

Demarcation

Webster defines *demarcation* as "the determining or marking off of boundaries or a separation of distinct boundaries."

*And it shall come to pass in the **last days**, saith God, I will pour out of my Spirit upon all flesh: and your sons and your daughters shall prophesy, and your young men shall see visions, and your old men shall dream dreams: and on my servants and on my handmaidens I will pour out in those days of my Spirit; and they shall prophesy; and I will shew wonders in heaven above, and signs in the earth beneath.*

Acts 2:17-19, Emphasis added

These words were spoken by the apostle Peter on the Day of Pentecost when people were first baptized with the Holy Spirit. He was quoting from Joel 2:28-30.

In 1 John 2:18, the apostle John says:

*Little children, it is the **last time**: and as ye have heard that antichrist shall come, even now are there many antichrists; whereby we know that it is the **last time**.* Emphasis added

Peter and John both spoke of the last days or last time, saying that we are in it. John said that we know we are in it because of the coming of antichrists.

With the outpouring of the Holy Spirit on the Day of Pentecost, God anointed about 120 believers and they went about performing signs, wonders and miracles. It stands to reason that Satan would immediately come against (anti) that anointing (Christ).

Christ is an English version of the Greek word *Christos*, which means "the Anointed One." When the hundred and twenty believers received the baptism with the Holy Spirit, they received the same anointing that Jesus received when John the Baptist baptized Him in the Jordan River, and the Spirit descended on Him like a dove (see John 1:32-33).

So two things happened in the beginning of this time period the Scriptures call "the last days" or "the last time": the outpouring of the Holy Spirit and the coming of the spirit of antichrist.

The Scriptures speak of the Church as the Body of Christ or the Body of the Anointed One, so those of us who are born-again (see John 3:3) are now the Anointed One in the earth. We are anointed ones. The book of Acts of the Apostles recorded in Scriptures makes it clear that the spirit of antichrist was continually attacking the anointed ones who were spreading the Gospel of the Kingdom in the first century. By the end of the first century, the attacks of this spirit of antichrist had taken their toll on the apostolic Church, which came into existence on the Day of Pentecost, as recorded in the 2nd chapter of Acts.

So the outpouring of the Holy Spirit on the Day of Pentecost and the coming of the spirit of antichrist were demarcations in history pertaining to God's dealing with mankind, more specifically with those chosen by Him to represent Him on the earth and to become like Him.

In our next teaching, we will look at some other demarcations that came about during the Church Age. ✛

Demarcation 2

*Little children, it is the **last time**: and as ye have heard that antichrist shall come, even now are there many antichrists; whereby we know that it is the **last time**.* 1 John 2:18, Emphasis added

The last time or last days, often referred to as "end-times," began on the Day of Pentecost, as recorded in the 2nd chapter of Acts, and has continued until the present day.

In history, there are certain events that were demarcations for various groups of people. The outpouring of the Holy Spirit on the Day of Pentecost was one such event. Another of these events occurred in the fourth century when the Roman emperor Constantine made Christianity the state religion. What had been a powerful apostolic Church in the first century then digressed into a dead religion, and the Dark Ages followed.

Another demarcation was when Martin Luther nailed his ninety-five thesis to the church house door in Wittenberg, Germany in 1517. In 1521 he was given an opportunity to recant, but refused, at the risk of his life. Thus, the Protestant Reformation was born, which began to restore truth and power to the apostolic Church that had been dormant, for the most part, for centuries.

There have been other such events in recent church history: the Welsh Revivals of 1859 and 1904, the outpouring of the Holy Spirit in Topeka, Kansas, around the turn of the twentieth century, the Azusa Street Revival in Los Angeles, California, in 1906, and the Charismatic Movement around the mid-twentieth century.

I believe we have entered another time of great significance in Church history. From the time that Israel came out of Egypt until Solomon began to build the Temple in Jerusalem was a period of 480 years (see 1 Kings 6:1). Forty is a biblical number for preparation. Israel spent forty years in the wilderness preparing to enter the Promised Land. Jesus spent forty days in the wilderness preparing for His ministry. Twelve represents government. There were twelve tribes of Israel. Jesus appointed twelve apostles that became the foundation of the apostolic Church in the first century (12 x 40 = 480).

So, it was 480 years from the time Israel came out of the bondage of slavery until Solomon began to build the Temple that became known for the manifested presence and glory of God, which was made possible by Israel's time of preparation and the government (Solomon's kingdom, which he inherited from his father, David) that was ordained by God. From the time that Martin Luther refused to recant his 95 Thesis in 1521 until 2001 was another period of 480 years. In 1521 the Church began to come out of the bondage of slavery to religion. I believe that in 2001 the Church entered into a time of preparation that will bring us to completion or fullness. God is birthing His Temple in us and, like the Temple that Solomon built, we are becoming known for His manifested presence and the glory of God.

We are becoming a people of worship. The Islamic attacks on the United States in 2001 appear to be an attempt by Satan to abort the birthing of this new time we are entering into, but I believe they were another line of demarcation, signifying a time of testing for the Church and the world, necessary to birthing this new time we are entering into.

True spiritual worship ushers in the presence and the glory of God. We are becoming a habitation of God through the Holy Spirit (see Ephesians 2:22).

Becoming a habitation of God through the Holy Spirit has not been an easy journey for us. God will not allow any flesh to glory in His presence (see 1 Corinthians 1:29). We have been going through a process (preparation) of dying to self so that we can live entirely for Him, becoming like Him. The end result will be a place of perfect rest and peace, positioning a people that will usher in the Kingdom (government) of God on earth as it is in Heaven. Glory to God!

There remaineth therefore a rest for the people of God.   Hebrews 4:9

And the peace of God, which passeth all understanding, shall keep your hearts and minds through Christ Jesus.   Philippians 4:7

✣

REVELATION = RESTORATION

He [Jesus] *saith unto them* [disciples], *But whom say ye that I am?*

And Simon Peter answered and said, Thou art the Christ, the Son of the living God.

And Jesus answered and said unto him, Blessed art thou, Simon Bar-jona: for flesh and blood hath not revealed it unto thee, but my Father which is in heaven. Matthew 16:15-17

And I will restore to you the years that the locust hath eaten, the cankerworm, and the caterpillar, and the palmerworm, my great army which I sent among you. Joel 2:25

In Matthew 16:15-17, Jesus is asking His disciples who they think He is. Peter speaks up and says, "You are the Anointed One, the Son of the living God."

Peter did not come to this conclusion intellectually. This knowledge was revealed to him by God. From that time on, Jesus began to talk about and move in the direction of the cross.

One man received the revelation of who Jesus was, and his ministry took a turn toward the primary purpose of why He was here on earth. Peter's revelation was a demarcation in the ministry of Jesus.

There are many Christians in the world today. Some are genuinely born-again and even baptized with the Holy Spirit. But only a few are discerning the time in which we live. These few are the remnant Joel spoke of (see Joel 2:32). This remnant is receiving the revelation that we are in a time of restoration, when the apostolic Church is coming to completion or fullness.

Joel 2:25 is part of a prophecy directed to Israel, but this passage of scripture has a double meaning. It is also a prophetic word to the Church and, more specifically, to the remnant that God is calling out of the church world at large, to manifest His glory in the earth.

The years that the locust, the cankerworm, the caterpillar and the palmerworm have destroyed are the years that religion has stolen from the apostolic Church that began in the first century. Joel 2:25 is a promise from God that He is going to restore those years to the Church.

Like Peter, the remnant has received and is receiving revelation from God. We are learning who we are and what it is we are to be about. Our purpose is to spearhead the greatest move of God the world has ever known. This great move of God will be much more than just another revival, like those of the past. It will be the completion of the apostolic Church that Paul spoke of in Ephesians and Jesus spoke of in Matthew 16:18.

Because we are now receiving this revelation, we have reached another demarcation in the history of the Church and of the world.

For the earth shall be filled with the knowledge of the glory of the LORD, as the waters cover the sea.   Habakkuk 2:14

✢

In That Day

In that day will I raise up the tabernacle of David that is fallen, and close up the breaches thereof; and I will raise up his ruins, and I will build it as in the days of old: That they may possess the remnant of Edom, and of all the heathen, which are called by my name, saith the LORD that doeth this. Amos 9:11-12, Emphasis added

James quotes this scripture in Acts 15:16-17, but instead of *Edom* the word *men* is used, and instead of *heathen* the word *Gentiles* is used.

The words *after this* in Acts and *in that day* in Amos refer to a specific time in history. The verses preceding Amos 9:11-12 make it clear that the rebuilding of the house of David comes after Israel is scattered among the nations. In AD 70 the northern ten tribes of Israel were already scattered among the nations. After the remnant of Israel, the Jews, revolted against Rome in AD 70, the rest of Israel was scattered among the nations, except for a very small remnant that remained in the area that became known as Palestine. In 1948 Israel was once again established as a nation and since that time Jews have been returning to the land from many nations.

In Luke 21:24 Jesus said, *"And they shall fall by the edge of the sword, and shall be led away captive into all nations: and Jerusalem shall be trodden down of the Gentiles, until the times of the Gentiles be fulfilled."*

When Jesus spoke these prophetic words, it seems clear to me that He was looking ahead to AD 70, when the Romans, for the most part, destroyed Jerusalem, and most of the Jews were dispersed among many nations. From that time until the Six Day War in June of 1967, most of Jerusalem was controlled in part or completely by various other nations. During the Six Day War Israel captured Jordanian-controlled East Jerusalem and more of the Old City, and on June 28th declared Jerusalem unified under Israeli control.

Prime Minister Ariel Sharon vowed that Jerusalem would remain the undivided, eternal capital of the Jewish people, and Prime Minister Benjamin Netanyahu has affirmed that determination. However, he purposed that the city remain open to all faiths, considering that Jews, Christians and Muslims all lay claim to it.

So Jerusalem was *trodden down by Gentiles* until 1967. Therefore I think it is safe to say that *after this* and *in that day* refers to a time after 1967.

The *times of the Gentiles* refers to the time from the Roman occupation until 1967, when nations other than Israel had control over Jerusalem. When Israel regained control of Jerusalem in 1967, I believe that period of time (*times of the Gentiles*) was fulfilled.

Even though all nations do not recognize Jerusalem as the capital of Israel and there are constant efforts at dividing Jerusalem, I suspect it will remain in Israeli control as Israel's capital just as Prime Ministers Sharon and Netanyahu have declared.

I believe the rebuilding of the Tabernacle of David refers to the present time. In David's time the presence of the Lord dwelt in that Tabernacle. Today God is manifesting His presence in the remnant that He is calling out and raising up to be a habitation of God through the Spirit (see Ephesians 2:22). God no longer dwells in buildings; now He dwells in people.

Hebrews 9:11 tells us that Christ (the Anointed One) became a high priest of things to come by a greater and more perfect tabernacle not made with hands. This Scripture goes hand in hand with the scriptures we have already read in Amos and Acts, and it is happening right now. Glory to God!

It is interesting to note the chapter and verse for this scripture in Hebrews and the first verse in Amos — *9/11*. Remember there were 480 years from Israel's deliverance from bondage in Egypt to the building of Solomon's Temple and 480 years from 1521 when Martin Luther refused to recant his 95 Thesis until September 11, 2001. Some think the attacks on *9/11* were the devil's attempt to abort the purpose of God for the United States and the world. Others think it was judgment on the United States. Still others think it was judgment on Islam. I believe it was a line of demarcation, signifying a time of testing for the Church, the United States and the world.

As a nation, the United States has stood by Israel, while most of the rest of the world has opposed Israel. At the same time, in the United States, as in many other countries, there is a remnant arising and becoming a habitation of God through the Spirit. I believe God has marked specific geographic locations where He will manifest models of His Church.

You may argue that God has dwelt in His people since believers were first born-again and baptized with the Holy Spirit, and you would certainly be right. But I believe what is happening today is going beyond the infilling of the Spirit. Haggai 2:9 confirms this:

The glory of this latter house shall be greater than of the former, saith the LORD of hosts: and in this place will I give peace, saith the LORD of hosts.   Haggai 2:9

✦

KINGDOM MANNA: Reading 6

In His Likeness

As for me, I will behold thy face in righteousness: I shall be satisfied, when I awake, with thy likeness.   Psalm 17:15

And God said, Let us make man in our image, after our likeness. So God created man in his own image, in the image of God created he him; male and female created he them.   Genesis 1:26-27

Psalm 17 is a prayer of David. In this prayer, he states that he has been tested and proven:

Thou hast proved mine heart; thou hast visited me in the night; thou hast tried me, and shalt find nothing; I am purposed that my mouth shall not transgress. Concerning the works of men, by the word of thy lips I have kept me from the paths of the destroyer.   Psalm 17:3-4

God tested David and found nothing lacking. David had decided that he would not sin by complaining or agreeing with his situation. Instead, he chose to agree with the Word of God, and in doing so, he kept himself from additional attacks of the devil implemented through his (David's) enemies.

David trusted God completely. We know this from verse 7: *Shew thy marvellous lovingkindness, O thou that savest by thy right hand them which put their trust in thee from those that rise up against them.*

David was in love with his Creator.

Keep me as the apple of the eye, hide me under the shadow of thy wings.   Psalm 17:8

Because David was an overcomer, being tested and passing the test, he knew he would one day awake in the likeness of God (see Psalm 17:15). Is that not the purpose of the tests and trials we face today?

When God first created man, He said, "*Let us make man in our image, after our likeness*" (Genesis 1:26). But then, in verse 27, He speaks only of man being created in His image. What happened to His likeness? The Hebrew word for *image* is *tselem*. It means, among other things, "resemblance or a representative." Adam resembled God and represented God on earth, but he was not exactly like God. Being created in God's image enabled Adam to operate on God's behalf. It had to do with doing rather than being.

The Hebrew word for *likeness* is *demuwth*. It means "like manner, like nature or like character." So to be made in God's likeness is to have God's nature and character. It is more about being than doing.

God's intention was to make man in His image and likeness, but Adam was initially created only in His image. God had knowledge of good and evil. Adam had no knowledge of good and evil. Therefore, he was not like God. Without a knowledge of good and evil, it was impossible for Adam to sin ... unless he chose to disobey the only commandment God had given him, which was to not eat of the fruit of the tree of the knowledge of good and evil (see Genesis 2:16-17).

How did the serpent tempt Eve? He told her that if she ate of the forbidden tree she would not die, as God had said, but would, instead, become like gods, knowing good and evil. He was implying that she and Adam would become like God.

Allow me to take this a little further. We have blamed the devil (serpent), blamed Eve and even blamed Adam for the mess mankind is in today, but didn't God say, *"Let us make man in our image, after our likeness?"* If Adam was not initially created after God's likeness, but only in his image, how was he to become like God? It looks to me like God set him up.

However, becoming like God and knowing good and evil was just the beginning. That knowledge brought death into the race of mankind. But, glory to God, He already had a plan to fix that. He, God Himself, would become the last Adam, Jesus. Then, He would indwell man as the Holy Spirit, giving man the power to be an overcomer. It would be the process of becoming an overcomer that would birth the character of God in mankind, causing the overcoming man to be in the image and likeness of God, not only with a knowledge of good and evil, but also with the character of God that is eternally good and overcomes evil. What an awesome plan! What an awesome God! ☥

STRONG MEAT

But strong meat belongeth to them that are of full age, even those who by reason of use have their senses exercised to discern both good and evil.   Hebrews 5:14

In our last reading, I pointed out that in Genesis 1:26 God spoke of making man in His own image and likeness, but then, in verse 27, where He actually created man, *likeness* is left out. We know from the Genesis account that God had knowledge of good and evil, but man did not. So, in that respect, man was not like God. The serpent pointed this fact out to Eve, persuading her to eat of the tree of the knowledge of good and evil. We tend to think that before they ate of the forbidden fruit, they knew good but had no knowledge of evil, when in fact, they knew neither good nor evil.

Adam and Eve initially had only one choice to make: whether or not to eat of the forbidden fruit. While it appears that they made the wrong choice, what they did manifested the words that God had spoken just before He created them. Before their eyes were opened to see good and evil, they were not like God. Afterward, they were. God Himself said, in Genesis 3:22, *"Behold, the man is become as one of us, to know good and evil."*

I've wondered many times why God would create man, knowing that man would fall and bring sin and death into the world. So I asked

Him, "God, why did You do that?" You see, I don't think it is necessary to wait until we get to Heaven to ask God the hard questions. If I am one of His sheep, if I know His voice (see John 10:3-5), and if I have the Holy Spirit leading me into all truth (see John 16:13), why shouldn't I ask God anything I want to know now? And why shouldn't I expect Him to answer me?

His Word declares:

If any of you lack wisdom, let him ask of God, that giveth to all men liberally, and upbraideth not; and it shall be given him.

James 1:5

Years have passed since I first asked God that question, and then suddenly one day I realized the answer. God wanted a people not only created in His image, but also created in His likeness.

Now, God knew that once man became like Him, knowing good and evil, man, because of his sinful nature, would choose evil over good. You see, while man was like God in the knowing of good and evil, he was not like God in character.

1 John 4:8 and 16 tells us that *"God is love."* So in order for man to become like God in character — becoming love, like God is love — God Himself had to become a man. What man was incapable of doing for himself, God did in the person of Jesus.

Man brought about a partial manifestation of the spoken word of God by his disobedience, but only God Himself could bring about the completion of His spoken word, which Jesus did by His obedience:

For as by one man's disobedience many were made sinners, so by the obedience of one shall many be made righteous.   Romans 5:19

40

When, on the cross, Jesus said, *"It is finished"* (John 19:30), He was saying, "I have done all that needs to be done in order for man to become like God."

After Jesus was resurrected and ascended into Heaven, the Holy Spirit came to indwell believers and guide them into all truth (see John 16:13). This guiding into all truth is a process that takes us through the many experiences of life, some of which are tests and trials. It is through these life experiences, especially the tests and trials, that God's character manifests in us, and we become mature believers (see Hebrews 5:14).

It is not enough to have the knowledge and wisdom of God. It is not enough to have the power of God. We must have His character. I can assure you that having God's character is worth whatever it cost us. I can even say: Having God's character is worth whatever it has cost mankind for the last six thousand years.

Only the almighty and loving God could devise such a plan. Is He awesome or what? ✝

THE TRIAL OF YOUR FAITH

*Wherein ye greatly rejoice, though now for a season, if need be, ye are in heaviness through manifold temptations: that **the trial of your faith**, being much more precious than of gold that perisheth, though it be tried with fire, might be found unto praise and honour and glory at the appearing of Jesus Christ: whom having not seen, ye love; in whom, though now ye see him not, yet believing, ye rejoice with joy unspeakable and full of glory: receiving the end of your faith, even the salvation of your souls. Of which salvation the prophets have inquired and searched diligently, who prophesied of the grace that should come unto you: searching what, or what manner of time the Spirit of Christ which was in them did signify, when it testified before hand the sufferings of Christ, and the glory that should follow.*

1 Peter 1:6-11, Emphasis added

Often, when we think of the word *temptation*, we may think of it in terms of being tempted to do something we shouldn't or something that is morally wrong. However, in this passage Peter uses the word *temptation* interchangeably with *trial*. He implies that the trial of our faith is a temptation.

Trials are tests. When our faith is tried or tested, there is the temptation to get out of faith and believe our circumstances. If we give in to this temptation, we will fail the test. If you think you have tried faith and it didn't work, the reality is that faith has tried you, and you failed the test.

When we begin to see the trials and tests that come our way as opportunities to overcome rather than as inconveniences or problems, we can then *greatly rejoice,* as Peter tells us to do in these scriptures. It is in the *greatly rejoicing* that we gain victory over the trial. The victory doesn't come when the trial goes away. The victory comes when we greatly rejoice. The going away of the trial is simply the manifestation of the victory that we already have.

When our faith prevails through the trial, we receive praise and honor and glory at the appearing of Jesus, the Anointed One (Christ). Instead of speaking of the appearing of Jesus, the Amplified Bible speaks of Jesus being *revealed,* which I think gives us a better idea of what Peter was saying here. When our faith prevails through the trial, Jesus and His anointing are revealed in us, enabling us to receive praise, honor and glory. Hallelujah!

When we receive *the end of our faith,* or in other words, when we overcome the trial, it is then easy to rejoice *with joy unspeakable and full of glory.* But remember, we don't receive the end of our faith when the trial is history; we receive the end of our faith by greatly rejoicing in the trial. Once we get the victory on the inside, there is no hindrance to unspeakable joy full of glory. [1]

When we walk in victory, during the trials of life, Jesus Himself will give us praise, honor and glory, as will other believers and, perhaps, even unbelievers. When people see us walking in the peace that passes all understanding (see Philippians 4:7) during the trials of life, they will take notice and, perhaps, want to know how we do it.

But having victory and peace is not the best part of being an overcomer. In the above passage, Peter equates the end of our faith to the

---

1. In Hebrew, the word for *glory* also translates as *goodness* and sometimes as *wealth.*

salvation of our souls. He then says that the Old Testament prophets would like to have understood and been partakers of this salvation (grace) that only we (the New Testament saints) can have and enjoy.

The salvation of our souls here is not talking about the initial experience of being born-again. It is talking about the ongoing process of being saved, of dying to self and becoming like Jesus, having the nature and character of God.

The Old Testament prophets prophesied the sufferings of Jesus that would make this possibility a reality, and they also prophesied the glory that would follow. The trial of our faith is to manifest that glory in us, bringing the knowledge of that glory to a lost and dying world (see Habakkuk 2:14). Hallelujah! ☩

KINGDOM MANNA: READING 9

PREDESTINED FOR GLORY

*For whom he did foreknow, he also did **predestinate** to be conformed to the image of his Son, that he might be the firstborn among many brethren. Moreover whom he did **predestinate**, them he also called: and whom he called, them he also justified: and whom he justified, them he also glorified.* Romans 8:29-30, Emphasis added

*According as he hath **chosen** us in him before the foundation of the world, that we should be holy and without blame before him in love: having **predestinated** us unto the adoption of children by Jesus Christ*

to himself, according to the good pleasure of his will. To the praise of the glory of his grace, wherein he hath made us accepted in the beloved.

Ephesians 1:4-6, Emphasis added

*For many are called, but few are **chosen**.*

Matthew 22:14, Emphasis added

*Ye have not **chosen** me, but I have **chosen** you, and ordained you, that ye should go and bring forth fruit, and that your fruit should remain: that whatsoever ye shall ask of the Father in my name, he may give it you.*

John 15:16, Emphasis added

*I exhort therefore, that, first of all, supplications, prayers, intercessions, and giving of thanks, be made for all men; for this is good and acceptable in the sight of **God our Saviour; who will have all men to be saved, and to come unto the knowledge of the truth.***

1 Timothy 2:1 and 3-4, Emphasis added

And I, if I be lifted up from the earth, will draw all men unto me.

Jesus in John 12:32, Emphasis added

God is no respecter of persons.   Acts 10:34

The subject of predestination has caused controversy among Christians for centuries. John Calvin may have been the first Protestant to teach on this subject. In studying the word *predestinated* or the modern English word *predestined*, there are basically two schools of thought that can be taken from the Greek. One is that God decides ahead of time

45

who will be saved and who will not. This idea eliminates all human choice in the matter. The other understanding is that, since God knows the end from the beginning, He already knows who will be saved and who will not.

Since God does know the end from the beginning, I think it is safe to say that He does know how each person's life will play out. But the scriptures that began this teaching tell us that God is *"no respecter of persons,"* that He desires for all people to be saved and come to knowledge of the truth, and that Jesus will draw all people unto Himself.

The word *chosen,* as used in John 15:16, is in the context of being appointed for service. Jesus chose His twelve disciples. They did not choose Him until after they were chosen *by* Him.

In Matthew 22:14, a stronger definition of the Greek word for *chosen* is *trusted.* Many are called, but few are trusted. We often think in terms of trusting God, but God is looking for individuals He can trust.

To be entrusted with a ministry, we first need to be trustworthy. For the Bride of Christ, becoming trustworthy involves a process of tests and trials that produce in us a dying to self and a complete trust in God. It is only as we trust God that we become trustworthy ourselves.

I believe those of us whom God is calling out today to be a part of the new remnant have been chosen or appointed by God to usher in something that will take the Church beyond anything we have known until now. We did not choose this service that we have been called to. Many of the adverse circumstances we have found ourselves in along the way are but part of the process necessary to bring us to a place of being trustworthy.

In the final analysis, we will become trustworthy because God does know the end from the beginning (see Isaiah 46:10), and He knows whom He can trust. All creation is groaning for the manifestation of the sons of God (see Romans 8:19). The process we have been going through and continue to go through is causing us to become mature sons. ✣

Predestined for Glory 2

*For whom he did foreknow, he also did **predestinate** to be conformed to the image of his Son, that he might be the firstborn among many brethren. Moreover whom he did **predestinate**, them he also called: and whom he called, them he also justified: and whom he justified, them he also glorified.* Romans 8:29-30, Emphasis added

*According as he hath **chosen** us in him before the foundation of the world, that we should be holy and without blame before him in love: having **predestinated** us unto the adoption of children by Jesus Christ to himself, according to the good pleasure of his will. To the praise of the glory of his grace, wherein he hath made us accepted in the beloved.*

Ephesians 1:4-6, Emphasis added

*For many are called, but few are **chosen**.*

Matthew 22:14, Emphasis added

*Ye have not **chosen** me, but I have **chosen** you, and ordained you, that ye should go and bring forth fruit, and that your fruit should remain: that whatsoever ye shall ask of the Father in my name, he may give it you.* John 15:16, Emphasis added

*I exhort therefore, that, first of all, supplications, prayers, intercessions, and giving of thanks, be made for all men; ... for this is good and acceptable in the sight of **God our Saviour; who will have all men to be saved, and to come unto the knowledge of the truth.***

1 Timothy 2:1 and 3-4, Emphasis added

And I, if I be lifted up from the earth, will draw all men unto me.
Jesus in John 12:32, Emphasis added

God is no respecter of persons. Acts 10:34

This third-day (millennium) of the Church (see 2 Peter 3:8) is going to bring about the restoration of and the completion of the apostolic Church that thrived in the first century. In order for this to come to pass, God has to have a remnant that doesn't fail or fall short of His fullness dwelling in them — individually and corporately.

I believe the life I am living has much more to do with His choosing me than with any choice I have made. He has orchestrated my life in such a way that I have repented for bad choices and made right choices. He has put pressure in the right places, steering me like a rudder steers a ship.

I can take no credit for any good that has come of my life or will come of my life. I am completely dependent upon Him. He is the Author and the Finisher of my faith (see Hebrews 12:2). While I do have choices to make, without Him I wouldn't have the sense to know what the right choices are. Even when I know what the right choices in my life are, He is the One who enables me to carry them out.

The truth that some of us have been chosen to be a part of the remnant that will spearhead the restoration and completion of the apostolic

Church doesn't make us any better than anyone else. In fact, the call on our lives is to one of service, rather than one of prominence. While our obedience to the call of God on our lives may exalt us in the eyes of other believers, we can never allow ourselves to think that we are, in any way, special or better than anyone else. After all, we did not do the choosing. We were chosen.

For ye see your calling, brethren, how that not many wise men after the flesh, not many mighty, not many noble, are called: for God hath chosen the foolish things of the world to confound the wise; and God hath chosen the weak things of the world to confound the things which are mighty; and base things of the world, and things which are despised, hath God chosen, yea, and things which are not, to bring to nought things that are: that no flesh should glory in his presence.

1 Corinthians 1:26-29

✣

KINGDOM MANNA: Reading 11

The Anointing and the Glory

And the LORD spake unto Moses face to face, as a man speaketh unto his friend.

And he [God] said, My presence shall go with thee, and I will give thee rest.

And he [Moses] *said unto him* [God], *If thy presence go not with me, carry us up not hence. For wherein shall it be known here that I and thy people have found grace in thy sight? Is it not in that thou goest with us? So shall we be separated, I and thy people, from all the people that are upon the face of the earth.*

And he [Moses] *said, I beseech thee, shew me thy glory.*

And he [God] *said, I will make all my goodness pass before thee, and I will proclaim the name of the* LORD *before thee.*

Exodus 33:11, 14-16 and 18-19

Moses had the promise of God. That promise was first given to Abraham. There was no question that Israel would possess the land of Canaan. But having the promise of God wasn't enough for Moses. Moses also wanted the presence of God.

Like Israel, we have the promises of God. His written Word is His covenant with us. When we receive the revelation of the promises of God in His Word and take action on those promises by operating in faith, we get results.

When Jesus stood up in the synagogue and read from the prophet Isaiah, He said, "The Spirit of the Lord is upon me because he has **anointed** me to preach the gospel to the poor, heal the brokenhearted, preach deliverance to the captives, recovering of sight to the blind and to free those that are bruised" (see Luke 4:18). The anointing enabled Jesus to operate in the power of God, and that same anointing enables us to operate in the power of God. It is the anointing that causes the promises of God to manifest in our lives and as we minister to others.

Moses was anointed to lead the Israelites out of Egypt and into the Promised Land. So the anointing is power. It is what enables us to do the things we are called to do. When God called Moses, He gave him the power to accomplish what he was called to do. But Moses wanted more. Moses wanted to know God. He wanted to commune with Him face to face. He wanted to see His glory. He wanted to experience His presence.

God's glory is His manifested presence. In Hebrew, the word that translates as *glory* also translates as *goodness*. So to experience God's *glory* is to experience His *goodness*. God's glory is His character, and his character is always good.

When we experience God's glory, it does something in us. Things that used to have great importance in our lives no longer matter very much. The realm of the natural takes a back seat to the realm of the Spirit. I have never experienced anything as wonderful as being in the presence of God. The more time I spend in His presence, the more I think like Him and become like Him. My character becomes like His character. His goodness becomes a part of me. I literally become that new person in the anointed Jesus that His Word says I am (see 2 Corinthians 5:17).

While we can operate in the anointing of God without being in His presence, there is something about being in His presence that better enables us to operate in His anointing. The more we think like Him, the more we love like Him, the easier it becomes to operate in His promises, bringing the Kingdom of God into earth as it is in Heaven.

So, yes, we need the promises, and we need to know our covenant. We need to continually study and feed on God's Word. But we also need His presence. We need to experience His glory. It is going to take both, the promises of God and the glory of God, for us to be filled with the fullness of God (see Ephesians 3:19), becoming all that He has created us to be. ✤

THE ANOINTED JESUS

How God anointed Jesus of Nazareth with the Holy Ghost and with power; who went about doing good, and healing all that were oppressed of the devil; for God was with him. Acts 10:38

I and my Father are one. Jesus in John 10:30

Jesus was anointed with the Holy Spirit, which gave Him power. That power enabled Him to go about doing good (healing, delivering, restoring, freeing, etc., see Luke 4:18) because God was with Him. Jesus had the anointing and the presence of God.

As we studied in our last reading, one can have the anointing without the presence, but the presence enables us to better walk in the anointing. The two go hand in hand, so that it is not always possible to distinguish between them.

I've been in meetings where people were healed sitting in their seat, without anyone laying hands on them or praying for them. This often happened in Kathryn Kuhlman's meetings and still happens in Benny Hinn's meetings. Some say it is because of the anointing. Others say it is because of the glory or manifested presence of God. Perhaps it is both. The anointing and the glory are very closely related.

As a young believer in the 1970s, I began reading books and listening to cassette tapes of the great faith teachers of that era. I experienced God's miraculous power and learned to operate in faith and the anointing of the Holy Spirit, the same anointing Jesus operated in.

I was baptized with the Holy Spirit in the summer of 1970. Within days of being baptized with the Spirit, I prayed for a sick person, and that person was healed. Since that time I have seen many healed. I've seen deliverances. I've even seen the dead raised. But the thing that has most enabled me to walk with God and in the Spirit has been His manifested presence in my life.

Around 2002 and 2003 I went through a period of time when the promises of God didn't seem to be working in my life. I reached a point when it looked like I was going to lose everything. At that point I told God that He could have it all. I said, "You can take my business, my house, my wife, and my dog, but I'm still going to obey You. No matter what it costs me, I will do whatever You say."

My situation didn't immediately turn around, but over the next two or three years I came to trust God more than ever before. Through that process, I spent much time praying in the Spirit. The presence and glory of God became very real to me, and that presence and glory has not only sustained me; it has changed me. It has brought me into a oneness with God that is greater than anything I have ever experienced. It has opened up the spiritual world to me and made it more real to me than the physical.

That was where Paul and Silas were walking when they were beaten and thrown into prison (see Acts 16:22-25). That was why, at midnight, they were singing and praising God so loudly that the other prisoners heard them.

Walking in the presence and glory of God enables you to walk above any circumstance that comes your way. When we walk in the Spirit, we walk above physical circumstances. And, glory to God, walking in that place enables us to change our physical circumstances (see Acts 16:26-34).

The Word of God does work. It always works. If it appears that it is not working, it is not because God is withholding something from us. God's intention was not to take my business, my house, my wife, or my dog. His intention was to get me to trust Him completely by bringing me into an intimate relationship with Himself.

In order for faith to work in our lives, we have to get it on the inside first. Once we have it inside, it will manifest on the outside. Once we have it in our spirit, it will manifest in the natural or physical world. That is why it is so important that we have the Word in us and that we continually walk in intimacy with God. ✣

PROPHETIC WORD 2

I have seen your suffering. I have witnessed your many trials. I have heard your heart cries reaching to the heavens and resounding in My ears. I am aware of your situation.

Know this: That I have a plan. Know that My desire for you and My plan for you is only good, for I am light. In light there is no darkness. Your situation only looks dark when you are focused on the situation. When you focus on Me, there is nothing to see but light.

Do you not trust me? If you know me as you claim to know Me, you will trust Me.

It is not a time to shrink back. It is not a time to become weary. It is the time to press in, to focus on Me and the many things I have promised you, the many things I have accomplished for you.

Why do you struggle? Why do you try to get Me to do what I have already done? Do you not see that the battle is already won, and we are the victors?

You are not called to be an army. You are not called to do battle. You are called and anointed to gather the spoils of battle. For I have won the battle. Yes, we are victors.

Can anything harm you? Can anything defeat you? Only if you allow it to. Only if you give in to it. Only if you focus on the problem and not on the solution.

Am I not the Solution to all of your problems? Am I not the One who has overcome? Lay down the struggle. Give it up. Rest in Me. There is no other way.

You must trust Me and you must walk with Me. You must walk in My counsel, for I am wisdom and I (and I alone) hold the key to your success.

Press in. Seek My counsel. Learn of My wisdom.

Do not allow yourself to become troubled about your circumstances. Trust Me. We are overcomers. We are victors. Have I not given you authority? Have I not given you My name? Use it. Use your faith. Trust Me, for My desire and plan for you is good only, with not even the slightest shadow of evil. Trust Me! Trust Me! Trust Me! ✝

SCRIPTURAL CONFIRMATION OF PROPHETIC WORD 2

For we know that the whole creation groaneth and travaileth in pain together until now. And not only they, but ourselves also, which have the firstfruits of the Spirit, even we ourselves groan within ourselves, waiting for the adoption, to wit, the redemption of our body. For we are saved by hope: but hope that is seen is not hope: for what a man seeth, why doth he yet hope for? But if we hope for that we see not, then do we with patience wait for it.

Likewise the Spirit also helpeth our infirmities: for we know not what we should pray for as we ought: but the Spirit itself maketh intercession for us with groanings which cannot be uttered. And he that searcheth the hearts knoweth what is the mind of the Spirit, because he maketh intercession for the saints according to the will of God.

And we know that all things work together for good to them that love God, to them who are the called according to his purpose. For whom he did foreknow, he also did predestinate to be conformed to the image of his Son, that he might be the firstborn among many brethren. Moreover whom he did predestinate, them he also called: and whom he called, them he also justified: and whom he justified, them he also glorified.

What shall we then say to these things? If God be for us, who can be against us?

He that spared not his own Son, but delivered him up for us all, how shall he not with him also freely give us all things? Who shall lay any thing to the charge of God's elect? It is God that justifieth. Who is he that condemneth? It is Christ that died, yea rather, that is risen again, who is even at the right hand of God, who also maketh intercession for us. Who shall separate us from the love of Christ? Shall tribulation, or distress, or persecution, or famine, or nakedness, or peril, or sword? As it is written, For thy sake we are killed all the day long [see Psalm 44:22, 2 Corinthians 4:11]; *we are accounted as sheep for the slaughter.*

Nay, in all these things we are more than conquerors through him that loved us. For I am persuaded, that neither death, nor life, not angels, nor principalities, nor powers, nor things present, nor things to come, nor height, nor depth, nor any other creature, shall be able to separate us from the love of God, which is in Christ Jesus our Lord.

Romans 8:22-39

Glory to God! ✠

KINGDOM MANNA: READING 15

GRACE

According to *Webster, grace* is, among other things, "a pleasing or attractive quality or endowment; favor or good will; a manifestation of favor; mercy, clemency, pardon; the freely given, unmerited favor and love of God; the influence or Spirit of God operating in humans to regenerate or strengthen them; a virtue or excellence of divine origin; moral strength."

In 2 Corinthians 12:7-9 the Apostle Paul says, *"And lest I should be exalted above measure through the abundance of the revelations, there was given to me a **thorn in the flesh**, the messenger of Satan to buffet me, lest I should be exalted above measure. For this thing I besought the Lord thrice, that it might depart from me. And he said unto me, My grace is sufficient for thee: for my strength is made perfect in weakness"* (Emphasis added).

In 2 Corinthians 12:6 Paul speaks of glorying in his infirmities. *Webster* defines *infirmity* as "a physical weakness or ailment, lack of strength, or moral failing." Many have speculated about what Paul's *thorn in the flesh* was. A popular opinion is that it was an ailment or sickness of some sort. However, Paul tells us exactly what it was: a messenger of Satan sent to buffet him.

Webster defines buffet as "to strike, as with the hand or fist; to contend against or battle; to force one's way by a fight, struggle, etc." Does this sound familiar to anyone reading this? It seems that everywhere I turn these days believers are suffering attack. Could it be we have all been sent messengers of Satan to buffet us?

Like Paul, many are focused on the attack and begging God to remove it. But what did the Lord say to Paul? *"My grace is sufficient for you. My strength is made perfect in weakness."* Was the Lord saying, as many people think, "Paul, you are just going to have to put up with this thorn in the flesh. Just grin and bear it. My grace is enough. What more do you want?"

This kind of religious mindset thinks that grace encompasses only being saved from sin so we can go to Heaven when we die. But grace is so much more than that! Grace entails everything that Jesus paid for when He was beaten, crucified and then became the firstborn from the dead. Grace is much more than forgiveness. Grace is empowerment! Grace is that which enables us to overcome.

So the Lord wasn't saying to Paul, "You're just going to have to put up with this messenger of Satan." No, he was saying, "Paul, why are you begging Me to do something about this? I've already done everything I can do. When I said, *'It is finished,'* I meant it is finished. *You* do something about this thorn in the flesh."

In the rest of 2 Corinthians 12:9, Paul says, *"Most gladly will I glory in my infirmities so the power of Christ may rest upon me."* In other words, "In my own strength I can do nothing, but I can do all things through Christ who strengthens me" (see Philippians 4:13).

We have been given God's grace. We have the power to persevere and overcome. We have the name of Jesus, and in that name is all the authority we need to be victorious. ✠

KINGDOM MANNA: Reading 16

Grace 2

And the Lord said, I will destroy man whom I have created from the face of the earth; both man, and beast, and the creeping thing, and the fowls of the air; for it repenteth me that I have made them. But Noah found grace in the eyes of the Lord. Genesis 6:7-8

In order to find something, usually you have to look for it. Noah must have been looking for God's grace. Verse 9 says that Noah was a just man and that he walked with God.

Since Noah walked with God, he probably had at least some idea that sin was about to take its toll on the earth. So, he was looking for grace in the eyes of the Lord.

When he found that grace, what did it do for him? Grace for Noah was information and instructions from the Lord. In verses 13 and 14 of Genesis chapter 6 God said to Noah, *"The end of all flesh is come before me; for the earth is filled with violence through them; and behold, I will destroy them with the earth. Make thee an ark of gopher wood; rooms shalt thou make in the ark, and shalt pitch it within and without with pitch."*

Noah's obedience to this information and instruction from God empowered him to survive the flood that brought about the destruction of everyone on earth except Noah and his family.

Not only do we have authority in the name of Jesus; His grace will also empower us with information and guidance. Sometimes just speaking to a situation or to the devil in the name of Jesus is enough. At other times we need wisdom and guidance to walk out God's plan and emerge victorious over our circumstances.

Sometimes it isn't the circumstance we need to overcome. The circumstances may be there to bring us to maturity and position us for the next step. In our next reading, I want us to begin to look at the life of Joseph, the eleventh son of Jacob and how his character was built through adversity. Not only was his character developed, but he was positioned to save the world from famine. ⚜

JOSEPH

Now Israel loved Joseph more than all his children, because he was the son of his old age: and he made him a coat of many colours.

Genesis 37:3

Jacob was the grandson of Abraham and the son of Isaac. He had two wives and twelve sons. The wife he loved the most, Rachel, was barren during the time that Jacob's first ten sons were born. In Genesis 30:22 we are told that God remembered Rachel and opened her womb. She bore a son and named him Joseph.

In Genesis 35:10 we are told that God changed Jacob's name to Israel. Then, in verses 11 and 12, God said to him, *"I am God Almighty; be fruitful and multiply; a nation and a company of nations shall be of thee, and kings shall come out of thy loins; and the land which I gave Abraham and Isaac, to thee I will give it, and to thy seed after thee will I give the land."*

Then, in verses 17 through 19, we are told that Rachel died giving birth to Israel's twelfth son, Benjamin, so it stands to reason that Israel would think more of Joseph than of his other eleven sons.

Israel's love for Joseph probably went to Joseph's head. He probably felt that he was, in some way, more important or special than his brothers. In Genesis chapter 37 we are told that Joseph was a tattle-tale, bringing information to his father about his brothers that they didn't want their father to know. So while Joseph was developing an ego about how special he was, his brothers were developing hatred toward him.

To add insult to injury, Joseph had two prophetic dreams. The interpretation of the first dream was that Joseph would reign over his brothers and his brothers would bow down to him. The second dream had the same interpretation, except that it included Joseph's father and mother bowing down to him as well. Naturally, when Joseph told these dreams to his brothers, they became even more offended. Not only did his brothers become offended, but Israel wasn't very happy with the second dream.

One day, while Israel's ten oldest sons were tending sheep some distance from home, he sent Joseph to see how they were doing. When the older sons saw Joseph coming, they decided to kill him.

One of the brothers, Reuben, didn't go along with this plan, so, instead, they sold Joseph to traveling merchants who took him to Egypt and sold him to Potiphar, the captain of Pharaoh's guard.

Before selling Joseph, his brothers took his coat of many colors given to him by his father and dipped it in animal blood, which deceived their father into thinking that Joseph had been killed and eaten by some wild animal. (Joseph was only seventeen when all this took place.)

Joseph had a prophetic anointing. God gave him dreams with obvious interpretations that many years later came to pass. Joseph's arrogance about his father's love for him and possibly his arrogance about his prophetic anointing compelled him to tell his brothers and father what he had dreamed. What Joseph didn't realize was that his arrogance was about to cost him many years with his family and cause him to endure much hardship.

There is more than one lesson to be learned here. For one thing, not everything we hear or receive from the Lord is to be told to others. We should always use discernment when sharing testimonies or prophecies.

But the greater lesson here is that Joseph's arrogance put in motion a series of events that actually brought his dreams to pass many years later. That series of events built character, patience and endurance in Joseph, and through it all, he learned to trust the God of his fathers. ✣

Joseph 2

Now Israel loved Joseph more than all his children, because he was the son of his old age: and he made him a coat of many colours.

Genesis 37:3

In our last KINGDOM MANNA, we looked at Joseph's beginnings as a young boy, loved by his father more than his brothers. Because of Joseph's immaturity, his prophetic anointing and Israel's love for him caused him to become puffed up with pride. Joseph's brothers grew to hate him and eventually sold him into slavery. However, these events positioned Joseph to fulfill his destiny and started a series of events that would prepare him for that destiny. Joseph's story is a great lesson for us today. I take great comfort in knowing that somehow, in God's bigger plan, even my shortcomings and failures will work out for my good and for the good of others. While this doesn't give me an excuse to fail, it is good to know that my loving and merciful heavenly Father works all things together for good to them that love God and are called according to His purpose (see Romans 8:28).

Much of the pain and suffering most of us have experienced in our lives were brought on by our own shortcomings and failures. However, not all adversity that comes against us is our fault. We do have an enemy whom Jesus described as one who kills, steals and destroys (see John 10:10). But, glory to God, Jesus also said that He had come that we might have life and have it more abundantly.

It is of utmost importance that we stay focused on Jesus and all He accomplished for us rather than on the attacks of the enemy or even our own shortcomings and failures. Yes, we have authority over adversity and the enemy in the name of Jesus! But not all adverse circumstances that we find ourselves in are there to harm us. I find that, more often than not, they are there to bring maturity to my life and to position me for a promotion in the Kingdom of God.

This was the case with Joseph. In our next teaching, we will look at the next event in a whole series of trials that Joseph endured. ✠

KINGDOM MANNA: Reading 19

JOSEPH 3

And Joseph was brought down to Egypt; and Potiphar, an officer of Pharaoh, captain of the guard, an Egyptian, bought him of the hands of the Ishmeelites, which had brought him down thither. And the Lord was with Joseph, and he was a prosperous man; and he was in the house of his master the Egyptian. And his master saw that the Lord was with him, and that the Lord made all that he did to prosper in

his hand. And Joseph found grace in his sight, and he served him: and
he made him overseer over his house, and all that he had he put into
his hand. And it came to pass from the time that he had made him
overseer in his house, and over all that he had, that the LORD blessed
the Egyptian's house for Joseph's sake; and the blessing of the LORD was
upon all that he had in the house, and in the field. And he left all that
he had in Joseph's hand; and he knew not ought he had, save the bread
which he did eat. And Joseph was a goodly person, and well favoured.

Genesis 39:1-6

Joseph had been sold into slavery by his brothers. For all he knew, he might never see his father or his homeland again. He could have thrown a big pity party and felt very sorry for himself. But the text here tells us the Lord was with Joseph and that he was a prosperous man because God made everything he touched to prosper. This tells me that Joseph didn't have time to feel sorry for himself. He was too busy working for his new master.

The text also says that Joseph found grace in his master's sight and served him. Not only was he working for his master; he was doing a good job; and he was looking for grace in his master's sight.

Joseph was a goodly or likeable person and well favored, meaning that he was liked by his master and probably by everyone in the household. So instead of complaining or becoming bitter or angry about what had happened to him, Joseph became a blessing in his new home. Even though he probably would rather have been back in Canaan with his father, God was with him where he was.

It didn't take Potiphar long to realize that Joseph was not only likeable and a hard worker, but that his household and business were prospering because of Joseph. God was with Joseph, and because God was with him, he was a blessed man. Because of the blessing that was on Joseph, Potiphar was being blessed too.

Potiphar was not a godly man, and he probably worshipped false gods. But God was blessing him because of Joseph.

Potiphar trusted Joseph so much that he put him in charge of his entire household and his business. He turned it all over to Joseph, a young Hebrew slave. How amazing! Potiphar no longer concerned himself with anything except what he ate. He went about his duties as captain of Pharaoh's guard and left everything else to Joseph.

1 Peter 5:6 says:

Humble yourselves therefore under the mighty hand of God, that he may exalt you in due time.

Joseph humbly undertook his duties as a slave, knowing that God was with him. Instead of expecting God to deliver him from his circumstances, he expected God to prosper him *in* his circumstances. As he worked, expecting God's blessing, he was looking for favor from his master. We know this because the text says that he found favor or grace in Potiphar's sight. If he found it, he must have been looking for it, expecting it.

The lesson I want to get across here is this: If we will stay focused on who we are and what has been provided for us in the finished work of Jesus, rather than focusing so much on our circumstances, God may use those very circumstances to promote us.

God blessed Joseph in a bad situation and caused him to be a blessing to everyone around him. He became ruler of his master's house and business, answering only to his master.

This wasn't the best God had for Joseph. It was just a temporary stop along the way. In our next reading, we will look at how Joseph got his next promotion. ✠

Joseph 4

And it came to pass after these things, that his master's wife cast her eyes upon Joseph; and she said, Lie with me. But he refused, and said unto his master's wife, Behold, my master wotteth not what is with me in the house, and he hath committed all that he hath to my hand; there is none greater in this house than I; neither hath he kept back anything from me but thee, because thou art his wife: how then can I do this great wickedness, and sin against God?   Genesis 39:7-9

When Joseph refused to commit adultery with his master's wife, she made it appear that he had tried to rape her. When Potiphar learned of the alleged incident, his trust in Joseph became history. He had Joseph thrown into Pharaoh's prison.

But the LORD was with Joseph, and shewed him mercy, and gave him favour in the sight of the keeper of the prison. And the keeper of the prison committed to Joseph's hand all the prisoners that were in the prison; and whatsoever they did there, he was the doer of it. The keeper of the prison looked not to any thing that was under his hand; because the LORD was with him, and that which he did, the LORD made it to prosper.   Genesis 39:21

Does this story sound familiar? Once again Joseph finds himself in a bad situation. Before he had been a slave, but now he was a prisoner. But, again, God prospered him and exalted him to the highest position in the prison under the keeper, and the keeper put complete trust in Joseph.

At this point in Joseph's life, he had endured two severe trials. First he had been sold into slavery by his own brothers. Then he had been falsely accused and thrown into prison.

Webster says a *trial* is "the act of trying, testing or putting to the proof." The apostle Peter said this about trials:

> *Wherein ye greatly rejoice, though now for a season, if need be, ye are in heaviness through manifold temptations: that the trial of your faith, being much more precious than of gold that perisheth, though it be tried with fire, might be found unto praise and honour and glory at the appearing of Jesus Christ.* 1 Peter 1:6-7

> *Beloved, think it not strange concerning the fiery trial which is to try you, as though some strange thing happened unto you: but rejoice, inasmuch as ye are partakers of Christ's sufferings; that, ye may be glad also with exceeding joy.* 1 Peter 4:12-13

A trial is a test. Tests are either passed or failed. Passing the tests that we encounter in our lives will refine our faith and trust in God, bringing us to maturity and positioning us for ministry.

Joseph passed the first two tests in his life. He had brought the first test on himself by his own arrogance. The second test came his way because he did the right thing. Regardless of why tests come, the important thing is that we pass them.

Joseph's next promotion was about to come, not through another test, but because of the prophetic gift he had received to interpret dreams. This gift had gotten him in trouble with his brothers, because of his arrogance. Now that he was more mature, God could use this gift to exalt him.

Humble yourselves therefore under the mighty hand of God, that he may exalt you in due time. 1 Peter 5:6

A man's gift maketh room for him, and bringeth him before great men.
Proverbs 18:16

KINGDOM MANNA: READING 21

JOSEPH 5

And it came to pass after these things, that the butler of the king of Egypt and his baker had offended their lord the king of Egypt. And Pharaoh was wroth against two of his officers, against the chief of the butlers, and against the chief of the bakers. And he put them in ward in the house of the captain of the guard, into the prison, the place where Joseph was bound. Genesis 40:1-3

We have studied how Joseph was falsely accused and thrown into prison. While there, God gave him favor with the keeper of the prison and exalted him to the highest position under the keeper.

In Genesis chapter 40, we find Pharaoh's chief butler and chief baker becoming prisoners and placed under Joseph's authority. One night each of them had a dream. Evidently both realized their dreams were not just random dreams but prophetic dreams. Keep in mind that these were not godly men. They were Egyptians. Still, they knew something of dreams with meanings. They were disturbed because neither knew the meaning of his dream.

Joseph noticed their downcast appearance and asked them why they looked so sad. This is a clue as to why Joseph had found favor with the keeper of the prison. He was evidently a very observant person, a needed attribute to be a ruler in a prison.

There is another interesting thing to note here. Back in chapter 39 and verse 21, it says, *"But the LORD was with Joseph* [in prison], *and shewed him mercy, and gave him favour in the sight of the keeper of the prison."* God is given credit for giving Joseph favor with the keeper of the prison.

I think sometimes we get the idea that God will give us favor with someone simply by causing that person to bless us in some way for no apparent reason. I am not suggesting that never happens, but I think most of the time God gives us favor by our using the talents and anointings we have. The manifestation of God's favor/blessing/provision is not always instant. It is usually due to the process of our implementing the talents/gifts/anointings we have been endowed with. To receive God's favor in a specific situation or in general in our lives, requires, at the very least, our obedience to God's Word and to the leading of the Holy Spirit, and, more than likely, it will require our using our talents and abilities.

Proverbs 18:6 says, *"A man's gift maketh room for him, and bringeth him before great men."* I have found that walking in God's favor usually requires something on my part. Since our talents, gifts and anointings all come from God, it is God who gives us the favor, so, of course, He also gets the credit.

When Joseph noticed that the two men were downcast and learned why, he told them (in Genesis 40:8), *"Do not interpretations belong to God? Tell me the dreams."* And he proceeded to tell them the corresponding interpretations.

The interpretation of the butler's dream was that in three days he would be restored to his former position in the palace of Pharaoh. Of course, the butler was pleased with this interpretation. Joseph took advantage of the situation, telling the butler his story of having been sold into slavery and then falsely accused and thrown into prison. He asked the butler to make mention of him to Pharaoh, probably hoping that Pharaoh would grant him a pardon and maybe even send him back to his homeland. But God had another plan. It was almost time for Joseph's next promotion.

As to the baker, the interpretation of his dream was not so good. Joseph told the baker that in three days Pharaoh would have him beheaded.

Both dreams came to pass just as Joseph had said, but when the chief butler was restored to his former position, he forgot about Joseph, and therefore Joseph remained in prison for two more years.

But God hadn't forgotten about Joseph. God had a plan. In order for that plan to be fulfilled, Joseph had to be promoted. It just wasn't quite time yet. Read on to learn about Joseph's next promotion. ✦

Joseph 6

And it came to pass at the end of two full years, that Pharaoh dreamed: and, behold, he stood by the river. And, behold, there came up out of the river seven well favoured kine [cows] *and fatfleshed; and they fed in a meadow. And, behold, seven other kine came up after them out of the river, ill favoured and leanfleshed; and stood by the other kine upon the bank of the river. And the ill favoured and leanfleshed kine did eat up the seven well favoured and fat kine. So Pharaoh awoke. And he slept and dreamed the second time: and, behold, seven ears of corn came up upon one stalk, rank and good. And, behold, seven thin ears and blasted with the east wind sprung up after them. And the seven thin ears devoured the seven rank, and full ears. And Pharaoh awoke, and, behold, it was a dream.*

And it came to pass in the morning that his spirit was troubled; and he sent and called for all the magicians of Egypt, and all the wise men thereof: but there was none that could interpret them unto Pharaoh.

Then spake the chief butler unto Pharaoh, saying, I do remember my faults this day.   Genesis 41:1-9

Suddenly the chief butler remembered Joseph. The time for Joseph's next promotion had come.

The chief butler told Pharaoh what had happened when he and the chief baker were in prison, how Joseph had interpreted their dreams. Pharaoh immediately sent for Joseph to be brought from the prison.

It is interesting to note here that this all happened very quickly or suddenly, and yet Joseph had been in prison two years since asking the chief butler to speak to Pharaoh on his behalf. In Revelation 22:7 and 12, Jesus says, *"Behold I come quickly."* Then, in verse 20, He says, *"Surely I come quickly."* He said those things to John more than a thousand, nine hundred years ago, definitely not a short period of time.

Where I live in the southern United States, we use the word *shortly*. If you were to ask me when I was coming to your house, I might answer, "Shortly." Shortly means in a short period of time. Quickly, however, doesn't necessarily have that same meaning. Quickly can mean suddenly. If you asked me when I was coming to your house, and I answered, "Quickly," I might mean that I would suddenly decide to come after ten years or so.

I have asked God for things and been told that they would come to pass, but the manifestation of those things sometimes did not occur for a very long time. When they did happen, they happened suddenly.

Some years ago I heard Randy Owen of the country music group Alabama being interviewed. The journalist doing the interview asked Randy how it felt to be an overnight success. Randy answered, "I don't know. Our overnight success took ten years." Alabama played at the Bowery in Myrtle Beach, South Carolina for ten years before scoring their first hit record. That first big hit quickly rose to the top of the charts, but it had taken time for them to gain popularity.

One good lesson we can learn from Joseph's story is not to become impatient when we have asked God for something or He tells us something is going to happen. As we have seen, there is often a process that has to take place to prepare us and position us for certain things to come to pass in our lives and ministries.

Now, Joseph was brought out of prison and into Pharaoh's presence. Pharaoh told Joseph the dreams he'd had, and Joseph was able to interpret them, but we will look closer at that in our next reading. ⚜

JOSEPH 7

And Joseph said unto Pharaoh, The dream of Pharaoh is one: God hath shewed Pharaoh what he is about to do. The seven good kine are seven years; and the seven good ears are seven years: the dream is one. And the seven thin and ill favoured kine that came up after them are seven years; and the seven empty ears blasted with the east wind shall be seven years of famine.

This is the thing which I have spoken unto Pharaoh: What God is about to do he sheweth unto Pharaoh. Behold, there come seven years of great plenty throughout all the land of Egypt: And there shall arise after them seven years of famine; and all the plenty shall be forgotten in the land of Egypt; and the famine shall consume the land; and the plenty shall not be known in the land by reason of that famine following; for it shall be very grievous. And for that the dream was doubled unto Pharaoh twice; it is because the thing is established by God, and God will **shortly** *bring it to pass.* Genesis 41:25-32, Emphasis added

In our last teaching I said that *shortly* is a southern term, but perhaps it is actually an Old English term. In the above scripture passage, God was warning Pharaoh that the interpretation of his dream was about to happen.

In the following verses, Joseph went on to give Pharaoh a plan to store up food during the seven years of plenty so they could survive the seven years of famine. Then, in verses 39 and 40, Pharaoh says to Joseph, *"Forasmuch as God hath shewed thee all this, there is none so discreet and wise as thou art: thou shalt be over my house, and according unto thy word shall all my people be ruled: only in the throne will I be greater than thou."*

Once again God exalted Joseph to second in command in the situation he was in. First it was in Potiphar's house, then in prison, and now he became the number two man to what was probably the most powerful king on earth at the time.

Through a process that was born of and carried out through adverse circumstances, Joseph went from being a young, arrogant seventeen-year-old Hebrew boy to ruling the most powerful nation on earth (under its king, of course).

In verse 36 we are told that Joseph was thirty years old when he stood before Pharaoh to interpret Pharaoh's dreams. Thirteen years had passed since Joseph's brothers had sold him into slavery. Through this thirteen-year process Joseph had grown to maturity and found himself in position to, not only save Egypt from starvation, but also to save the entire region (including his father and the brothers who had sold him into slavery).

It would be at least seven more years before God would reunite Joseph with his family, and the rest of the story is that God was positioning, not only a man, but also a people. Joseph's family would move to Egypt, where they would become a great nation, one day spoiling Egypt of her wealth and returning to Canaan to establish the nation of Israel.

What an awesome plan! Glory to God! ✣

PATIENCE

That ye be not slothful, but followers of them who through faith and patience inherit the promises. Hebrews 6:12

For ye have need of patience, that, after ye have done the will of God, ye might receive the promise. Hebrews 10:36

Knowing this, that the trying of your faith worketh patience. But let patience have her perfect work, that ye may be perfect and entire, wanting nothing. James 1:4

Webster says that *patience* is, among other things, "quiet, steady perseverance or diligence." Patience is not the goal or desired result. Patience is that quality that will get you to the goal or desired result.

In Luke 21:19, Jesus says that in patience we possess our souls. In other words, if we are patient, we will control our minds. Sometimes people use the word *soul* instead of *spirit* but your soul is not your spirit. Your soul is your mind.

When trouble or adverse circumstances come your way, do you find yourself questioning God, questioning His Word, or even questioning yourself (your ability to meet the challenge before you)? Or do you patiently trust in Him, trust in His goodness and mercy, trust in who you are in Him?

We have been studying Joseph's life and how he persevered through severe trials until eventually he found himself prepared and positioned for greatness. We are on a journey in this life. If we preserve with faith and patience, that journey will take us to where God wants us to be. We were all created with a purpose, and God knows how to get us from where we are to where He wants us to be.

Many times the word *saved* is used to refer to that point in a person's life when he or she accepts Jesus as Lord and Savior and is born again. But if you study the Scriptures, you will learn that the term *saved* rarely means that initial born-again experience. It usually means the on-going process of being saved.

Saved from what? Saved from ourselves. In 1 Corinthians 15:31, the apostle Paul says, *"I die daily."* The process of continually being saved is one of continual dying to ourselves so we can live for Christ, or live in the anointing (see Galatians 2:20). In other words, walk in the Spirit. When we walk in the Spirit, we do not fulfill the lust of the flesh (see Galatians 5:16).

Like Joseph, walking in the flesh can get us in a lot of trouble. But also like Joseph, if we will trust God in the adverse circumstances that living in this world can bring our way, we will become the overcomers He desires us to be. We will continue on the journey toward our purpose for being on this planet, and I assure you each one of us has purpose.

When we continually walk in the Spirit, we will, like Joseph, not only bring blessing to every circumstance we find ourselves in, but we will also overcome the adverse circumstances in our lives and continue on to greatness. ✠

Greatness

Before I formed thee in the belly I knew thee; and before thou camest forth out of the womb I sanctified thee, and I ordained thee a prophet unto the nations. Jeremiah 1:5

God, who lives in eternity and not in time, knows the end from the beginning. He is never surprised. Just as He knew Jeremiah before he was conceived, He also knew you and me before we were conceived. He knew the paths our lives would take.

In Matthew 20:16, Jesus said that many are called but few are chosen. Jeremiah was chosen. His destiny was sealed before he was even conceived. The Amplified Bible makes this a little clearer than the King James Version:

Before I formed you in the womb I knew and approved of you [as my chosen instrument], and before you were born I separated and set you apart, consecrating you: and I appointed you as a prophet to the nations.

Jeremiah 1:5, AMP

If you are chosen, you did not do the choosing. The Bible is full of examples of chosen ones like Jeremiah. And, like Jeremiah, chosen ones are destined for greatness. However, greatness doesn't necessarily mean attaining a high position. Greatness in the Kingdom of God is simply doing what He created us to do and being what He created us to be.

Jesus said, *"He that believeth on me, the works that I do shall he do also; and greater works than these shall he do; because I go unto my Father"* (John 14:12). I think we can safely say this is a definition of greatness.

Ye know that the princes of the Gentiles exercise dominion over them, and they that are great exercise authority upon them. But it shall not be so among you: but whosoever will be great among you, let him be your minister; and whosoever will be chief among you, let him be your servant: even as the Son of man came not to be ministered unto, but to minister, and to give his life a ransom for many.

Jesus in Matthew 20:25-28

So, greatness in the Kingdom of God is not about position. It is about serving, about ministering to others. The more we die to self and walk in love toward others and in the Spirit, the more we will walk in greatness.

God's purpose for us may be to exalt us to a high position, like Jeremiah or Joseph. But even then our purpose for being in that high position will be to serve others.

Here in the United States, our form of government, as instituted by our founding fathers, is a republic. Often it is referred to as a democracy, but it was originally set up as a constitutional republic. In a republic, representatives are elected by the people to govern. But the elected officials are not there to *rule over* the people. They are there to *serve* the people. We are supposed to be a government of the people, by the people, and for the people.

God's Kingdom works much the same way. The higher the position God exalts one to, the greater servant that one is to become.

Humble yourselves therefore under the mighty hand of God, that he may exalt you in due time.   1 Peter 5:6

✠

Being a Blessing

And now I exhort you to be of good cheer: for there shall be no loss of any man's life among you, but of the ship. For there stood by me this night the angel of God, whose I am, and whom I serve, saying, Fear not, Paul; thou must be brought before Caesar: and, lo, God hath given thee all them that sail with thee.   Acts 27:22-24

The apostle Paul was a prisoner en route to Rome aboard a ship. A violent storm was threatening to destroy the ship (which it eventually did). God sent an angel to Paul to comfort and encourage him, reassuring him that he would not perish in the storm. Not only did the angel comfort Paul; he told him that no one on the ship would lose his life. So Paul comforted all onboard with the message the angel had given him. Sure enough, verse 44 tells us that all escaped to dry land.

As we have studied Joseph we have seen how Potiphar was blessed because of Joseph. Potiphar was not a godly man. In fact, he most likely served false gods. Yet, because Joseph was in Potiphar's household, everything Potiphar had was blessed. Later in life, because Joseph was in Egypt, all of Egypt was blessed and saved from famine. In the account of Paul being shipwrecked, we see this same principal at work. Because of Paul's presence on that ship loaded with prisoners, no one's life was lost.

I believe this same principal applies to any believer who is walking in the blessing of God. We should expect our families to be blessed because we are blessed. If we are employed, we should expect our employer to be blessed. Wherever we live, we should expect our communities and even our nation to be blessed.

We are not seeking God's blessing. We are blessed because of who we are (provided we belong to God). That blessing should affect every situation we find ourselves in and everyone we are involved with.

Of course, those around us can choose to receive or not receive the blessing. With Joseph, Potiphar received it, but his wife didn't. Because she lived in the household, she enjoyed the benefits of the blessing, but she made a very bad choice that cost Potiphar his servant (Joseph), who was bringing the blessing to his household and business.

As the ship that Paul was on broke apart, the soldiers decided to kill the prisoners so they couldn't escape, but the officer in charge stopped them. Had the soldiers killed the prisoners, they, too, probably would have lost their lives. Because of the blessing that Paul walked in, the officer in charge believed him and forbade the soldiers from killing anyone. As a result, no one onboard that ship died in the storm.

Christ hath redeemed us from the curse of the law, being made a curse
for us: for it is written, Cursed is every one that hangeth on a tree:

that the blessing of Abraham might come on the Gentiles [nations] *through Jesus Christ.* Galatians 3:13-14, Emphasis added

The Blessing

Christ hath redeemed us from the curse of the law, being made a curse for us: for it is written, cursed is every one that hangeth on a tree: that the blessing of Abraham might come on the Gentiles through Jesus Christ; that we might receive the promise of the Spirit through faith.

Galatians 3:13-14

Often we hear Christians say, "Be blessed," or "Have a blessed day." Sometimes people say, "God bless you." If you are a citizen of the United States, you have probably sung the beautiful song "God Bless America." The indication is that God's blessing is something we are seeking or something we want God to bestow upon us. The truth is that when Jesus, on the cross, said, *"It is finished"* (John 19:30), the blessing was released. So, we don't have to seek God's blessing or wait on God's blessing to come on us. God has already made provision for us to be blessed. We already have God's blessing.

Like everything else we receive from God, we must appropriate His blessing in our lives by faith. That is why I often end my letters and emails with *Stay in the blessing.* How do we stay in the blessing? By operating in faith continually.

Some ministers give the impression that you can give to receive a blessing, but if we are already blessed (and we are), that just isn't true. However, giving can activate the blessing in your life if you are giving in faith.

No farmer sows just to be sowing. A farmer sows to reap a harvest. When you give to a ministry, to an individual or to a local church, you should expect a multiplied return on your giving. It is not that you give to get, but God has built into the system a means for you to increase and continue to give.

What enables us to give in the first place is the truth that we are blessed. Sowing finances is only one way to give. There are many other ways to give.

In Mark 16:15 Jesus said, *"Go ye into all the world, and preach the gospel to every creature."* *Gospel* means "good news." The Gospel is the blessing of God. So Jesus was telling us to go into the entire world and preach the blessing to everyone.

In 1 Corinthians 2:4, the apostle Paul says, *"And my speech and preaching was not with enticing words of man's wisdom, but in demonstration of the Spirit and of power."* So Paul not only preached the Gospel; he demonstrated it.

We are the blessed of God, so we should not only be talking about the blessing of God; we should be demonstrating it. We have the ability to make a difference in the situations and circumstances that we come in contact with. We aren't blessed just so we can enjoy life; we are blessed to be a blessing. So, stay in the blessing. ✝

Walking in the Blessing

Now the LORD had said unto Abram, Get thee out of thy country, and from thy kindred, and from thy father's house, unto a land that I will shew thee: and I will make of thee a great nation, and I will bless thee, and make thy name great; and thou shalt be a blessing: and I will bless them that bless thee, and curse him that curseth thee: and in thee shall all families of the earth be blessed. Genesis 12:1-3

Abram, whose name God changed to Abraham, was a descendant of Shem, Noah's son. Abram was the son of Terah, who was born in Ur of the Chaldees. Ur was most likely in modern-day southern Iraq. The Bible tells us that Terah took his son, Abram, his daughter-in-law, Sarai, and his grandson, Lot (Abraham's nephew), and left Ur with the intention of going to Canaan (see Genesis 11:31).

We don't know why Terah did this. Perhaps God told him to or perhaps he just decided to for some other reason. We don't know what Terah's relationship with God was or if he had one at all. However, we do know that he didn't get to Canaan. He settled in Haran and died there.

After Terah's death, God spoke to Abram and told him to leave Haran and his kinfolks. God's instructions to Abram were, *"Go to a land I will show you."* Abram took his wife, Sarai and his possessions (including servants) and traveled until he came to Canaan. Then the Lord appeared to Abram and said, *"Unto your seed I will give this land"* (Genesis 12:7). Abram believed what God told him and traveled to the land God showed him. However, it would be many years before the great nation God spoke of would come into existence. In fact, Abram would not live to see it come to pass.

Abram was blessed because he believed God's promise to him, not because he saw the promise come to pass. When God spoke the word to Abram and Abram received it, the blessing of God began working in Abram's life. Romans 4:3 tells us that because Abraham believed God, he was a righteous man. Abraham was a type and shadow of the New Testament Church. Like Abraham, we, too, are righteous because we believe God. It is our faith in the promises of God and the finished work of Jesus that makes us righteous. Because of Jesus, the blessing of Abraham has come on us (see Galatians 3:13-14).

God changed Abram's name to Abraham. *Abraham* means "father of many nations." This is another type and shadow of the Church. When we are born again, we become new creatures in Christ Jesus (see 2 Corinthians 5:17) and take on His name (see Ephesians 3:15). Every time Abraham heard his name spoken, he was reminded of the promise of God to him. Everyone that addressed him was calling him *Father of Many Nations!* That must have been a real faith builder!

An interesting thing to note here is that even though Abraham believed God and obeyed Him by going to the land that God showed him, he could not see how God's promise to him would be fulfilled. Abraham was old and his wife (whose name God changed from Sarai to Sarah, meaning princess) was past the age of childbearing. So God did an interesting thing to confirm to Abraham that His promise would come to pass. God was about to cut a covenant with Abraham. ✠

WALKING IN THE BLESSING 2

Now the LORD had said unto Abram, Get thee out of thy country, and from thy kindred, and from thy father's house, unto a land that I will shew thee: and I will make of thee a great nation, and I will bless thee, and make thy name great; and thou shalt be a blessing: and I will bless them that bless thee, and curse him that curseth thee: and in thee shall all families of the earth be blessed. Genesis 12:1-3

In the 15th chapter of Genesis, we are told that God appeared to Abram in a vision and said, *"Fear not, Abram: I am thy shield and thy exceeding great reward."* Abram had already experienced this. God had made him a wealthy man and had caused him to be victorious over his enemies. The blessing of God was already working in Abram's life. Still, Abram couldn't understand how God's promise to make him the father of many nations would come to pass. So one night God brought Abram to a place where he had a clear view of the heavens and told him to count the stars. Of course, there were too many to count. God said, *"So shall thy seed be."* In the very next verse is a statement that was quoted by Paul in Romans 4:3, *"And he [Abram] believed in the LORD; and he [God] counted it to him for righteousness."*

But then Abram did an interesting thing. He asked God for some kind of a confirmation that the word He had spoken would indeed come to pass. We were just told that Abram believed God, or exercised faith in

God, and that because of Abram's faith God considered him a righteous man. But here we find Abram asking God for a confirmation concerning what He (God) had already said. And God seemed okay with that. He didn't seem to consider it doubt or unbelief. I believe it was because God wanted to establish another type and shadow of the New Testament Church. He literally wanted to establish a type and shadow of the New Covenant.

God's confirmation to Abram was a blood covenant. He established this covenant with the blood of a heifer, a female goat, a ram, a turtledove and a pigeon (see Genesis 15:9-11). Evidently Abram understood blood covenants and that they were the most sacred and binding agreements between individuals, families, people groups or nations. Because Abram cut this blood covenant with Almighty God, he opened the door for Jesus to cut a blood covenant with the Father (God) that would establish an eternally-binding agreement between them.

The thing that excites me about that covenant is that it includes me! I belong to the Body of Christ. I am one with Him. So the covenant is between God and me, just as much as it is between God and Jesus. When we, the Church, grasp the fullness of that covenant, the devil is finished. Glory to God! ✝

Walking in the Blessing 3

Now the LORD had said unto Abram, Get thee out of thy country, and from thy kindred, and from thy father's house, unto a land that I will shew thee: and I will make of thee a great nation, and I will bless thee, and make thy name great; and thou shalt be a blessing: and I will bless them that bless thee, and curse him that curseth thee: and in thee shall all families of the earth be blessed. Genesis 12:1-3

And he [God] said unto him [Abram], Take me an heifer of three years old, and a she goat of three years old, and a ram of three years old, and a turtledove, and a young pigeon. And he took unto him all these, and divided them in the midst, and laid each piece one against another: but the birds divided he not. And when the fowls came down upon the carcases, Abram drove them away. Genesis 15:9-11

The picture here is that of a covenant being cut between God and Abram. The word *covenant* means *"to cut."* If you can picture this in your mind, there was a lot of blood. Birds came to feed on the carcasses, but Abram drove them away. This was not unlike what happens today. As soon as a new believer enters the Kingdom of God, that person finds himself/herself involved in a struggle that attempts to rob them of the covenant he/she has just entered into.

After Abram drove the birds away, he fell into a deep sleep. Then the Bible tells us that a horror of great darkness fell upon Abram. In this dreadful situation, God spoke to Abram. God told him that his seed would be in bondage to another nation for a period of four hundred years, but that He (God) would bring them out of bondage and establish them in the Promised Land. This is another type and shadow of the Church. As believers, we go through times of testing and trials, as God brings us out of bondage, establishes His character in us, and positions us for greatness.

In Genesis 15:17-18, we are told that a smoking furnace and a burning lamp passed between the pieces of animal carcass, confirming the blood covenant God established with Abram that night in the land of Canaan. Then God said, *"Unto thy seed have I given this land, from the river of Egypt unto the great river, the river Euphrates."* The people of Israel have never yet occupied all that land, but they will. Why? Because of the covenant that God cut with Abram thousands of years ago in a land called Canaan. It was an everlasting covenant and all the promises of that covenant will come to pass.

My point is this: When we enter the Kingdom of God, by being born again, the blessing of God comes on us. Abraham walked in that blessing by faith, just as we walk in the blessing by faith. When we walk in the blessing by faith, that blessing begins to work in our lives immediately. However, coming into the fullness of that blessing is a process that takes time.

The process has to do with our dying to self and maturing in the Lord. We have to increase on the inside to be able to handle increase on the outside. It may also have to do with circumstances lining up with our faith.

Walking in the blessing has everything to do with living according to Kingdom principles, walking in love and in faith. The blessing is not dependent upon or affected by the world's system or the world's economy. The blessing works, period, and we are the blessed, period! Glory to God! ✢

Establishing the Blessing

Now the LORD had said unto Abram, Get thee out of thy country, and from thy kindred, and from thy father's house, unto a land that I will shew thee: and I will make of thee a great nation, and I will bless thee, and make thy name great; and thou shalt be a blessing: and I will bless them that bless thee, and curse him that curseth thee: and in thee shall all families of the earth be blessed. Genesis 12:1-3

We have been studying the blood covenant God cut with Abram to confirm the promise He had made to Abram. Interestingly, the next thing Abram did was fall into doubt and try to make the covenant come to pass on his own. Because Sarai was past the age of childbearing, Abram decided to help God a little and have a son by Sarai's servant, Hagar. It is very interesting to me that even though Abram messed up, it didn't change God's covenant with him. Abram's failure did cause some problems, but God just continued right on bringing the covenant to pass. This should be an encouragement to anyone in the Body of Christ who has messed up. Our failures don't change the covenant we have with God. If we will simply admit the wrong we have done, running to God instead of from Him, we can get back on track and continue running our race.

The secret to walking in the covenant we have with God is to believe it. God established it, and it was not established on our ability to perform. It was established on God's Word.

For if Abraham were justified by works, he hath whereof to glory; but not before God. For what saith the scripture? Abraham believed God, and it was counted unto him for righteousness.

Romans 4:2-3

We can't do anything to earn the blessing of God. We are blessed because of the covenant we have with God. So why do we not all walk one hundred percent in the blessing all the time? I can assure you this. The problem is not with God or with His covenant. And it is not because God is sovereign and sometimes decides to go against His own Word, His own promises or His own covenant and allow sickness or poverty or some other problem in our lives. God is sovereign, but His sovereignty does not allow Him to lie (see Titus 1:2 and Hebrews 6:18). So if the blessing is not working in our lives, it is not because of anything God has done or allowed to happen. Then guess who the responsibility lies with? It lies with you and me.

Some Christians refuse to believe this. They would rather believe that God chooses to withhold His covenant at times. They distort the truth and believe that sickness, disease, poverty and other problems are in some way a blessing from God. While it is true that all things work together for our good (see Romans 8:28), James tells us that we are tempted (or tested) when we are drawn away because of lust (see James 1:14). Drawn away from what? Drawn away from God's promises, from His Word and from His covenant. Lust is simply pressure, and pressure is a thief designed to get our focus off of our covenant and onto our circumstances.

The thief cometh not, but for to steal, and to kill, and to destroy: I am come that they might have life, and that they might have it more abundantly. Jesus in John 10:10

So if the blessing is not being established in our lives, it has to be because we are not walking in faith, or something is hindering our faith. We all have the same measure of faith (see Romans 12:3), and our success depends on how we use that faith.

To walk in faith is to rest in the finished work of Jesus (see Hebrews 4:9-11). It is to trust God completely. Trusting God completely enables us to walk in the covenant we have with Him because of the finished work of Jesus. Glory to God! ⚜

ESTABLISHING THE BLESSING 2

Now the Lord had said unto Abram, Get thee out of thy country, and from thy kindred, and from thy father's house, unto a land that I will shew thee: and I will make of thee a great nation, and I will bless thee, and make thy name great; and thou shalt be a blessing: and I will bless them that bless thee, and curse him that curseth thee: and in thee shall all families of the earth be blessed. Genesis 12:1-3

In our last teaching we looked at the covenant God cut with Abram. That covenant is still in effect today because God kept His end of the agreement, even though Abram had difficulty keeping his.

A few years ago I thought I trusted God, until I experienced some severe tests and trials. I discovered that I only trusted God in part, and He was requiring complete trust. My lack of trust caused those things to manifest in my life due to pressure I had given into. My focus was in the wrong place.

Actually, I was being double-minded. James tells us that a double-minded man is unstable in all his ways (see James 1:8). I thought I trusted God, but I was still trying to work out problems on my own (in the flesh).

There is a remnant on the earth today that God is calling out of organized religion, out of tradition, and out of double-mindedness, to establish the blessing of God, first of all, in their own personal lives, then, corporately, as the true Church and, finally, on the earth. Jesus is building His glorious Church, and it will be without spot, wrinkle or any such thing. It will be holy and without blemish (see Ephesians 5:27).

In other words, Jesus is establishing the blessing of Abraham on earth. That's what the glorious Church is. It is a people blessed by God, walking in faith that works by love, establishing the blessing of Abraham on earth. It is not about our being blessed so we can have more "stuff." It is about bringing the Kingdom of God on earth as it is in Heaven (see Matthew 6:10 and Luke 11:2).

Is that not why Jesus went to the cross?

Christ hath redeemed us from the curse of the law, being made a curse for us: for it is written, Cursed is every one that hangeth on a tree: **that the blessing of Abraham might come on the Gentiles [nations]** *through Jesus Christ.* Galatians 3:13-14, Emphasis added

Now, let me make one more point. While many of the tests and trials that believers experience are the result of being drawn away from the Word, as James 1:14 says, every test and trial we experience is not necessarily because of some failure on our part. Let's look at the response Jesus gave to a question one of His disciples asked concerning a man who was born blind.

And as Jesus passed by, he saw a man which was blind from his birth. And his disciples asked him, saying, Master, who did sin, this man, or his parents, that he was born blind?

Jesus answered, Neither hath this man sinned, nor his parents; but that the works of God should be made manifest in him. John 9:1-3

We can open the door to tests and trials in our lives, but every test and trial may not be because of some failure on our part. We do have an enemy, and it is our enemy's nature to steal, kill and destroy. While it can be helpful to know why certain things come against us, the more important thing is how we respond to the things that come against us (or others). Jesus responded by working the works of the Father (see John 9:4). In the verses following John 9:1-4, we are told that Jesus restored the blind man's sight. We, too, should be about working the works of our Father, establishing the blessing of Abraham.

Verily, verily, I say unto you, He that believeth on me, the works that I do shall he do also; and even greater works than these shall he do; because I go unto my Father. And whatsoever ye shall ask in my name, that will I do, that the Father may be glorified in the Son. If ye shall ask any thing in my name, I will do it. Jesus in John 14:12-14

Glory to God! ✞

The Righteousness of Faith

*For the promise, that he should be the heir of the world, was not to Abraham, or to his seed, through the law, but through **the righteousness of faith**.*

Therefore it is of faith, that it might be by grace; to the end the promise might be sure to all the seed; not to that only which is of the law, but that also which is of the faith of Abraham; who is the father of us all. Romans 4:13 and 16, Emphasis added

But Thomas, one of the twelve, called Didymus, was not with them when Jesus came [after His resurrection]. *The other disciples therefore said unto him, We have seen the Lord.*

But he said unto them, Except I shall see in his hands the print of the nails, and put my finger into the print of the nails, and thrust my hand into his side, I will not believe.

Then after eight days again his disciples were within, and Thomas with them: then came Jesus, the doors being shut, and stood in the midst, and said, Peace be unto you. Then saith he to Thomas, Reach hither thy finger, and behold my hands; and reach hither thy hand, and thrust it into my side: and be not faithless, but believing.

And Thomas answered and said unto him, My Lord and my God.

Jesus saith unto him, Thomas, because thou hast seen me, thou hast believed: blessed are they that have not seen, and yet have believed.

John 20:24-29, Emphasis added

The covenant God established with Abraham was established by faith. Had it been established by the law, man would have been responsible for the outcome of the covenant (which he was incapable of). The covenant had to be established on the promises of God, with God alone responsible for its success.

Thomas wanted to see in order to believe. Therefore, his faith was based on what he saw rather than on the Word of God. To walk by sight is to walk by something other than the blessing. That is why Jesus said, *"Blessed are they that have not seen, and yet have believed"* (John 20:29).

Faith in God's Word is a more substantial proof than anything that can be seen. Things that can be seen can change, fail or vanish, but God's Word (covenant) never changes, fails or ceases to exist.

For God made promise to Abraham, because he could swear by no greater, he sware by himself, saying, Surely blessing I will bless thee, and multiplying I will multiply thee.

Wherein God, willing more abundantly to shew unto the heirs of promise the immutability of his counsel, confirmed it by an oath: That by two immutable things, in which it was impossible for God to lie, we might have a strong consolation, who have fled for refuge to lay hold upon the hope set before us: Which hope we have as an anchor of the soul, both sure and stedfast, and which entereth into that within the veil; whither the forerunner is for us entered, even Jesus, made an high priest for ever after the order of Melchisedec.

Hebrews 6:13-14 and 17-20

The Melchisedec priesthood had no beginning or end (see Hebrews 7:1-3). Therefore the covenant that God made with Jesus, which is the fulfillment of the Abrahamic covenant, is without beginning or end. Jesus, who was slain from the foundation of the world (see Revelation 13:8), is our eternal High Priest (see Hebrews 7:24-25).

It is by faith that we receive the blessing:

Christ hath redeemed us from the curse of the law, being made a curse for us: for it is written, Cursed is every one that hangeth on a tree: that the blessing of Abraham might come on the Gentiles through Jesus Christ; that we might receive the promise of the Spirit through faith.

Galatians 3:13-14

It is by faith that we walk in the blessing:

For we walk by faith, not by sight. 2 Corinthians 5:7

And we are carriers of the blessing:

And I will make of thee a great nation, and I will bless thee, and make thy name great; and thou shalt be a blessing: and I will bless them that bless thee, and curse him that curseth thee: and in thee shall all families of the earth be blessed. Genesis 12:2-3

✠

KINGDOM MANNA: READING 34

CARRIERS OF THE BLESSING

Now the LORD had said unto Abram, Get thee out of thy country, and from thy kindred, and from thy father's house, unto a land that I will shew thee: and I will make of thee a great nation, and I will bless thee, and make thy name great; and thou shalt be a blessing: and I will bless them that bless thee, and curse him that curseth thee: and in thee shall all the families of the earth be blessed.

So Abram departed, as the LORD had spoken unto him; and Lot went with him: and Abram was seventy and five years old when he departed out of Haran. And Abram took Sarai his wife, and Lot his brother's son, and all their substance that they had gathered, and the souls that they had gotten in Haran; and they went forth to go into the land of Canaan; and into the land of Canaan they came. Genesis 12:1-5

Abram's father, Terah, had died in Haran, leaving his inheritance to Abram and his two brothers, Nahor and Haran. When Abram left Haran to go to Canaan, in obedience to the Lord, he was already a wealthy man.

Abram arrived in Canaan during a famine, so he settled in Egypt temporarily. His wife, Sarai, was a very good looking woman. Abram, fearing that the Egyptians would kill him and take Sarai, told Sarai to pretend to be his sister (actually she was his half-sister). When Pharaoh, king of Egypt, learned of this beautiful woman that had come into his kingdom, he had her brought into his palace. Pharaoh treated Abram very well because of Sarai, giving him sheep, oxen, donkeys, camels and servants.

Pharaoh didn't realize he was dealing with people who were blessed by the Almighty God. Even though Abram was operating in fear rather than faith in this situation and being deceptive, he and his wife were carriers of the blessing that had come on them because of Abram's obedience to God's initial instructions to him. Even though Pharaoh didn't know that Sarai was Abram's wife, the blessing she carried protected her from violating her marriage covenant and becoming the wife of Pharaoh:

And the LORD *plagued Pharaoh and his house with great plagues because of Sarai Abram's wife. And Pharaoh called Abram, and said, What is this that thou hast done unto me? Why didst thou not tell me that she was thy wife? Why saidst thou, She is my sister? so I might have taken her to me to wife.* Genesis 12:17-19

Pharaoh was deceived by Abram and innocent of any wrongdoing in this situation. However, the blessing Abram carried protected Sarai, at great expense to Pharaoh. Saints, God protects His own. That's why we don't have to retaliate against our enemies. That's why we should pray for our enemies. When someone comes against you, they are coming against the covenant of blessing you have with Almighty God, putting themselves in a very dangerous position. It is God's desire that everyone be saved and come to knowledge of the truth (see 1 Timothy 2:4), and that should be our desire too. It is very possible that if we don't pray for our enemies they could come to a very bad end. I have actually seen this happen, when non-believers have come against believers. In fact, I have even seen it happen when believers came against other believers.

After Pharaoh realized the situation, he sent Abram and Sarai on their way. Evidently Pharaoh didn't take back all the "stuff" he had given Abram. Verse 2 of the next chapter tells us that Abram was very rich in cattle, silver and gold.

The blessing of the LORD, it maketh rich, and he addeth no sorrow with it.   Proverbs 10:22

Jesus was crucified, so the blessing of Abraham could come on the Gentiles (nations) (see Galatians 3:14). Saints, as carriers of that blessing, it is always at work in our lives, bringing increase and protecting us. That blessing has an effect on all that we come in contact with. We are blessed to be a blessing. ✠

KINGDOM MANNA: Reading 35

Blessing = Promise + Obedience

Now the LORD had said unto Abram, Get thee out of thy country, and from thy kindred and from thy father's house, unto a land that I will shew thee: and I will make of thee a great nation, and I will bless thee and make thy name great; and thou shalt be a blessing.

And Abram took Sarai his wife, and Lot his brother's son, and all their substance that they had gathered, and the souls that they had gotten in

Haran; and they went forth to go into the land of Canaan; and into the land of Canaan they came. Genesis 12:1-2 and 5

And he [Abram] *believed in the* LORD; *and he* [God] *counted it to him* [Abram] *for righteousness.* Genesis 15:6

In Genesis 12:1-2, Abram received instructions and promises from God, which he obeyed, because he believed God, and God considered Abram's belief (faith) as righteousness. Therefore, Abram became a blessed man, carrying that blessing wherever he went and being a blessing. Saints, is it not the same with us today? It is our faith in the promises (the written Word) of God and our obedience to the leading of the Holy Spirit that enables us to walk in the blessing, being carriers of that blessing and being a blessing.

Christ hath redeemed us from the curse of the law, being made a curse for us: for it is written, Cursed is every one that hangeth on a tree: that the blessing of Abraham might come on the Gentiles through Jesus Christ; that we might receive the promise of the Spirit through faith.
Galatians 3:13-14

We walk in the same blessing that Abraham had, only we have a better covenant because of the finished work of Jesus. Hallelujah!

We have the promises (the written Word) of God. If we are baptized with (immersed into) the Holy Spirit, we also have the teaching, guidance and power of the Holy Spirit at our disposal. Should we find ourselves unable to access all that, we have also been baptized with fire (see Matthew 3:11). The fire of adversity will bring us to the place of total surrender and complete trust, changing our character, enabling us to walk in all the power and authority of the name of Jesus.

The promises + obedience = blessing.

Let's continue on and look a little deeper into this subject, for it is of the utmost importance that we stay in the blessing! ✞

BLESSING = PROMISE + OBEDIENCE 2

And Melchizedek king of Salem brought forth bread and wine: and he was the priest of the most high God. And he blessed him and said, Blessed be Abram of the most high God, possessor of heaven and earth: and blessed be the most high God, which hath delivered thine enemies into thy hand. And he [Abram] gave him [Melchizedek] tithes of all.

Genesis 14:18-20

In the verses preceding the above scripture, we are told of a battle that Abram won against some enemies. After that battle, he was met by Melchizedek, King of Salem, at the valley of Shaveh. The 7th chapter of Hebrews tells us that Melchizedek was a priest of God, without beginning of days or end of life. His priesthood is eternal. Melchizedek immediately recognized the blessing that Abram carried.

Notice that Melchizedek blessed Abram, and then Abram gave Melchizedek tithes. Abram didn't tithe in order to get a blessing. He tithed because of the blessing. How often today is it taught the other way around? We are taught that we must tithe in order to be blessed, which puts saints back under the Law and in bondage, nullifying the blessing in their lives. When New Testament believers give tithes and/or offerings, it should be by the leading of the Holy Spirit and not out of any obligation or in order to get a blessing. We are already blessed because we believe God, and we prove our faith in Him by our obedience to the Holy Spirit.

I do believe that we can and should give expecting a return on our giving (see Luke 6:38), but we should not give in order to be blessed. We are already blessed, and our giving is an expression of gratitude for that blessing. The Holy Spirit will lead us as to when, where and how much to give.

Under the New Covenant, we don't owe God a tenth, and we don't pay Him anything. It grieves me (and I think it grieves the Holy Spirit) to hear saints of God use the term *pay their tithes*. You pay for something you purchase, and you can't buy anything from God. The truth is you have been purchased by Him. If you were purchased by Him, guess what? You belong to Him, as does everything you have and everything you are.

I asked the Lord once, "How much of the money in my wallet is Yours?"

He quickly said, "All of it."

Well, if all of it is His, and if I am led by the Holy Spirit, then I should do with it whatever the Holy Spirit leads me to do. I know from experience that He will lead me to give some of it into the work of the ministry, some of it to the poor and some of it just to be a blessing to someone else.

We are the blessed, and the purpose of everything we have and everything we are is to be a blessing. It all belongs to God, not just a tenth or any other amount that is less than one hundred percent.

Every man according as he purposeth in his heart, so let him give; not grudgingly, or of necessity: for God loveth a cheerful giver. And God is able to make all grace abound toward you; that ye, always having all sufficiency in all things, may abound to every good work: as it is written, He hath dispersed abroad; he hath given to the poor: his righteousness remaineth for ever. Now he that ministereth seed to the sower both minister bread for your food, and multiply your seed sown, and increase the fruits of your righteousness: being enriched in every thing to all bountifulness, which causeth through us thanksgiving to God.

2 Corinthians 9:7-11

This scripture describes a blessed person who is also being a blessing. That's us, saints. That's who we are, and who we are determines what we do. It's not the other way around. Stay in the blessing. ✣

KINGDOM MANNA: Reading 37

Carriers of the Blessing 2

Christ hath redeemed us from the curse of the law, being made a curse for us: for it is written, Cursed is every one that hangeth on a tree: that the blessing of Abraham might come on the Gentiles through Jesus Christ; that we might receive the promise of the Spirit through faith.

Galatians 3:13-14

Saints, we have been studying the blessing and how we are carriers of that blessing. One of the greatest examples of this I know of is my friend, DeCarol Williamson. DeCarol is the founder of FCN, a Christian television and radio network, which at the time of this writing is covering all of the Americas, the Caribbean and Spain, reaching one hundred million homes twenty-four hours a day, seven days a week. They are actually reaching the entire world via the Internet.

Recently the Lord told DeCarol to go to Rwanda and establish a facility there to broadcast into other parts of Africa, as well as India and China. At the time he received instructions to go to Rwanda, genocide was taking place in that nation. Rwandans were killing Rwandans. Several times DeCarol bought a plane ticket to go, but the Lord said to him, "Not yet."

Finally, one day the Lord said, "Go." Obviously the timing of DeCarol's trip to Rwanda was of great importance, and his obedience to the leading he was getting from the Holy Spirit not only insured his success but protected his life. The end result was that DeCarol purchased nine acres of land on top of a mountain in Rwanda. God had to change the laws of the nation so that he could do that, for Rwanda previously hadn't allowed foreigners to buy property. After DeCarol established his television facility there, Rwanda became one of the safest places on earth. Amazing!

Why did all of this happen? He simply heard and obeyed God as a carrier of the blessing, and a nation changed for the better in the process. As a result DeCarol has been invited by the leaders of other African nations to come and talk with them. And this is just the beginning. Yet to be seen is how great an impact FCN will have on Africa, India and China.

If the obedience of one believer can have such an effect on the nations of the world, imagine what the obedience of one hundred believers or one thousand or one million believers would be. We can literally bring the Kingdom of God on earth as it is in Heaven, which is what Jesus taught us to pray for. Saints, Jesus didn't waste words. When He spoke it, teaching us to pray it, I have no doubt that He knew it would come to pass.

All glory to God! ☦

Protecting the Blessing

Finally, my brethren, be strong in the Lord, and in the power of his might. Put on the whole armour of God, that ye may be able to stand against the wiles of the devil. For we wrestle not against flesh and blood, but against principalities, against powers, against the rulers of the darkness of this world, against spiritual wickedness in high places. Wherefore take unto you the whole armour of God, that ye may be able to withstand in the evil day, and having done all, to stand.

Stand therefore, having your loins girt about with truth, and having on the breastplate of righteousness; And your feet shod with the preparation of the gospel of peace; Above all, taking the shield of faith, wherewith ye shall be able to quench all the fiery darts of the wicked. And take the helmet of salvation, and the sword of the Spirit, which is the word of God: praying always with all prayer and supplication in the Spirit, and watching thereunto with all perseverance and supplication for all saints. Ephesians 6:10-18

Putting on the whole armor of God is not so much something we do, as it is a way of life. It is actually a description of who we are as the blessed. So how do we protect that blessing?

By having our loins wrapped in a girdle of Truth (see Ephesians 6:14): Our loins are the part of our body between our hips and ribs and is considered to be the seat of physical strength and generative power. In other words, our strength and power should always be protected by the truth. Jesus is the Truth (see John 14:6).

By having on a breastplate of righteousness (see Ephesians 6:14): The breastplate covers the heart. By thinking right, doing and being right, by knowing our rights as the blessed citizens of the Kingdom of God, our heart is protected. Our life issues out of our heart, thus sustaining our life.

By having our feet shod with the preparation of the Gospel of Peace (see Ephesians 6:15): The Amplified Bible makes this verse much clearer. "*And having shod your feet in preparation [to face the enemy with the firm-footed stability, the promptness, and the readiness produced by the good news] of the Gospel of peace.*" The biblical definition of *peace* is "completeness or wholeness." It literally means "nothing missing and nothing broken." Health and prosperity are part of the blessing, and as soldiers of the Kingdom, we need to be in good physical health, prospering in every area of our lives.

By taking the shield of faith to stop the fiery darts of our enemy (see Ephesians 6:16): Our faith is our defense, perhaps against the attacks of the devil, but more likely against wrong thinking and fleshly attitudes, which are intended to rob us of the blessing.

By taking the helmet of salvation (see Ephesians 6:17): The Greek word for *salvation* here is *sozo*, which is not referring to the initial experience of being born again (which is spiritual). It is referring to the salvation of our soul, or mind, which is an ongoing process as we renew our minds to the Word of God (see Romans 12:2). It is literally changing our thinking.

By the Sword of the Spirit, which is the Word of God (see Ephesians 6:17): We must stay in the Word, study the Word and receive revealed knowledge from the Word by the Holy Spirit. Realizing that Word indwells us, we must allow it (Him/Jesus) to separate us from the wrong thinking and fleshly attitudes of the old man (see Hebrews 4:12).

By praying always in the Spirit, not only for ourselves, but also for all saints (see Ephesians 6:18): We pray as we are led by the Holy Spirit and in tongues. We cover each other with prayer. It is comforting to know that others are praying for me. It is even more comforting to know that the Spirit is praying for me (see Romans 8:26-27) and that Jesus Himself is making intercession for me (see Romans 8:34 and Hebrews 7:25).

Do you get the idea that God wants us to stay in the blessing, that He wants us to prosper in every area of our lives? We can do much to protect the blessing in our lives, but even if we fail in some area, there are believers, the Holy Spirit and Jesus Himself taking up the slack for us. Bless the name of the Lord forever! ✛

KINGDOM MANNA: Reading 39

A Description of the Blessed

Praise ye the Lord. Blessed is the man that feareth the Lord, that delighteth greatly in his commandments. His seed shall be mighty upon earth: the generation of the upright shall be blessed. Wealth and riches shall be in his house: and his righteousness endureth for ever. Unto the upright there ariseth light in the darkness: he is gracious, and full of compassion, and righteous.

A good man sheweth favour, and lendeth: he will guide his affairs with discretion. Surely he shall not be moved for ever: the righteous shall be in everlasting remembrance. He shall not be afraid of evil tidings: his heart is fixed, trusting in the LORD.

Psalm 112:1-7

As he is, so are we in this world.   1 John 4:17

When Jesus walked this earth as a man, He knew who He was. As a Jew, He was a descendant of Abraham. Because He was a descendant of Abraham, He walked in the blessing of Abraham. It was that blessing that enabled Him to do the things He did, including going to the cross and becoming a curse for us, so that the blessing of Abraham could become available for everyone. This fulfilled God's promise to Abraham that He would be the father, not only of the Jews, but also of many nations (see Genesis 17:4 and Galatians 3:13-14). So, it is the finished work of Jesus that enables us to become a people walking in the blessing of Abraham.

The apostle Peter described us this way:

But ye are a chosen generation, a royal priesthood, an holy nation, a peculiar people; that ye should shew forth the praises of him who hath called you out of darkness into his marvelous light: which in time past were not a people, but are now the people of God: which had not obtained mercy, but now have obtained mercy.   1 Peter 2:9-10

We are not blessed because of what we have or by our abilities and talents. It is the blessing of God that enables us to receive the things we have and to utilize our abilities and talents. Psalm 112 is not something we do to receive the blessing; it is a description of what we can have and do because we are blessed.

Realizing we are blessed and utilizing that blessing enables us to trust God completely, and it is only when we trust God completely that we walk in perfected love. Perfected love allows no place for fear of any kind in our lives (see 1 John 4:18). When there is no fear in our lives, we have no need to retaliate against wrong done to us. Hence, there is no need to harbor unforgiveness against anyone for any reason.

Because we are blessed, we become a blessing. Wherever we go and whatever we do, we carry that blessing with us. As we walk out our lives in obedience to God, being led by His Spirit, we become a testimony to His goodness and glory. Our presence on this earth can not only change individual lives; it can change families, people groups and entire nations.

Jesus taught us in the 5th chapter of Matthew to love our enemies and to bless them. The only reason we can do this is because we are blessed. That blessing removes all fear and enables us to trust God completely and walk in the love that He is (see 1 John 4:16).

The more we walk in this love, the more we will look and act like Psalm 112. This is who we are, and as the people of God, this is where we are going, as we become the glorious Church, without spot, wrinkle or any such thing, holy and without blemish (see Ephesians 5:27). All glory to God! ✠

FOCUSING ON PROTECTING THE BLESSING

Finally, my brethren, be strong in the Lord, and in the power of his might. Put on the whole armour of God, that ye may be able to stand against the wiles of the devil. For we wrestle not against flesh and blood, but against principalities, against powers, against the rulers of the darkness of this world, against spiritual wickedness in high places. Wherefore take unto you the whole armour of God, that ye may be able to withstand in the evil day, and having done all, to stand.

Stand therefore, having your loins girt about with truth, and having on the breastplate of righteousness; and your feet shod with the preparation of the gospel of peace; above all, taking the shield of faith, wherewith ye shall be able to quench all the fiery darts of the wicked. And take the helmet of salvation, and the sword of the Spirit, which is the word of God: praying always with all prayer and supplication in the Spirit, and watching thereunto with all perseverance and supplication for all saints. Ephesians 6:10-18

We have studied ways to protect the blessing in our lives, mentioned in the above passage of scripture. However, in the past I have read this portion of scripture and focused more on the attacks of the enemy than on the ways to prevent or overcome those attacks. I think this is a real temptation that all believers face.

There is no question that attacks will come. In Mark's Gospel, we are told that Peter became concerned about giving up everything to follow Jesus. Jesus assured him that he would be well compensated for all he had given up, but then Jesus said an interesting thing: He said the compensation would come with persecutions (see Mark 10:28-30).

Webster's Dictionary defines persecute as "to pursue with harassing or oppressive treatment, to annoy or trouble persistently." Webster says persecution is "a program or campaign to exterminate, drive away or subjugate a people because of their religion, race or beliefs."

Persecution, regardless of how it comes, is the work of the devil. Peter tells us in his letter to believers in Pontus, Galatia, Cappadocia, Asia and Bithynia: *"Be sober, be vigilant; because your adversary the devil, as a roaring lion, walketh about, seeking whom he may devour"* (1 Peter 5:8). Then, in verse 9, he tells us to resist the devil, remaining steadfast in the faith.

We should note here that Peter didn't say the devil **is** a roaring lion. He said he masquerades **as** a roaring lion. Then he tells us to resist him by continuing steadfast in the faith. How do we do that? By staying focused on the Word rather than on the enemy's attacks.

Smith Wigglesworth was a great English healing evangelist whose ministry flourished toward the end of the nineteenth century and the first half of the twentieth century. In one of the biographies I have read on his life, the story is told that he was awakened one night to find the devil himself standing in the corner of his bedroom. Wigglesworth looked at the devil and said, "Oh, it's only you." He then turned over and went back to sleep. [2]

I don't say this to minimize the danger the devil represents. He may only be masquerading as a roaring lion, but he is seeking someone to devour. That is why we must stay focused on the Word and on the authority we have in the name of Jesus.

2. Wilson, Julian, *Wigglesworth: The Complete Story* (Tyrone, GA, Authentic Publishing, 2002)

We must also be led by the Holy Spirit. The Spirit knows what is going on behind the scenes. The Spirit can see things that we may not be able to see in the natural. He will lead and guide us as to how to pray, when to pray and exactly what to pray. This is why the baptism with the Holy Spirit is so important to the believer. We can pray in tongues, not even knowing what we are praying and be assured that the Spirit is praying a perfect prayer for us.

Praying always with all prayer and supplication in the Spirit, and watching thereunto with all perseverance and supplication for all saints. Ephesians 6:18

KINGDOM MANNA: Reading 41

Focusing on Protecting the Blessing 2

Finally, my brethren, be strong in the Lord, and in the power of his might. Put on the whole armour of God, that ye may be able to stand against the wiles of the devil. For we wrestle not against flesh and blood, but against principalities, against powers, against the rulers of the darkness of this world, against spiritual wickedness in high places. Wherefore take unto you the whole armour of God, that ye may be able to withstand in the evil day, and having done all, to stand.

Stand therefore, having your loins girt about with truth, and having on the breastplate of righteousness; and your feet shod with the preparation of the gospel of peace; above all, taking the shield of faith, wherewith ye shall be able to quench all the fiery darts of the wicked. And take the helmet of salvation, and the sword of the Spirit, which is the word of God: praying always with all prayer and supplication in the Spirit, and watching thereunto with all perseverance and supplication for all saints. Ephesians 6:10-18

In our last teaching I made this statement concerning the above Scripture: In the past I have read this portion of Scripture and focused more on the attacks of the enemy than on the ways to prevent or overcome those attacks. And I concluded: I think that is a real temptation all believers face. The Word tells us through the apostle Paul that one of the primary ways of overcoming our enemy is by praying in the Spirit. He even tells us the Spirit prays for us with groanings that cannot be uttered.

Likewise the Spirit also helpeth our infirmities: for we know not what we should pray for as we ought: but the Spirit itself maketh intercession for us with groanings which cannot be uttered. And he that searcheth the hearts knoweth what is the mind of the Spirit, because he maketh intercession for the saints according to the will of God. And we know that all things work together for good to them that love God, to them who are the called according to his purpose. Romans 8:26-28

What are these *"all things"* that Paul is talking about here? Is it everything that happens to us, or is it the things Paul mentions in Ephesians 6:10-18, along with the things he mentions in Romans 8:26-27 about the Spirit praying for us?

Where is your focus? Is it on the things God has provided that enable us to overcome our enemy, or is it on the attack? While we should be ever watchful and wise concerning the ways of our enemy, our focus should be continually on the things that overcome.

General George Patton won a tank battle with the Germans in North Africa during World War II. The Germans were led by the infamous Erwin Rommel, who had written a book on tank warfare. In a movie made about General Patton, after the battle was won, he looked out over the desert and said, "Rommel, you fool, I read your book." Patton knew his enemy, but instead of allowing that knowledge to put him on the defense, he used that knowledge to mount an offensive battle that overcame his enemy.

The devil is defeated. Jesus won the battle over him and then sat down at the right hand of the Father in Heaven (see Hebrews 10:12-13). In reality, the battle has already been won, so we are not fighting, so much as we are taking the spoils of battle.

It is time we change our focus from what our enemy can do to what Jesus has already done. That is how we fight the good fight of faith (see 1 Timothy 6:12).

Wherefore take unto you the whole armour of God, that ye may be able to withstand in the evil day, and having done all, to stand.

Ephesians 6:13

Prosperity

Beloved, I wish above all things that thou mayest prosper and be in health, even as thy soul prospereth. 3 John 2

Webster's Dictionary defines *prosperity* as "a successful, flourishing, or thriving condition, especially in financial respects." In our recent studies of the blessing of Abraham, I noted that even before God promised Abraham that his descendants would become a great nation and that he would be the father of many nations, God made him wealthy and gave him success over his enemies.

Psalm 35:27 tells us that God has pleasure in the prosperity of His servant. Psalm 35 is a psalm of David, and the servant David spoke of was himself. David realized that his prosperity brought pleasure to God.

Our prosperity is essential to our ability to establish God's covenant or the blessing on earth. Deuteronomy 8:18 says, *"But thou shalt remember the LORD thy God: for it is he that giveth thee power to get wealth, that he may establish his covenant which he sware unto thy fathers, as it is this day."* So, God gives us power to get wealth, and He takes pleasure in our prosperity. God is no respecter of persons (see Acts 10:34), so if He did it for David, and if he did it for the Israelites, He will do it for us too.

Jesus went to the cross so that the blessing of Abraham might come on us (the Gentiles or nations) (see Galatians 3:13-14). So why are more Christians not prosperous? Why have many of us struggled in this area? Could it be due to wrong thinking?

John's third epistle was written to Gaius. After his greeting, the first thing John said to Gaius was a wish for him to prosper and be in health. But John added a condition to his wish for Gaius to prosper and be in health. He said, *"Even as your soul prospers."*

We are triune, beings made up of spirit, soul and body. We are a spirit, we have a soul, and we live in a body. Our soul is our mind, which houses our will, our emotions and our intellect. So how is it that our soul needs to prosper in order for prosperity to manifest in our lives?

And be not conformed to this world: but be ye transformed by the renewing of your mind.   Romans 12:2

Our soul prospers when we renew our minds to the Word of God. Renewing the mind to God's Word will change wrong thinking into right thinking. Right thinking will produce righteousness in our lives.

But seek ye first the Kingdom of God and his righteousness; and all these things shall be added unto you.   Jesus in Matthew 6:33

Righteousness is not only doing and being right; it is having rights. As citizens of the Kingdom of God, we have every right to the blessing of Abraham. When we walk in the blessing of Abraham, we will be prosperous, and by being prosperous, we will establish God's covenant on earth.

When we proclaim the Gospel and bring people into the Kingdom, then disciple them and teach them to walk in the blessing, God's covenant is established or manifested on earth.

Imagine what would happen if believers would simply walk in the blessing of Abraham and proclaim the Gospel or the blessing to others. Many new converts would be brought into the Kingdom and then taught to do the same.

The devil knows this, and that's why he fights the prosperity of believers. He has even convinced some that poverty is somehow desirable and makes one holy. I don't mean to offend anyone whose religion teaches this, but that's ignorance gone to seed. God does not take pleasure in the poverty of His people; He takes pleasure in the prosperity of His people. If God owns the cattle on a thousand hills (and He does, see Psalm 50:10), why would He want His children to be poor? It is time we renew our minds by the Word of God, make right our wrong thinking, and become the prosperous people God intends for us to be.

If you were prospecting for gold, wouldn't it be nice to have a map showing where to dig? The Word of God is our map, and the Holy Spirit is our Scout, leading us to the spot marked on the map. Hallelujah! ☩

KINGDOM MANNA: Reading 43

True Prosperity

The thief cometh not, but for to steal, and to kill, and to destroy: I am come that they might have life, and that they might have it more abundantly.   Jesus in John 10:10

True prosperity is abundance in every area of our lives. It includes much more than finances. It includes mental and physical health, relationships, and our position in society, the business world, ministry and more. However, prospering in these areas is not the blessing of Abraham that we have been studying. Prospering in these areas is the result of the blessing of Abraham. Abraham was not blessed because he was wealthy; he was wealthy because he was blessed.

The blessing is simply the empowerment to succeed. By the same token, the curse is the empowerment to fail. When Jesus was made a curse for us (see Galatians 3:13-14), He enabled us to walk free of any curse. He, therefore, empowered us to walk in the blessing.

When we walk in the blessing, the blessing goes with us wherever we go. We literally become a blessing that will change the environment around us.

I know that everyone won't receive us and, as a result, some will not benefit from the blessing that we carry, but I also know that love never fails (see 1 Corinthians 13:8) and that our faith (in the blessing) will overcome (see 1 John 5:4-5). Hallelujah!

True prosperity comes from God. We receive it by trusting in Him. We trust in Him by believing His Word.

The world has a kind of prosperity, but Proverbs 10:22 indicates that there is sorrow attached to the world's brand of prosperity:

The blessing of the LORD, it maketh rich, and he addeth no sorrow with it.   Proverbs 10:22

Before Adam fell, he lived in continual blessing in the Garden of Eden. His work was not hard or toilsome. He was not a planter but a gatherer. God planted the garden, and Adam simply gathered the fruit of it, as he had need.

Often I hear people speaking of working for a living, but the blessing of God enables us to once again become gatherers instead of workers. Until all things are restored, we may still sweat a little, but we don't earn our living by the sweat of our brow (as God told Adam he would do after he had brought the curse upon himself). We live by our faith in the blessing, and our increase comes from God, not from our abilities or hard work.

Do we still work? Of course. And I have worked plenty hard at times. But renewing our thinking in this area will enable us to prosper beyond our means or expectations, in every area of our lives.

We are the blessed. We can't lose for winning. We can't go under for going over. Glory to God! ✠

KINGDOM MANNA: Reading 44

Totally Dependent on God

And the children of Israel did eat manna forty years, until they came to a land inhabited; they did eat manna, until they came unto the borders of the land of Canaan. Exodus 16:35

And the Lord said, I have surely seen the affliction of my people which are in Egypt, and have heard their cry by reason of their taskmasters; for I know their sorrows; and I am come down to deliver them out of the hand of the Egyptians, and to bring them up out of that land unto a good land and a large, unto a land flowing with milk and honey;

unto the place of the Canaanites, and the Hittites, and the Amorites, and the Perizzites, and the Hivites, and the Jebusites.

Exodus 3:7-8

Now the LORD had said unto Abram, Get thee out of thy country, and from thy kindred, and from thy father's house, unto a land that I will shew thee. And I will make of thee a great nation, and I will bless thee, and make thy name great; and thou shalt be a blessing: and I will bless them that bless thee, and curse him that curseth thee: and in thee shall all families of the earth be blessed. Genesis 12:1-3

And these all, having obtained a good report through faith, received not the promise: God having provided some better thing for us, that they without us should not be made perfect. Hebrews 11:39-40

All the promises of God in him [Jesus] *are yea, and in him amen unto the glory of God by us.* 2 Corinthians 1:20

Are you seeing a pattern here? Are you getting the bigger picture? Is your vision being expanded to the panoramic view?

God made Abraham a promise and established a covenant relationship with him. While that covenant promise benefitted him much in his lifetime, Abraham didn't see the complete fulfillment of it in his lifetime. The fulfillment of it would be realized by his descendants and many others that would become his descendants by faith, eventually bringing about the restitution of all things (see Acts 3:21).

Did the fact that Abraham didn't see the fulfillment of God's promise to him in his lifetime cause that promise to be any less true? Of course not!

122

Abraham was blessed by God. The blessing of Abraham was really the blessing of God on Abraham's life. This is the same blessing we carry today, but now it is a more powerful blessing because we are on the other side of the cross and the resurrection of Jesus. While this blessing empowered Abraham to get more "stuff" and to die a very rich man, the purpose of all that "stuff" was to establish the Kingdom of God on earth:

But thou shalt remember the LORD thy God: for it is he that giveth thee power to get wealth, that he may establish his covenant which he sware unto thy fathers, as it is this day. Deuteronomy 8:18

Abraham was one piece of a puzzle that God has been assembling for six thousand years. Israel was and is another piece of that puzzle. Even Jesus, in His first coming to earth, was a pivotal piece of that puzzle. Since His first coming, the picture has been getting clearer and clearer, as more and more pieces fall into place. What we are seeing today is clearer than the generation before us saw. That is why it is so important that we realize we cannot camp out in past revelation. We must continue to build upon it ... until we see the completed picture.

Our focus has to be on the Kingdom and the completion or perfection of the Kingdom on earth. First, the Kingdom must be completed or perfected in us individually and corporately, and then it will be manifested on earth in such a way as to impact all nations. Only then will the promise that God made to Abraham be fulfilled:

As for me, behold, my covenant is with thee, and thou shalt be a father of many nations. Genesis 17:4

Abraham could not bring the promise of God to pass in his lifetime. All he could do was obey and believe God. And the same is true with us. Like Israel in the wilderness, we are totally dependent upon God to fulfill His promises. ✝

Totally Dependent on God 2

Now the Lord *had said unto Abram, Get thee out of thy country, and from thy kindred, and from thy father's house, unto a land that I will shew thee. And I will make of thee a great nation, and I will bless thee, and make thy name great; and thou shalt be a blessing: and I will bless them that bless thee, and curse him that curseth thee: and in thee shall all families of the earth be blessed.*   Genesis 12:1-3

And these all, having obtained a good report through faith, received not the promise: God having provided some better thing for us, that they without us should not be made perfect.   Hebrews 11:39-40

All the promises of God in him [Jesus] *are yea, and in him amen unto the glory of God by us.*   2 Corinthians 1:20

The pattern these scriptures show us is a process. In order to see and understand that process, we must see the bigger picture, the panoramic view.

I am a citizen of the United States, and our society has become one of instant everything. We have microwave ovens to quickly heat and cook our food. We go to fast-food restaurants. And we want instant success.

My parents married very young and started out in an upstairs apartment, living over their landlord. When I was very young, they lived with a relative for a while and then bought a very small three-bedroom house with one bath. We had a washing machine but no dryer. Wet clothes were hung on a clothesline in the backyard. I was fourteen years old before they built their dream house, which my mother was able to live in until she moved to another dimension (Heaven).

Before the most recent recession, perhaps the worst in the history of the United States, young couples in this country married, expecting to start out with everything, much more than their parents accumulated over many years. Often, starting out that way meant going deeply into debt, and many are suffering the consequences now.

As citizens of the Kingdom of God I think we probably all like getting instant answers to our prayers, but I have found that, more often than not, the manifestation of the promises of God in my life require a process that takes time. Like Joseph, I have to be prepared and positioned for increase and promotion.

In the bigger scope of things, the Kingdom of God coming on earth as in Heaven works the same way. We are in a process that will play out on God's timetable. It is just as He has planned, but He cannot manifest it in fullness or completely until the appointed time.

We may be the generation that will see the full manifestation of the Kingdom coming on earth as in Heaven, or we may be just another piece of the puzzle, fulfilling our purpose, but not experiencing God's completed purpose for mankind in our lifetime on earth.

While Abraham became very wealthy, he died without seeing the promise God had made him come to pass. Abraham was a part of the process that would one day bring that promise to pass. Even when his descendants took possession of the land of Canaan, they, too, were a part of the process, and not the complete fulfillment of it.

When Jesus went to the cross, enabling the blessing of Abraham to come on the nations, He, too, was but another piece of the puzzle. However, He was a pivotal piece of that puzzle that made it possible for us to get a glimpse of and a taste of the fulfillment of the promise God made to Abraham four thousand years ago. Surely we were born for such a time as this! ⚜

KINGDOM MANNA: Reading 46

What is the Promise?

And these all, having obtained a good report through faith, received not the promise: God having provided some better thing for us, that they without us should not be made perfect.   Hebrews 11:39-40

And when Abram was ninety years old and nine, the LORD appeared to Abram, and said unto him, I am the Almighty God; walk before me, and be thou perfect. And I will make my covenant between me and thee, and will multiply thee exceedingly. And Abram fell on his face: and God talked with him, saying, As for me, behold, my covenant is with thee, and thou shalt be a father of many nations.   Genesis 17:1-4

God made a promise to Abraham and then cut a covenant with him to guarantee that promise. He blessed Abraham, who became a carrier of that blessing. Part of that promise/blessing was concerning his immediate descendants, who became the nation of Israel, but the full blessing was for all nations. Jesus went to the cross so the blessing of Abraham could come on the nations (Gentiles) (see Galatians 3:13-14), enabling all to receive the **promise of the Spirit.**

John the Baptist called Jesus, "*he which baptizeth with the Holy Ghost*" (John 1:33). Jesus said, "*But ye shall receive power, after that the Holy Ghost [Spirit] is come upon you: and ye shall be witnesses unto me both in Jerusalem, and in all Judea, and in Samaria, and unto the utter most part of the earth*" (Acts 1:8). On the Day of Pentecost, when the Spirit was given and the Church was born, the apostle Peter said, "*For the promise is unto you, and to your children, and to all that are afar off, even as many as the Lord our God shall call*" (Acts 2:39).

The writer of Hebrews told us this:

> But this man [Jesus], *after he had offered one sacrifice for sins for ever, sat down on the right hand of God; from henceforth expecting till his enemies be made his footstool. For by one offering he hath **perfected** for ever them that are sanctified. Whereof the Holy Ghost also is a witness to us: for after that he had said before, This is the covenant that I will make with them after those days, saith the Lord, I will put my laws into their hearts, and in their minds will I write them.*

> Hebrews 10:12-16, Emphasis added

The Law was given to show man his need for a Savior, but man, in his fallen state, could not obey the Law. Even if he did, somehow, by sheer determination, do the right things, there was still the issue of his heart, which was evil. Obedience to the Law was not enough to bring perfection. It took a changing of the heart, which was not possible before Jesus became sin for us, enabling us to be perfected:

> *For the law made nothing perfect, but the bringing in of a better hope did; by the which we draw nigh unto God.*   Hebrews 7:19

So, by receiving the Holy Spirit we are born again (see John 20:22), which enables us to see the Kingdom (see John 3:3) and receive the blessing (see Galatians 3:13-14). By being baptized with the Holy Spirit, which is a separate event from receiving the Holy Spirit, we receive power to carry and proclaim the blessing to the world (see Acts 1:8), establishing the Kingdom on earth as it is in Heaven. But the promise of the Spirit is not the completion of the promise God made to Abraham; it is the means to the completion of that promise.

When Jesus offered Himself as the sacrifice for sin, He perfected those who are sanctified (see Hebrews 10:14). Who are those who are sanctified? They are simply those whom God has chosen to become like Him.

So, the promise that the covenant guarantees is perfection, not only for us individually, and not only for the Church corporately, but for all things (see Revelation 21:1-3).

Abraham died without reaching it. Israel has not yet reached it. The Church (while we are already there positionally) has not yet reached it experientially. But we will. Glory to God! ✣

What is the Promise? 2

And these all, having obtained a good report through faith, received not the promise: God having provided some better thing for us, that they without us should not be made perfect.   Hebrews 11:39-40

And when Abram was ninety years old and nine, the LORD appeared to Abram, and said unto him, I am the Almighty God; walk before me, and be thou perfect. And I will make my covenant between me and thee, and will multiply thee exceedingly. And Abram fell on his face: and God talked with him, saying, As for me, behold, my covenant is with thee, and thou shalt be a father of many nations.

Genesis 17:1-4

Christ hath redeemed us from the curse of the law, being made a curse for us; for it is written, Cursed is every one that hangeth on a tree: that the blessing of Abraham might come on the Gentiles through Jesus Christ; that we, might receive the promise of the Spirit through faith.

Galatians 3:13-14

In our last teaching, we noted that the promise of the Spirit is not the completion of the promise God made to Abraham. It is the means to the completion of that promise. The completion of that promise is perfection. Jesus said:

> *Be ye therefore perfect, even as your Father which is in heaven is perfect.*
>
> Matthew 5:48

Perfection is the nature or character of God. The Law reveals the character of God, and when we obey the Law, not just out of duty or determination, but because it is who we are (it is written in our minds as a result of having been put in our hearts, see Hebrews 10:16), we are perfected. We become like God.

A thorough study of the Genesis account will reveal that Adam was created in the image of God (being His representative on earth) but not in the likeness of God (possessing His character). Why? Because image can be created, but character has to be developed. While the first Adam was made in the image of God, it took the last Adam (Jesus, see 1 Corinthians 15:45) to enable a people to become the likeness of God, possessing His character.

While on the cross, Jesus said, *"It is finished."* There is nothing else required for us to be perfected. His position is that it is a done deal and that should be our position as well. However, there is the process of walking out this truth in our daily lives, which is actually a process of bringing us into perfection.

Jesus is the Author and the Finisher of our faith (see Hebrews 12:2). Only He could position us for perfection, and only He can bring us to perfection. We are, therefore, totally dependent on Him. It is only by His mercy that this is even possible, and only by His grace that we can attain it.

The feasts of the Old Testament are a picture of the New Testament Church. Passover has to do with receiving the Holy Spirit and being born again, made possible by the crucifixion and resurrection of Jesus. Pentecost has to do with being baptized with the Holy Spirit and the Church Age. Tabernacles has to do with God dwelling with and in His people in fullness, bringing them to perfection. We have experienced Passover and Pentecost. In this, the third day (millennium) of the Church (see 2 Peter 3:8), we will experience Tabernacles as we transition from the Church Age into the Kingdom Age. The promise God made to Abraham will be fulfilled and brought to completion or perfection. Surely we were born for such a time as this! All glory to God! ✝

KINGDOM MANNA: READING 48

THE CHOICE

And, behold, one [a young man] *came and said unto him* [Jesus], *Good Master, what good thing shall I do, that I may have eternal life?*

And he [Jesus] *said unto him, Why callest thou me good? There is none good but one, that is, God: but if thou wilt enter into life, keep the commandments.*

He [the young man] *saith unto him, Which?*

Jesus said, Thou shalt do no murder, thou shalt not commit adultery, thou shalt not steal, thou shalt not bear false witness, honour thy father and thy mother: and, thou shalt love thy neighbour as thyself.

The young man saith unto him, All these things have I kept from my youth up: what lack I yet?

Jesus said unto him, If thou wilt be perfect, go and sell that thou hast, and give to the poor, and thou shalt have treasure in heaven: and come and follow me.

But when the young man heard that saying, he went away sorrowful: for he had great possessions.　　　　　　　　Matthew 19:16-22

Then said Jesus unto his disciples, Verily I say unto you, that a rich man shall hardly enter into the kingdom of heaven. And again I say unto you, it is easier for a camel to go through the eye of a needle, than for a rich man to enter into the kingdom of God.

When his disciples heard it, they were exceedingly amazed, saying, Who then can be saved?

But Jesus beheld them, and said unto them, With men this is impossible; but with God all things are possible.　　　　Matthew 19:23-26

At first reading this story might seem to be in contradiction to our recent study of the blessing. Didn't God say that He gives power to get wealth to establish His covenant (see Deuteronomy 8:18)? But here we have Jesus saying it is almost impossible for a rich man to enter the Kingdom. Even Jesus' disciples were perplexed by these words.

You must remember that these were Jewish businessmen who most likely knew and understood the Abrahamic covenant. They were not poor boys. While they had left their businesses to follow Jesus, they hadn't given up their businesses to follow Him. After the crucifixion, the fishermen in the group went back to their fishing boats, so they still owned them. Perhaps others had continued with their businesses in their absence.

Even Jesus was a businessman, a carpenter by trade, and I would be very surprised if He wasn't very successful at it. So why would He make such a statement? And why would He tell the rich man he had to sell everything and give it all to the poor?

In the last two KINGDOM MANNA's we established that perfection was the promise God made to Abraham. Jesus told the rich man that being perfect depended on his selling everything, giving the money to the poor and following Him. But was the issue here possessions? I think not. It appears to me the issue here was the man's heart. There is nothing wrong with having possessions. The problem arises when possessions have us. Money or wealth is not evil. Money can do much good. It is the love of money that is not only evil; it is the root of all evil (see 1 Timothy 6:10).

Why is this? Because the love of money reveals the condition of the heart. You cannot serve God and money (see Matthew 6:24 and Luke 16:13).

Why do people love money? Because they are self-centered and selfish individuals. Money fuels that selfishness. It can provide pleasure, comfort and protection. It can buy power and friends (but not true friends). It gives one a sense of self-sufficiency and self-worth. Self, self, self! Self is the enemy of God. Self says, "I can do it without God. I can get it without God." Self has to die in order for us to truly serve God or to even know Him.

So the question is not, "Does money have us?" The question is, "Does God have us?" Even poor people can be very self-centered and selfish.

In order to be perfected we must be God-centered and godly, not self-centered and selfish. To be God-centered is to have God's character with His laws in our hearts and written on our minds (see Hebrews 10:16). The Promised Land that Abraham was promised by God was much more than a geographical location. It was a state of being. It was and is perfection. ✤

THE CHOICE 2

And, behold, one [a young man] *came and said unto him* [Jesus], *Good Master, what good thing shall I do, that I may have eternal life?*

And he [Jesus] *said unto him, Why callest thou me good? There is none good but one, that is, God: but if thou wilt enter into life, keep the commandments.*

He [the young man] *saith unto him, Which?*

Jesus said, Thou shalt do no murder, thou shalt not commit adultery, thou shalt not steal, thou shalt not bear false witness, honour thy father and thy mother: and, thou shalt love thy neighbour as thyself.

The young man saith unto him, All these things have I kept from my youth up: what lack I yet?

Jesus said unto him, If thou wilt be perfect, go and sell that thou hast, and give to the poor, and thou shalt have treasure in heaven: and come and follow me.

But when the young man heard that saying, he went away sorrowful: for he had great possessions. Matthew 19:16-22

Then said Jesus unto his disciples, Verily I say unto you, that a rich man shall hardly enter into the kingdom of heaven. And again I say unto you, it is easier for a camel to go through the eye of a needle, than for a rich man to enter into the kingdom of God.

When his disciples heard it, they were exceedingly amazed, saying, Who then can be saved?

But Jesus beheld them, and said unto them, With men this is impossible; but with God all things are possible.　　　　　　Matthew 19:23-26

In our last teaching, we noted that money is not evil. It is the love of money fueled by selfishness that is not only evil, but also the root of all evil.

The thing Jesus required of the rich young man revealed his heart. Because of the condition of his heart, he obviously made the wrong choice. The young man didn't realize that had he given up all to follow Jesus, he would have received much more in return (see Mark 10:29-31). How sad!

While we can choose to serve and obey God, the walking out of that choice is not something we can accomplish. We are totally dependent upon God to bring it to pass in our lives.

Jesus made it possible. Because of Jesus, God already considers us perfect (see 2 Corinthians 5:21), but in order to experience that perfection we must have a change of mind. And that is only possible when we have a change of heart:

This is the covenant that I will make with them after those days, saith the Lord, I will put my laws into their hearts, and in their minds will I write them.　　　　　　Hebrews 10:16

Receiving the Holy Spirit and being born again is but the door into the process of becoming like God, possessing His nature and character. Character cannot be created. Character has to be developed. God knows how to get us from where we are to where we are going. Jesus is the Author and the Finisher of our faith (see Hebrews 12:2).

The destination of our journey, which is perfection, will culminate in this, the third day (millennium) of the Church, which is the "*after those days*" mentioned in Hebrews 10:16. *Those days* refers to the first two days (two-thousand years) of the Church. The first two days of the Church were the fulfillment of Pentecost. The third day of the Church will be the fulfillment of Tabernacles, which is our destiny, glory to God!

Brethren, I count not myself to have apprehended: but this one thing I do, forgetting those things which are behind, and reaching forth unto those things which are before, I press toward the mark for the prize of the high calling of God in Christ Jesus. Let us therefore, as many as be perfect, be thus minded: and if in any thing ye be otherwise minded, God shall reveal even this unto you. Nevertheless, whereto we have already attained, let us walk by the same rule, let us mind the same thing.

Philippians 3:13-16

KINGDOM MANNA: Reading 50

The Transfer of Wealth

*A good man leaveth an inheritance for his children's children: and **the wealth of the sinner is laid up for the just.***

Proverbs 13:22, Emphasis added

He that by usery and unjust gain increaseth his substance, he shall gather it for him that will pity the poor.   Proverbs 28:8

For I was envious at the foolish, when I saw the prosperity of the wicked.   Psalm 73:3

The blessing of the LORD, it maketh rich, and he addeth no sorrow with it.   Proverbs 10:22

Have you ever wondered why the wicked seem to prosper, while the righteous seem to struggle? Has that ever bothered you? Did you know that the wicked rich have a call of God on their lives? They are called to store up wealth for the righteous. Once you realize that truth, you will no longer be envious of the prosperity of the wicked. Instead, you will begin to expect their wealth to be transferred to the righteous.

We have already studied how the blessing produces prosperity, and we have studied how the covenant we have with God and the Holy Spirit enables us to walk in the blessing. This is something we grow into. We saw that process in motion, as we studied the life of Joseph. Through the process of trials and victories, Joseph was placed in a position that gave him control over all the wealth of Egypt. Because of that position of authority, Joseph himself became a wealthy man and was a blessing, not only to Egypt, but also to other nations. He was able to save many from famine, including his own father and brothers.

Many of us today have been and are going through a process as well. If we will continue growing and maturing, overcoming by faith and walking in victory, I believe we, too, will prosper and reach a season in our lives at which we no longer experience lack or just barely getting by. Instead, we will have abundance in every area of our lives, which will enable us to be a blessing to many. Not only will we be a blessing; we will use our wealth and authority to establish God's covenant on earth (see Deuteronomy 8:18) and bring His kingdom on earth as it is in Heaven:

Be not deceived; God is not mocked: for whatsoever a man soweth, that shall he also reap. For he that soweth to his flesh shall of the flesh reap corruption; but he that soweth to the Spirit shall of the Spirit reap life everlasting. And let us not be weary in well doing: for in due season we shall reap, if we faint not. Galatians 6:7-9

KINGDOM MANNA: Reading 51

The Transfer of Wealth 2

Be not deceived; God is not mocked: for whatsoever a man soweth, that shall he also reap. For he that soweth to his flesh shall of the flesh reap corruption; but he that soweth to the Spirit shall of the Spirit reap life everlasting. And let us not be weary in well doing: for in due season we shall reap, if we faint not. Galatians 6:7-9

*A good man leaveth an inheritance for his children's children: and **the wealth of the sinner is laid up for the just.***

Proverbs 13:22, Emphasis added

He that by usery and unjust gain increaseth his substance, he shall gather it for him that will pity the poor. Proverbs 28:8

The blessing of the LORD, it maketh rich, and he addeth no sorrow with it. Proverbs 10:22

The wicked may prosper for a season, but eventually they will reap the fruit of their wickedness. And if we continue sowing to the Spirit, without giving up (fainting), we will receive life that is everlasting.

One of *Webster's* many definitions of *life* is "the force or principle that makes or keeps something or someone alive." To sow to the Spirit entails everything that makes us alive and keeps us alive. To sow to the Spirit causes our soul (mind) to prosper, and as our soul prospers, we will prosper in every area of life — if we continue without giving up (see 3 John 2).

However, I believe there is coming a time when there will be a supernatural or spiritual transfer of wealth from the Babylonian or world system into the Kingdom of God. I believe it will happen very quickly. While it will more than likely be the result of things that have been in motion for a long time, it will seem to happen almost overnight.

This won't be the first time it has happened. When the Israelites came out of bondage in Egypt, they went from being slaves to being a wealthy nation in one night:

Who hath heard such a thing? Who hath seen such things? Shall the earth be made to bring forth in one day? Or shall a nation be born at once? For as soon as Zion travailed, she brought forth her children.

Isaiah 66:8

The nation of Israel was born in one day and came out of Egypt with great wealth. And that wasn't the first time someone had come out of Egypt with great wealth. Remember Abram? It also wasn't the last time God plundered Egypt to prosper His people. In 1967 Egypt, along with other nations, came against Israel with plans to push the Jews into the sea. Instead, in just three days, tiny Israel conquered the invading armies, captured Jerusalem, and then spent three more days cleaning up, sending the Egyptians walking home across the desert, minus their weapons.

What God has done in the past He can do again. He wants us to be a blessing, establishing His covenant and Kingdom on earth, and He will place the necessary means in our hands to accomplish His purposes and plans.

It is time for us to declare it, to prophesy it, and to speak it into existence. We have been and continue to be prepared to receive it. Surely we were born for such a time as this! ✠

KINGDOM MANNA: READING 52

FROM NOT ENOUGH TO JUST ENOUGH TO MORE THAN ENOUGH

And the LORD said [to Moses], I have seen the affliction of my people which are in Egypt, and have heard their cry by reason of their taskmasters; for I know their sorrows; and I am come down to deliver them out of the hand of the Egyptians, and to bring them up out of that land unto a good land and a large, unto a land flowing with milk and honey. Exodus 3:7-8

And I will give this people favour in the sight of the Egyptians: and
it shall come to pass, that, when ye go, ye shall not go empty: but every
woman shall borrow of her neighbour, and of her that sojourneth in
her house, jewels of silver, and jewels of gold, and raiment: and ye shall
put them upon your sons, and upon your daughters; and ye shall spoil
the Egyptians.   Exodus 3:21-22

Not only did God bring the Israelites out of Egypt as a wealthy nation; He sent them on a journey to a wealthy place. He brought them out of Egypt with supernatural wealth and protection and led them through the wilderness with His visible glory as a cloud by day and column of fire by night. What an awesome experience that must have been! And yet, they complained continually and didn't trust Moses or God.

Then, when they arrived at the Promised Land, only two men out of the whole nation thought they could take the land and defeat the inhabitants who were dwelling there. After all the miracles they had seen God perform, they acted with fear and refused to take the land God had promised them. They even wanted to return to Egypt. So God sentenced the entire adult generation (except for Joshua and Caleb, who believed God and wanted to take the land) to wander in the wilderness until they died. He then started over with a new generation that would enter the land.

In Egypt the Israelites had been in bondage and had suffered much lack. In the wilderness, they had only enough to survive. (The manna would last only one day, except for the day before the Sabbath.) While their provision was supernatural, it was only enough. It wasn't until the next generation went into the Promised Land that they had abundance.

Is that not the same process many of us have been through and continue to go through? We start in bondage to sin and many times in poverty and lack. We accept Jesus, are delivered from the bondage of sin, get some revelation on the blessing that is ours, and begin to walk in it. But, it seems, we reach a point where we are barely getting by. We may even receive supernatural provision from time to time, but we still have just enough. The Word tells us we can have abundance, but it always seems to be just out of our reach. So how do we get from just enough to more than enough? The same way we get anything else from God, by faith and obedience.

First of all, we must believe that God wants us living in abundance. *Webster* defines *abundance* as "an extremely plentiful or over-sufficient quantity or supply; overflowing fullness; affluence; wealth." In other words, abundance is too much. Glory to God!

In John 10:10, Jesus said, *"I am come that they might have life, and that they might have it more abundantly."* In the 14th and 15th chapters of John's account of the Gospel Jesus tells us that we can have whatever we ask of Him, if we abide in Him, His words abide in us, and we obey His commands.

God wants us living in abundance, but nothing in the Kingdom of God is automatic. There are conditions to receiving from God. First of all, we must believe him. That comes by abiding in His Word and having His Word abiding in us.

According to *Webster*, to *abide* is "to stay, continue or dwell." We literally must live in the Word of God, and His Word must live in us. We must become one with the Word to the point that faith is not something we have to work at or something to be acquired; it becomes a part of us. It is who we are. We are people of faith. We are the blessed. Glory to God! ✠

From Not Enough, to Just Enough, to More than Enough 2

And the LORD said [to Moses], *I have seen the affliction of my people which are in Egypt, and have heard their cry by reason of their taskmasters; for I know their sorrows; and I am come down to deliver them out of the hand of the Egyptians, and to bring them up out of that land unto a good land and a large, unto a land flowing with milk and honey.*

Exodus 3:7-8

And I will give this people favour in the sight of the Egyptians: and it shall come to pass, that, when ye go, ye shall not go empty: but every woman shall borrow of her neighbour, and of her that sojourneth in her house, jewels of silver, and jewels of gold, and raiment: and ye shall put them upon your sons, and upon your daughters; and ye shall spoil the Egyptians.

Exodus 3:21-22

For as many as are led by the Spirit of God, they are the sons [mature children] *of God.*

Romans 8:14

Israel's prosperity (success) depended on their obedience to the commands or instructions they received from God. We, too, must walk in obedience, not only to the written Word, but also to the leading of the Holy Spirit, in order to be successful in every area of our lives.

We must see ourselves as God sees us, as carriers of the blessing. And we must follow the leading of the Holy Spirit. He knows where the bargains are and where the wealth is. He knows how to position us to receive whatever it is we need in order to accomplish whatever it is we are called and anointed to do. It can come naturally, or it can come supernaturally. He is our supply. He is our provision. He is more than enough. Bless the Lord!

My God shall supply all your need according to his riches in glory by Christ Jesus.   Philippians 4:19

Notice that *need* in this Scripture is singular and not plural. We have only one need, and that is to be one with our Creator and Lord. To be one with Him means there is no difference in Him and us. Yes, He is the head, and we are the Body, but one without the other cannot exist. We are only complete (perfect) in Him, and He will only be completed (perfected) in us:

Behold, I cast out devils, and I do cures to day and to morrow, and the third day I shall be perfected.   Jesus in Luke 13:32

This is a prophetic scripture that has more than one application. While Jesus may have been referring to His crucifixion and resurrection, the stronger application of this scripture refers to the third day (millennium) of the Church, which we are now entering. It is in this third day that we will be perfected, because in this third day He will be perfected in a people, bringing about the glorious Church that Paul spoke of in

Ephesians 5:27. Saints, there is no lack in perfection. To be one with Him is to have all our need supplied. We are in a process of going from just enough to more than enough. Glory to God! ✠

OUR SUPPLY

My God shall supply all your need according to his riches in glory by Christ Jesus. Philippians 4:19

But seek ye first the kingdom of God, and his righteousness; and all these things shall be added unto you. Matthew 6:33

In Paul's letter to the Philippians, he said, *"My God shall supply all your need."* How many times have you heard this misquoted as "My God shall supply all your needs"? But *need* is not plural here; it is singular. We only have one need, and that is to know Him intimately, becoming one with Him. Everything else we need is in that relationship. When we become one with Him, everything He is and everything He has is available to us.

To become one with Him in an intimate relationship is to experience His riches in glory, or the riches of His glory (see Ephesians 3:16). The word that translates as *glory* also translates as *goodness* and *wealth*. So God supplies our need, which is intimacy with Him, according to His riches in His glory/goodness/wealth, by Christ (the Anointed) Jesus.

We are one with Jesus (see John 17:21-22), and therefore we share in His anointing. It is because of our participation in His anointing that we experience intimacy with God because of or according to the riches that are in His glory/goodness/wealth.

In other words, it is all about Him. Nothing else matters. When our lives are entirely wrapped up in and dependent on Him, He becomes entirely wrapped up in and dependent on us. Yes, God needs us. He is love (see 1 John 4:8 and 16), and love needs someone to love. That's why He has established an everlasting covenant relationship with us that can never be broken. And that's why He is all we need.

To seek first the Kingdom of God and His righteousness is to seek Him. Everything we need is in Him. We've got to stop reading the Bible as a how-to book and start reading it as a love letter from our Beloved. Yes, there are many instructions and promises in the Bible, but it is only as we comprehend it in the context of an intimate relationship with Him that it comes alive in us and produces life:

In the last day, that great day of the feast [this was the Feast of Tabernacles and is a type and shadow of where we are and what we are coming into historically and prophetically at the present time], *Jesus stood and cried, saying, If any man thirst, let him come unto me, and drink. He that believeth on me, as the scripture hath said, out of his belly shall flow rivers of living water.*   John 7:37-38

My beloved is mine, and I am his. He brought me to the banqueting house, and his banner over me was love.

Song of Solomon 2:16 and 4

Bless the Lord! ✠

A Prayer for Your Success

(Please note that the terms *man* or *men* are not used in this teaching in the context of gender, but, rather, in the context of mankind, which includes men and women.)

For this cause I bow my knees unto the Father of our Lord Jesus Christ, of whom the whole family in heaven and earth is named.

Ephesians 3:14-15

When we were born into the family of God, we received His name — Jesus, in the Greek, or Yeshua, in the Hebrew. We have every right to walk in and use the authority and power in that name.

That he should grant you, according to the riches of his glory, to be strengthened with might by his Spirit in the inner man.

Ephesians 3:16

Our inner man is the real us. It is our spirit man. We are not human beings that have a spirit; we are a spirit that has a soul (mind) and lives in a body. Our spirit is strengthened by His Spirit, according to the riches of His glory. That is why the baptism with the Holy Spirit is not an option for the believer; it is a necessity. This is where we get the strength to be mighty men of God.

But the baptism with the Spirit is not an end in and of itself. It is a beginning. It is the beginning of the coming of the Lord in us, in fullness, bringing us to maturity so the sons (mature children) of God can be manifested on earth (see Romans 8:19). This process will not only manifest Christ in us (see Colossians 1:25-29), but will cause the knowledge of His glory to be known throughout the earth (see Habakkuk 2:14). Glory to God!

That Christ may dwell in your hearts by faith. Ephesians 3:17

Christ is the English version of the Greek word *Christos*, which means *the Anointed One*. Since we are partakers of that anointing, we can say that Christ means *the Anointed One* and His anointing. So the same anointing that Jesus has, which is also our anointing, lives in our hearts (inner man, spirit) by faith. We receive His anointing by faith.

The anointing is not something we can see, so we must accept it by faith. However, we can see and feel the results of that anointing. Glory to God!

That ye, being rooted and grounded in love, may be able to comprehend with all saints what is the breadth, and length, and depth, and height; and to know the love of Christ, which passeth knowledge, that ye might be filled with all the fulness of God. Ephesians 3:17-19

Faith works by love (see Galatians 5:6), and God is love (see 1 John 4:8 and 16), therefore it is absolutely necessary for us to be well rooted and completely grounded in love. This makes it possible for us to understand the width, length, depth and height (that's all of it) and to know the love of the Anointed One and His anointing.

The word *know* here implies intimacy. Adam knew Eve and she conceived (see Genesis 4:1). To know the love of Christ is to have an intimate relationship with Him. Out of that intimacy comes a complete understanding of His love, of who He is and who we are in Him. That kind of understanding only comes from the Spirit, and it passes knowledge. It cannot be understood with the intellect alone. It can only be known by revelation, which grows out of intimacy.

The result of knowing the love of Christ is that we become filled with all the fullness of God. All the fullness of God means all the fullness of God! *All* means all there is. Glory to God!

Are you grasping this? We are filled with *all* the fullness of God! What else is there? What more could we want or need? Nothing is impossible for us! We lack nothing! We need nothing! It can't get any better than that! Truly He is our only need, and truly He is more than enough! Hallelujah! ☩

A Prayer for Your Success 2

In our last teaching, we looked at a prayer the apostle Paul prayed for the Church at Ephesus (which is also a prayer for our success today). However, we didn't complete that prayer. What we read was wonderful, but listen to this. It gets even better ... if that's possible. And it is!

Now unto him that is able to do exceeding abundantly above all that we ask or think, according to the power that worketh in us, unto him be glory in the church by Christ Jesus throughout all ages, world without end. Amen. Ephesians 3:20-21

He is able to do far more than we can ask or even think of! Think about that. What can you think of? How much can you ask for? He's able to do more! How? According to the power that works in us. That would be the power of the Holy Spirit, the name of Jesus, the anointing of Jesus, the very character and love of God Himself. Hallelujah!

Unto Him be glory/goodness/wealth (the word that translates as glory also translates as goodness and wealth) in the Church. The Church is the Body of Christ on earth. Because the Father, Son and Holy Spirit are one, and we are one with them, when Paul says *"unto him,"* he is saying unto the Father, Son and Holy Spirit and unto us. So we could say, "Unto us be glory/goodness/wealth." How? By knowing (having an intimate relationship and being one with) God by the anointed Jesus.

You see, we are not only the Body of Christ. Today there is a remnant that is becoming the Bride of Christ. Meditate on that for a while.

Now listen to this: He is not only able to do far more than we can ask or think now, but throughout all ages, world without end. How many ages are there, and how long will they continue? I don't know how many ages there are, but I know they will continue forever. The world will never end.

As we walk more and more in the manifestation of this prayer that Paul originally prayed for the Ephesians, know that what is taking place in us and through us and because of us has no end. Our future is not doom and gloom. Our future is the eternal Kingdom of God on earth as it is in Heaven and wherever else we may travel and dwell in the universe during eternity, which has no beginning and no end. Hallelujah!

Bless the Lord! All glory to God! Hallelujah! Hallelujah! Hallelujah! ✤

BEING AN OVERCOMER

In the world ye shall have tribulation: but be of good cheer; I have overcome the world. Jesus in John 16:33

For whatsoever is born of God overcometh the world: and this is the victory that overcometh the world, even our faith. Who is he that overcometh the world, but he that believeth that Jesus is the Son of God?

1 John 5:4-5

Webster says that *overcome* means "to get the better of in a struggle or conflict; conquer; defeat. To prevail over opposition, a debility, temptations, etc. To gain the victory; win; conquer." Breaking the word down, to overcome something means to come over it. Not just to get on top of it but to get on top of it and then go on over it, to get beyond it.

Look at *Webster's* definition again. You can't get the better of something or someone in a struggle or conflict without there being a struggle or conflict. You can't prevail over opposition without experiencing opposition. You can't gain a victory without facing a battle.

Battles are not usually won in a day. Some take years. I have come to realize that overcoming my flesh, the world and the devil is a continuing process. I haven't yet arrived. Therefore I must say with the apostle Paul, *"I die daily"* (1 Corinthians 15:31).

In the United States and many other countries today we have become instant societies. We want everything right now. I remember when the first McDonald's came to my hometown as a young boy. The owner of a local barbecue restaurant made the statement that McDonald's wouldn't last long. He said people wouldn't go for that *fast food*. But guess what? McDonald's is still there, and the barbecue restaurant is long gone.

We want everything to happen right now because we don't like to wait. Have you ever heard the saying, "If something is worth having, it is worth waiting for?" The Scriptures teach:

But they that wait upon the LORD shall renew their strength; they shall mount up with wings as eagles; they shall run, and not be weary; and they shall walk, and not faint. Isaiah 40:31

Each of us has a purpose, and God has a plan for our lives. If we will allow patience to work in our lives (see Luke 21:19), possessing our souls (see James 1:4), we will one day be able to say with Paul, *"I have fought a good fight, I have finished my course, I have kept the faith"* (2 Timothy 4:7). Glory to God! ✠

WAITING ON THE LORD

But they that wait upon the LORD shall renew their strength; they shall mount up with wings as eagles; they shall run, and not be weary; and they shall walk, and not faint. Isaiah 40:31

In our last teaching, I used this scripture in the context of patiently waiting for the Lord, referring to the process that we go through to become overcomers, mature and positioned for ministry. However, a more correct translation of the word *wait* in this scripture is to wait upon the Lord much like a waiter waits on a table. Some other scriptures that use this Hebrew word for *wait* refer to the priests that served in the Temple, waiting (or serving) at the altar. So we could read the scripture like this: "They that *serve* the Lord shall renew their strength."

Webster says *to serve* means "to act as a servant; to wait on a table, as a waiter; to render assistance, be of use, help; to go through a term of service, such as a soldier, senator, juror, etc.; to have a definite use (this cup will *serve* as a sugar bowl); to be favorable, suitable or convenient, such as being on time; to render obedience, respect or reverence to God; to contribute to or promote as to *serve* a cause; to treat in a specific manner; to gratify the desires, wants, needs of another; to mate with."

So the word *wait* here implies actively ministering to (serving) others while being intimate with God. It is not a passive waiting, expecting

God to do something. It is an active relationship that entails our walking out the covenant we have with God, which has two aspects. The vertical aspect of that covenant is between God and us. The horizontal aspect is between us and all other believers.

If this is our focus, rather than the adverse circumstances we sometimes find ourselves in, we will get through and overcome the adverse circumstances. The life that is within us, which is the life of the Lord Himself, will issue out of us, and we will overcome in spite of our circumstances.

I have found that when challenges come my way (I don't even like to call them trials anymore), I don't begin to question God as to what has gone wrong. I just continue to serve Him, primarily through thanksgiving, praise and worship born out of the deep, passionate love I have for Him, and to serve my fellow believers in the Body of Christ. Many times I have seen circumstances change without taking any other action.

If we have missed something that has opened the door to the challenge we find ourselves in, the Spirit of God will reveal that to us as we continue to serve Him. Then we can simply make the necessary adjustment and continue on.

Now, in the next reading, let's look at Paul and Silas in Macedonia and how they overcame a severe challenge by continuing to serve the Lord. ✠

WAITING ON THE LORD 2

But they that wait upon the LORD shall renew their strength; they shall mount up with wings as eagles; they shall run, and not be weary; and they shall walk, and not faint.　　　　　　　　　　Isaiah 40:31

And the multitude rose up together against them: and the magistrates rent off their clothes, and commanded to beat them. And when they had laid many stripes upon them, they cast them into prison, charging the jailor to keep them safely: who, having received such a charge, thrust them into the inner prison, and made their feet fast in the stocks. And at midnight Paul and Silas prayed, and sang praises unto God: and the prisoners heard them. And suddenly there was a great earthquake, so that the foundations of the prison were shaken: and immediately all the doors were opened, and every one's bands were loosed.

　　　　　　　　　　　　　　　　　　Acts 16:22-26

Paul and Silas were arrested for preaching the Gospel. They were stripped and severely whipped. With their backs ripped open and bleeding, they were thrown into the most secure part of the prison and left bound, probably lying on their mutilated backs.

We might picture them lying there, hurting, complaining and questioning God: "God, we were doing what You told us to do. We were preaching. We came here because of a man in a vision. What happened? What went wrong? Did we miss You somewhere? Did we misunderstand the meaning of the vision? Did we somehow get out of Your will? Is there some secret sin in our lives that we don't even know about that brought this on us?"

But, no! That is not the way it happened! Paul and Silas were lying there praying and praising God. These guys were either insane, or there was something going on inside of them that was more real to them than the circumstances they found themselves in.

I don't think they were being noble. I don't think Paul said to Silas, "Silas, we are in a predicament here. Not only are our backs ripped open and we're in a lot of pain, but we may get an infection that will kill us here in prison in a foreign country. They have taken our passports and visas, and they won't let us call the embassy. But, Silas, we've got to be strong. Instead of complaining, let's try praying and singing praises to God."

I just don't think it happened that way. Paul and Silas were so passionate about serving the Lord and so in love with the Lord that the most natural thing for them to do in that situation was to pray and praise God. It just came out of them.

You don't get to that place by being self-centered and seeking the American dream. You get there by dying to self, becoming a servant in the Kingdom and staying in love with your Creator. You get there by trusting Him completely and believing His Word rather than believing what your five physical senses are telling you.

Is that not what happened with Paul and Silas? As they were praying (probably in the Spirit) and praising God, there was an earthquake. Their chains fell off, and the doors of the prison swung open. In fact, all the prisoners' chains fell off, and all the cell doors were opened. This is another example of how walking in the blessing affects those around us.

The other prisoners had done nothing to deserve their freedom, and yet they could have walked out of the prison at that point.

In verses 27 and 28 we are told, *"And the keeper of the prison awaking out of his sleep, and seeing the prison doors open, he drew out his sword, and would have killed himself, supposing that the prisoners had been fled. But Paul cried with a loud voice, saying, Do thyself no harm: for we are all here."* Why did the prisoners not escape? The blessing Paul and Silas walked in made it possible for every prisoner to escape, but the Lord prevented it so the jailer and his household could be saved.

The rest of chapter 16 tells us how the jailer took Paul and Silas to his home and dressed their wounds. He and his household accepted salvation that night and were baptized. Did it ever occur to you that the jailer might have been the man Paul saw in the vision who was saying, *"Come over here"* (Acts 16:9-10)? What an awesome God we serve! ✛

KINGDOM MANNA: Reading 60

WAITING ON THE LORD 3

But they that wait upon the LORD shall renew their strength; they shall mount up with wings as eagles; they shall run, and not be weary; and they shall walk, and not faint. Isaiah 40:31

Let's look at this word *wait* or the phrase *wait upon the Lord* from yet another perspective before we move on. In Hebrew the word is *qavah.* It means "to expect, gather, collect or to bind together."

As a child, I had a rock collection. I had searched for these rocks, **expecting** to find them. Having found them, I placed them on a board, in a sense binding them together. They had been individual rocks, scattered over the landscape, but I put them in order on a board, and they became connected. They were no longer individual rocks. They were now a collection of rocks. They had been many, but now they were one rock collection, and I was the creator and owner of that collection. Are you getting the picture?

We were individual people, lost in the world. Then we became individual believers, born from above (born again). Now we are becoming a collective people, the Body of Christ compacted and fit together into one with Him and with each other (see Ephesians 4:16), chosen (found) by Him and selected to be His Bride. He has placed us where He purposed us to be, in covenant with Him and with each other and is bringing us into the unity of the faith. As we get to know Him better and better, we are becoming like Him in character, *"unto a perfect man, unto the measure of the stature of the fulness of Christ"* (Ephesians 4:13).

To be in covenant is to be bound together. Perhaps the primary way to bind something together is to twist it together. Think about wicker furniture. The wicker material is in individual strands until it is twisted together and becomes one piece of furniture.

It is interesting to note that the word *wicker* is very much like and related to the word *wicked*. *Wicked*, like many other scriptural words, has become, for many, a very religious term, but it simply means "twisted." Wicked thinking is twisted thinking, and we usually use it in a negative sense. However, when we look at it in the context of Isaiah 40:31, it has a very positive application. While a wicked person is bound to evil, we are bound to the Lord and to each other.

We could say a wicked person is one with evil. Actually, that person is evil. So it is with a righteous person. Jesus has made us the righteousness of God (see 2 Corinthians 5:21), twisting our lives together with

His so that we are no longer an individual, but have become one with Him. We are righteous because He is righteous. You could say we are one and the same with righteousness.

Isn't that what Jesus prayed for us, that we would be one with each other, one with Him and one with the Father, as He is one with the Father (see John 17:20-23)? It is in this oneness (unity of the faith) that we are enabled to renew our strength, mount up with wings as eagles, run and not be weary and walk and not faint.

This is not something we can do individually. It is only possible as we become one collectively, realizing that it is He who has called us out of the world, having chosen us to be in Him before the foundation of the world (see Ephesians 1:4).

It seems *waiting upon the Lord* is more something He has done than something we do. And, saints, the end result of Isaiah 40:31 will ultimately be our physical, mortal bodies putting on immortality (see 1 Corinthians 15:53). This is a three-part process, just as we are a three-day (millennium) Church. Our spirit becomes alive when we are born from above. Our soul (mind) is renewed to the Word of God, and we become like Him in character. Then our physical bodies put on immortality, not only restored to the life Adam had before the fall, but going beyond Adam's experience and becoming like God, knowing good and evil, but walking in love, as the Lord lives His life in and through us. ✛

The Steps of a Righteous Man

The steps of a good man are ordered by the Lord: and he delighteth in his way. Though he fall, he shall not be utterly cast down: for the Lord upholdeth him with his hand.   Psalm 37:23-24

Blessed be the God and Father of our Lord Jesus Christ, who hath blessed us with all spiritual blessings in heavenly places in Christ: according as he hath chosen us in him before the foundation of the world, that we should be holy and without blame before him in love.

        Ephesians 1:3-4

My daddy told me that I was asking questions about spiritual things when I was three years old. He said they were questions that he couldn't answer, so he did a wise thing: He placed me in God's hands. He told the Lord, "I don't know how to raise this boy, so You are going to have to raise him."

In my teen years, I put that prayer to the test. Then, in the spring of 1970, at the age of nineteen, I accepted Jesus as my Lord and Savior and was genuinely and dramatically born again. A few weeks later, I was baptized with the Holy Spirit.

In Matthew 20:16 Jesus said, *"Many be called, but few chosen."* I know I was *chosen.*

How many three-year-olds ask questions about spiritual matters? Where did that come from, if not from the Holy Spirit already at work in my young life?

1 Timothy 2:4 tells us that God wants all men to be saved and come to knowledge of the Truth. Acts 10:34 tells us that God is no respecter of persons. And yet it seems and there are many scriptures that say some are chosen by God. Guess what? If you were chosen, you did not do the choosing.

We all know the story of how Paul (whose original name was Saul) was knocked off his horse and blinded on the road to Damascus. I've heard teachings on the Holy Spirit that contended that the Holy Spirit is a gentleman and will not force Himself on anyone. Try telling that to Paul.

In the 9th chapter of Acts the Lord told Ananias to go and pray for Paul to receive his sight. In verse 15, the Lord said, *"Go thy way: for he is a **chosen** vessel unto me, to bear my name before the Gentiles, and kings, and the children of Israel: For I will shew him how great things he must suffer for my name's sake"* (Emphasis added). If a person is chosen (and many of you reading this are), it stands to reason that your steps are and have always been ordered by God. Jesus has made us the righteousness of God (see 2 Corinthians 5:21). If we were chosen by God before the foundation of the world (see Ephesians 1:4), then He was ordering our steps even before we accepted His righteousness.

Have we made bad choices in our lives? Of course we have. Have we reaped pain and suffering for our bad choices? I know I have. And yet, somehow, in the bigger picture, God has used all of that to bring us to where we are and to equip us for ministry. When He chose us before the foundation of the world, He knew every mistake we would make.

We have all fallen, as Psalm 37 says, and yet God has upheld us, saved us and brought us to where we are today. Isn't it good to know that He is the Author and Finisher of our faith (see Hebrews 12:2)? Glory to God! ✢

Prophetic Word 3

"Come up here. Come up here," says the Lord. "Come and see as I see. Come and see what I see."   Revelation 4:1, My Paraphrase

Some of you are seeing that this is a new day and that I am doing a new thing, but you aren't yet seeing it as I see it. You've had a glimpse, and you've tasted that which is good, but what you have tasted has turned bitter in your stomach (see Revelation 10:7-11).

There is much that you don't yet understand, much that you don't yet know. Don't try to make the new fit into the old. As new wine will burst old wineskins, the new wine that I am pouring will not, cannot, be contained by the old.

The enemy of your soul is waging a war of containment. He knows, he understands that unless he can contain you and hold you where you are, unless he can stop you in your tracks, he will see his demise (see Luke 10:17-24, Matthew 24:27-37, Mark 13:25-26 and Hebrews 12:1-3).

"Come up here. Come up here," says the Lord. "Come and see as I see. Come and see what I see."   Revelation 4:1, My Paraphrase

As the Spirit was giving me this word, I thought it would be longer. But like many of the praise and worship choruses I write, it is short, but complete.

I don't usually give scripture references in prophecies, but I have written this as the Spirit gave it to me. I encourage you to read these scripture references, re-read them and then read them several more times.

If you are like me, you have probably read these scriptures, applying them to some future time and/or future event. Put that mindset aside, and read them in light of where we are right now in the course of prophetic history. These words were not only for the apostle John or for some past or future generation. They are for us, the remnant, the first-fruits of the third day Church (see 1 Peter 3:8) that is appearing on the horizon of time as we know it.

This new day that we are entering into, this new thing that is being prophesied, is more about being than about doing. It is more about who we are becoming than what we are doing. Of course, what we are becoming will, in many ways, determine what we do, but if we allow our focus to get on the doing rather than the being, we will miss what the Spirit is saying to the Church.

I could expound much on the above scriptures and, indeed, there has already been much teaching done that is available to those who are interested. But I am believing that as you read these scriptures anew, you will begin and/or continue to receive revealed knowledge from the Spirit of God concerning the time in which we live.

Certainly we live in the most exciting time in all of history so far, and certainly we were born for such a time as this. Glory to God! ✝

PROPHETIC WORD 4

"Do you not know that I have been crucified since before the foundation of the world? Do you not know that I knew you before the foundation of the world was laid, before I spoke the worlds into existence? Do you not know that I chose you, I trusted you, I predestined you to be who you are, where you are, fulfilling My plan for your life long before anything that is in the realm of the physical existed?

"For, you see, I dwell in eternity, where time has no relevance. I knew you then, just as I know you now. I know the end from the beginning and all the in-between. There is nothing that surprises me, nothing that startles me, nothing that catches me off guard, for I am all-knowing and all-seeing.

"Why is it that you have a hard time trusting Me, when I have you in the palm of My hand? Why is it that you have a hard time relating to Me, when my love for you has no beginning and no end?

"Ah, but there are those of you who are trusting Me and relating to Me, walking with Me and in My ways, one with Me. There are those of you whom I am calling out to know Me in My fullness, not only in part, as some know Me, or in name only, as many know Me. For there are those of you who are after My own heart, and My heart is continually toward you, revealing Myself to you and taking you from glory to glory.

"And we are just beginning. The day just ahead (see 2 Peter 3:8) is beyond anything you can ask or think (see Ephesians 3:20), a glorious day, filled with awe and wonder, with power and strength, with the fullness of My glory.

"The sons of God are about to manifest in the earth, and you are among those the world will look at with awe and wonder, seeing your power and strength, being drawn to you because of My glory in and on and around you continually (see Romans 8:19).

"For you have stepped over into eternity, where the plowman overtakes the reaper, and the treader of grapes overtakes him who sows seed, a time of fullness of blessing, a time when harvest is continual (see Amos 9:13).

"I have prepared you. I have positioned you. I have anointed you. You are chosen. I trust you because I know you, and I know that which I have invested in you. I am love, and love never fails. My love is being perfected in you. Therefore you never fail.

"There is none like you because there is none like Me. You are my handiwork, my expression of all that I am in the earth.

"Do you not think I will finish all that I have started? Surely I will," says the Lord, the Almighty. ✠

THE PLOWMAN AND THE REAPER

Behold, the days come, saith the LORD, that the plowman shall overtake the reaper, and the treader of grapes him that soweth seed; and the mountains shall drop sweet wine, and all the hills shall melt.

Amos 9:13

This prophetic word is clearly for physical Israel, but I believe it is also for spiritual Israel (the true Church). While the days spoken of here could be referring to ages to come, I think it is speaking of a specific day, the third-thousand-year day of the Church. And, saints, we are there!

I was born again and baptized with the Holy Spirit during the Charismatic/Word/Faith Movement of the 1960s and 70s here in the United States. As a young believer, I read books by Kenneth Hagin. I heard Kenneth Copeland preach in my hometown before many knew him. These and others taught me much in those early days of my walk with the Lord, and as a result, I experienced and witnessed many miracles.

Without the revealed knowledge I received as a direct result of the teachings of these and others, I might not have survived the trials that came my way as a young believer, husband and father. I learned much about standing in faith, praying the prayer of faith, the authority in the name of Jesus, the power of confession, sowing and reaping, etc. I thank God for the ministries of those who taught me, but, saints, this is a new day.

In 1999 the Lord spoke to me and said, "It is time to get more involved in ministry." At the time, I had a successful paint contracting business, which I had built up over a period of some fourteen years. I joined Full Gospel Business Men's Fellowship International and began leading praise and worship at chapter meetings and FGBMFI functions. Then I became worship leader at a local church.

Almost immediately I began having financial difficulty. By 2002, I found myself in deep financial trouble. Even though I had that good paint contracting business and was working hard, I wasn't able to make enough profit. Something seemed to be continually happening to rob me of what I needed. I found myself deeply in debt.

I did everything I knew to do. I prayed, as best as I knew how to pray, in faith. I confessed the right things that lined up with my understanding of the Word of God. I took authority over the situation in the name of Jesus, and I continued sowing time and finances, expecting a return on my giving, but nothing seemed to be working.

One day I told the Lord, "I don't know why this isn't working. I'm doing everything I know to do. I know Your voice, and I know I am walking in obedience to all You have told me to do. I will continue to obey You, even if it costs me everything." For a short time after that, things seemed to turn around, but then everything went downhill even faster ... until it appeared I might actually lose everything.

About 4:00 AM one morning in the summer of 2003, I was lying on my couch at home unable to sleep. As I was praying in the Spirit, I heard the Lord say, "Put the ball back in My court."

I said, "Lord, I didn't know I was carrying the ball, but I put it back in Your court. I quit. I'm not doing another thing until You do something."

Four months earlier, while I was in Lisbon, Portugal with Miguel Escobar (a traveling revivalist who has ministered in more than sixty nations), the Lord spoke to me and told me to get out of the painting business. I told Him I would do it, but He had to tell my wife. When I got back home, I went to work as usual, and didn't tell anyone what the Lord had said. That summer night at 4:00 AM, at the same time the Lord was speaking to me on the couch, He woke my wife Cathy and told her that I was to get out of the painting business. Later that morning, we discussed what we had heard, and a few weeks later I gave my business to my sons and quit contracting.

You may be wondering what all of this has to do with Amos 9:13. Let me share a little more testimony with you in the next reading that will tie it together. ✠

KINGDOM MANNA: READING 65

THE PLOWMAN AND THE REAPER 2

Behold, the days come, saith the LORD, that the plowman shall overtake the reaper, and the treader of grapes him that soweth seed; and the mountains shall drop sweet wine, and all the hills shall melt.

Amos 9:13

In Reading 64 I shared testimony about how just the opposite of Amos 9:13 seemed to be taking place in my life between 1999 and 2003. A pivotal moment came when at 4:00 AM one morning in the summer of 2003 the Lord spoke to me and said, "Put the ball back in My court."

Looking back on that night I now realize that even though I was doing, praying and confessing the right things, I didn't completely trust God. There was still a lot of me (self) involved. Complete trust is only possible when everything is completely surrendered to Him. When we find that place of complete surrender and trust, we discover that place of rest the writer of Hebrews wrote so much about. I no longer work for God. Now I work *with* Him. You see, I don't have a ministry. It is His ministry, and I am a partner with Him in His ministry.

I used to give, expecting to be blessed and receive a return on my giving. Now I give because I am blessed. I don't give to receive abundance. I have abundance, therefore I can give. Yes, my sowing produces a harvest, but I no longer sow to reap; I sow because I can and I want to, out of the harvest I have already reaped because of the covenant I have with Him.

The covenant I have with God means that everything He has and everything He is now belongs to me. It is out of that abundance that I give, whether it is time, finances or simply love. By the same token, everything I have and everything I am now belongs to Him. When I give to Him, I am actually giving what is already His, and when I receive from Him, He is giving me what is already mine. Does this sound like the plowman overtaking the reaper, and the treader of grapes overtaking him that sows seed?

You see, this life we live, this walk we walk isn't about doing; it is about being. What we do does not determine who we are. Who we are determines what we do. Because of who we are, we are in a continual cycle where the reaper overtakes the sower. In other words, we reap where we have not sown and possess what we have not built, just as Israel acquired houses already built and fields with crops when they took possession of Canaan.

You can't give to get something that is already yours, any more than you can give something that already belongs to the one you are giving it to. Do you think that maybe Jesus had this in mind when He prayed in the 17th chapter of John's account of the Gospel: *"That they all may be one; as thou, Father, art in me, and I in thee, that they also may be one in us: that the world may believe that thou hast sent me. And the glory which thou gavest me I have given them; that they may be one, even as we are one: I in them, and thou in me, that they may be made perfect in one; and that the world may know that thou hast sent me, and hast loved them, as thou hast loved me"* (John 17:23)?

Much past teaching has put the emphasis on doing, but in this third day of the Church we are realizing that results come when we understand who we are. When Jesus said on the cross, *"It is finished,"* He was, in essence, saying there is nothing else to be done. When we are born from above (born again), enabling us to see the Kingdom and become one with Him, we no longer have to deal with lack of any kind. We are now walking into our destiny, as we renew our minds to His Word and enable Him to live His life in and through us. Is this not a place where the plowman is overtaking the reaper and the treader of grapes is overtaking the sower? Yes, it is a place of continual harvest. Glory to God! ✤

KINGDOM MANNA: Reading 66

The Plowman and the Reaper 3

Behold, the days come, saith the LORD, that the plowman shall overtake the reaper, and the treader of grapes him that soweth seed; and the mountains shall drop sweet wine, and all the hills shall melt.

Amos 9:13

Realizing that we are the blessed, not because of what we have, but because of the covenant we are in, has changed the way I look at a lot of things. It hasn't necessarily changed my understanding of the Word concerning sowing and reaping, prayer, faith and confession, but it has definitely built upon my understanding, giving me a more complete understanding. Through this process of getting a more complete understanding, I have begun to see the bigger picture. Saints, it is not about us. It is all about the Kingdom. It is not about my dreams and desires. It is about the Kingdom. It is not even about my business, ministry or family. It is about the Kingdom. What did Jesus say?

Seek ye first the kingdom of God, and his righteousness; and all these things shall be added unto you. Matthew 6:33

It is a matter of priorities. It is a matter of where our focus is. It is a matter of realizing who we are and who we are becoming. We are becoming who He has already made us to be. We are the blessed, and as carriers of that blessing, we are in a continual cycle of reaping what we have not sown, enabling us to sow, so that others can reap. Glory to God! Did you get that? What a plan! What an awesome, exciting and glorious life we are living, all because of Him, all because of what He has purposed and done. That is why it is all about Him. Without Him we would not be. We are literally an extension of Him. We are His Body. He is the Head, and we are the Body.

We are one in Him, just as He and the Father are one (see John 17:23). Just as we are in Him, He is in us, the hope of glory becoming the manifestation of glory (see Colossians 1:27). All creation is waiting for us to be revealed (see Romans 8:19), and we will be revealed in this third day. Hallelujah!

We are almost there. The Kingdom of God is coming in earth as it is in Heaven.

So what is there to fret about? What is there to worry about? I literally don't have a care in the world. I have nothing to lose because the outcome does not depend on me. It depends on Him. It has been settled since before the foundation of the world. He is love, and love never fails (see 1 Corinthians 13:8). I am one with Him. Therefore I am love, and I never fail. Are you getting it? It is not about what we do or don't do. It is all about who and whose we are.

He that findeth his life shall lose it: and he that loseth his life for my sake shall find it.   Matthew 10:39

KINGDOM MANNA: Reading 67

The Kingdom of God

Seek ye first the kingdom of God, and his righteousness; and all these things shall be added unto you.   Jesus in Matthew 6:33

For the kingdom of God is not meat and drink; but righteousness, and peace, and joy in the Holy Ghost.   Romans 14:17

The kingdom of God is within you.   Jesus in Luke 17:21

The wind bloweth where it listeth, and thou hearest the sound thereof, but canst not tell whence it cometh, and whither it goeth: so is every one that is born of the Spirit.   Jesus in John 3:8

Except a man be born again, he cannot see the kingdom of God.

Jesus in John 3:3

A king is an absolute ruler. Everything in a kingdom is either decreed by the king or permitted by the king. Anything else is illegal, and anyone involved is subject to suffer the consequences of being in rebellion against the king.

A king gets his authority or position by being born into the right family and inheriting the throne, by being appointed by another king or, in the case of Saul and David in Israel, being appointed by God, or by taking the kingdom by force. A kingdom is not a democracy or a republic. It is not for the people, by the people and of the people. It is for the king, by the king and of the king. The quality of life within the kingdom is at the discretion of the king, for a king**dom** is the **dom**ain of the king.

In the Kingdom of God, God is the King. However, He didn't acquire His kingship by any of the above means. He is King because He created the Kingdom.

In order to be a part of God's Kingdom we must, first of all, be born again or born from above, born of the Spirit. Then we must seek His Kingdom and His righteousness.

Often we think of righteousness as a moral code, and certainly, doing the right thing is a part of righteousness. To live peacefully under a government, we must obey the laws of that government. However, the other side of righteousness is the possibility that we may have rights. Because we are part of a country or area that is under a ruling government, we can exercise any rights given to us by that government. Such is the case with the Kingdom of God.

God has granted us certain rights in His Kingdom. These rights are found in the Bible. We often call them the promises of God. In order to access these promises or rights, we must know them, first of all, and then operate them according to the laws and principles of the Kingdom. The primary Kingdom principle needed to exercise our rights in the Kingdom of God is faith. *"Without faith it is impossible to please God"* (Hebrews 11:6).

Nothing in the Kingdom of God is automatic. Faith is required. God doesn't respond to your need. He responds to your faith. That is why crying, begging and pleading doesn't impress God. Faith impresses God. Romans 12:3 tells us that we have all been given *"**the** measure of faith."*

Those of us who are born again have the same faith. It is not more faith that we need. What we need to do is to operate in the faith that we already have. We operate in that faith by working the principles of the Kingdom. What are the principles of the Kingdom? It will take much more study to even briefly look into that part of the Kingdom of God. So let's get started in the next reading. ✠

KINGDOM PRINCIPLES

Verily, verily, I say unto thee, Except a man be born again, he cannot see the kingdom of God.   Jesus in John 3:3

In order to understand Kingdom principles, we must first be able to see or have a revelation of the Kingdom of God. The condition that enables us to do that is being born again or born from above. This is a spiritual experience that changes us on the inside.

Every true believer is born again. If you say you are a believer or a Christian and are not born again, you are just practicing religion. You are no different than anyone else practicing any of the other religions of the world. You are lost.

As a young boy, growing up in a denominational church, I don't recall ever hearing the term *born again*. All I was told was that I needed to join the church, which I did when I was twelve.

I believed in the existence of God, because my parents and Sunday school teachers taught me to believe in the existence of God. I was taught that Jesus died on the cross to save me from my sins, but I was clueless as to why He had to do that, and no one seemed to be able to explain it to me. I had been taught to pray to God, but had no idea that prayer could be a two-way conversation.

I was a very serious young man and took my religion very seriously, but, at best, I was a carnal Christian because I knew nothing of the Spirit. Obviously the Spirit was drawing me because I kept asking questions that no one seemed to be able to answer. It just seemed to me that there had to be more. I didn't understand why we didn't see miracles. I didn't understand why we just prayed for the sick to be blessed or comforted and never prayed for them to be healed.

I remember watching Oral Roberts on television on Sunday mornings before going to church. Back in those days he filmed his tent meetings. I saw those long lines of people Oral laid his hand on and prayed for. I saw those who appeared to get healed. When I asked about Oral Roberts, I was told that he was a fake, that he had an electric buzzer in his hand, and people only thought they got healed. Can you imagine that? It was the blind leading the blind. My parents, teachers and pastors just didn't know any better.

Eventually the questions led me to believe that perhaps everything I had been taught was wrong. As a teenager I reasoned, "They lied to me about Santa Clause. Maybe all this stuff about God is a lie too." By the time I was eighteen, I no longer believed in the existence of God.

But the Holy Spirit kept drawing me. Glory to God! Let me share with you in the next reading my *born-again* experience. ✣

BORN AGAIN

Verily, verily, I say unto thee, Except a man be born again, he cannot see the kingdom of God.   Jesus in John 3:3

In the spring of 1970 I was nineteen. God sent a former disc jockey from New York to High Point, North Carolina, where I lived at the time. This former disc jockey had emceed the Beatles at Shea Stadium and had partied with Bob Dylan and the Rolling Stones. I wasn't sure why he was coming to High Point, but I thought he might be interesting to hear.

On Monday and Tuesday of that week, he was on the local television station for thirty minutes each day. He was telling how he had been born again and had left the world of sex, drugs and rock-n-roll. From the moment I heard him, I couldn't get enough. It was as if a fire began to burn in my gut, and flames shot up through my chest. I kept thinking, "This guy is talking about Jesus, and I've heard about Jesus all my life. But this one is different. This one is real!"

This former DJ was Scott Ross, who, in more recent years, has worked for the Christian Broadcasting Network in Virginia. I heard Scott speak in person on Wednesday night of that week. As my girlfriend and I left the place where he was speaking, I turned to her in the car and said, "That guy has got what I've been looking for."

I heard him again the next night. At the end of the service that night, I said to Jesus, "Lord, I've made a mess of my life. I want You to take over and be Boss from now on." Suddenly, I changed on the inside. A joy I can't describe flooded my entire being. I knew that I knew that I knew that Jesus was the Truth I had been looking for.

My point is this: If you are born again, you know you are born again. You are different from those who are not yet born again. Your thoughts are continually about the things of God. Your experience of being born again may be different from mine, but if you are truly born again, it is every bit as real as mine.

I remember reading Pat Robertson's book, *Shout It from the Housetops* [3] about how he came to start the Christian Broadcasting Network back in the days when housetops had television antennas on them. Pat told, in the book, that even though he believed in the existence of God, he suddenly realized one day that he didn't know God personally. He had never been born again. He prayed and asked God for the experience. God answered that prayer while Pat was sitting in a restaurant, and from that moment on, no one could take the experience away from him or ever convince him that it didn't happen.

I have heard it said that a person with an experience is never at the mercy of a person with an argument. Praise the Lord! It's true.

Are people that are born again perfect? No. But we are in a process of being perfected, if we are seeking the Kingdom. We should never be satisfied with just being born again. We should continually be seeking the Kingdom of God and His righteousness. There is no other way. The Kingdom of God is at hand! ✛

---

3. Alachua, FL., Bridge/Logos, 1972

Born Again 2

There was a man of the Pharisees, named Nicodemus, a ruler of the Jews: the same came to Jesus by night, and said unto him, Rabbi, we know that thou art a teacher come from God: for no man can do these miracles that thou doest, except God be with him.

Jesus answered and said unto him, Verily, verily, I say unto thee, except a man be born again, he cannot see the kingdom of God.

John 3:1-3

The term *born again* has almost become a religious cliché. It is often used to describe Christians who have a personal relationship with God, separating them from Christians who only adhere to religious doctrines or a certain Christian denomination. Often it is used to describe a group of Christians who have become known as Evangelical Christians. I'm not exactly sure who these Evangelical Christians are, but they are spoken of a lot today in the political and social arenas of the United States.

I have heard *born again* used and have used it myself when preaching an evangelistic message, inviting the lost to accept Jesus as their Lord and Savior. We think of it as a condition for salvation, a spiritual experience that changes one on the inside. But the experience of being *born again* has a broader purpose, an even greater purpose than the initial experience of salvation. To be born again is to become that new creature that the apostle Paul spoke of in 2 Corinthians 5:17, which enables us to see the Kingdom of God. In John 3:3, Jesus says that being **born again** is necessary if we are to **see the Kingdom of God**.

Have you ever tried to talk with someone about spiritual things, and they just could not hear (understand) anything you were saying? Most likely that person was not **born again**. The Kingdom of God is a spiritual Kingdom, and unless a person is **born again,** they have no understanding or comprehension of the Kingdom or of the Spirit.

But the natural man receiveth not the things of the Spirit of God: for they are foolishness unto him: neither can he know them, because they are spiritually discerned.   1 Corinthians 2:14

If you are born again, your whole way of thinking is changing. The way you see things, the way you comprehend things, is changing. As a result, the way you behave is changing. You no longer reason like the world reasons. Things that matter to the world no longer matter to you. Probably you are finding or have found new friends because you no longer have much in common with the old ones.

In essence, you have changed kingdoms. You still live in the world, but you no longer belong to the world. You now belong to (can see and experience) the Kingdom of God.

Being born again can make family relationships difficult. In Matthew 10:34-36, Jesus said, *"Think not that I am come to send peace on earth: I came not to send peace, but a sword. For I am come to set a man at variance against his father, and the daughter against her mother, and the daughter in law against her mother in law. And a man's foes shall be they of his own household."*

This is why, in the 7th chapter of 1 Corinthians, Paul instructs that unbelieving spouses are sanctified by the believing spouse. However, if the unbelieving spouse wants to leave, he tells the believing spouse to let the unbeliever go. In such cases, he says the believer is free to remarry (see 1 Corinthians 7:15).

> *What fellowship hath righteousness with unrighteousness? And what communion hath light with darkness?* 2 Corinthians 6:14

If you are born again, you now live in the Kingdom of God, and the Kingdom of God is in you (see Luke 17:21). You are different from the world, and so the world no longer understands you.

The only place in the four biblical accounts of the Gospel that Jesus speaks of being born again is in the 3rd chapter of John. However, throughout the four Gospels He speaks many times of the Kingdom of God or the Kingdom of Heaven. The purpose of being born again is to see, know and experience the Kingdom. Being born again is not just saying a sinner's prayer, so that we can one day go to Heaven. It is far more than that! Glory to God! ✝

KINGDOM MANNA: Reading 71

A Seer

*Except a man be born again, he cannot **see** the kingdom of God.*

Jesus in John 3:3, Emphasis added.

Webster's Dictionary describes a *seer* as "a person who sees or an observer; a person who prophesies future events or a prophet; a person endowed with profound moral and spiritual insight or knowledge; or a wise person or sage who possesses intuitive powers." A person who is born again has the ability to see the Kingdom of God. This doesn't necessarily mean that everyone who is born again does see the Kingdom of God, but without being born again you cannot see the Kingdom of God. I think you must be looking for the Kingdom in order to see it. You must be seeking it (see Matthew 6:33).

Some people think being born again is just a means to go to Heaven when you die, but being born again is much more than that. Being born again enables you to walk out your salvation in the here and now. In order to walk out that salvation, you must see the Kingdom of God (know, understand and experience it). So, in a sense, everyone who **sees** the Kingdom is a **seer**. If you are seeing the Kingdom, you have the ability to know, understand and experience the spiritual realm. You can see into the Spirit.

When you are seeing into the Spirit or spiritual realm, what you are seeing is foreign to those who cannot see the Kingdom. That is why it is futile to try to bring unity to the Christian church at large. Many who sit in pews every Sunday and many who speak from pulpits every Sunday are not born again and cannot know, understand or experience spiritual matters. Even many who are born again are not seeking the Kingdom. Therefore, they cannot walk in unity with those who are. Only the true Church, the true Body of Christ, can be unified, and that is the work of the Holy Spirit. I am not saying we don't have a part to play in bringing unity, but there will be no real unity except in the Spirit.

The 3rd chapter of John is the only place recorded in the four biblical accounts of the Gospel where Jesus spoke of being born again, but He spoke many times of the Kingdom of God or the Kingdom of Heaven. He called the Gospel *"the gospel of the kingdom"* (Matthew 4:23, 9:35,

24:14 and Mark 1:14). While it is imperative that we be born again, I think the emphasis in John 3:3 is on seeing the Kingdom. Without seeing the Kingdom we will not be of much use to the Kingdom.

So, in a sense, we can all be seers. However, there are those called and chosen for the five-fold ministry function of prophet. Among those prophets, some are seers, sort of watchmen on the wall, positioned there to guide and protect the Body of Christ through the use of their anointing or special gift, to see into the spiritual realm. This gift is not to elevate the seer to some celebrity position, but is to encourage, build up, sometimes bring correction, guide and protect the Body of Christ.

You may not be called to the ministry of seer, but if you are seeing the Kingdom, you, too, can be used by God to encourage, build up, sometimes bring correction, guide and protect the Body of Christ, as the need arises and as the Spirit leads. And you can see much that the natural man (the person who is not born again) has no knowledge of. ✝

KINGDOM MANNA: Reading 72

KINGDOM PRINCIPLES 2

For the kingdom of God is not meat and drink; but righteousness, and peace, and joy in the Holy Ghost.   Romans 14:17

Therefore take no thought, saying, What shall we eat? or, What shall we drink? or, Wherewithal shall we be clothed? (For after all these things do the Gentiles seek:) for your heavenly Father knoweth that ye have need of all these things. But, seek ye first the kingdom of God, and his righteousness; and all these things shall be added unto you.

Jesus in Matthew 6:33

The Kingdom of God is not meat and drink or, in other words, it is not the daily necessities of life. The Kingdom of God is righteousness, peace and joy in the Holy Spirit. If we seek righteousness, peace and joy in the Holy Spirit, **all these things** — the daily necessities of life — will be added to us.

To enter into the Kingdom of God is to enter into covenant with God. We have been bought with a price. Therefore, we no longer belong to ourselves. We belong to God and to His Kingdom. We are His servants. Everything we have and everything we are now belongs to Him.

Under the Old Testament Law, God required tithes and offerings, but under the New Testament or New Covenant, He requires it all — everything.

In Luke 6:38, Jesus said, *"Give, and it shall be given unto you."* When we give our entire selves to the Kingdom, God gives His entire self to us. Everything He has and everything He is now belongs to us. Psalm 50:10 says that God owns the cattle on a thousand hills. Then, in verse 12, He says, *"For the world is mine, and the fullness thereof."*

God owns it all, everything. There is no lack in the Kingdom of God. Therefore, when we come into covenant with Him, there is no longer any lack in our lives. Everything we need He has already provided. All we have to do is access it or receive it, and we do that by faith. We believe God. We believe the covenant we have with Him. We study His Word to know what our rights (righteousness) are, what belongs to us according to what He has said in His Word, the Bible.

When we know what belongs to us, according to His Word, we add to that knowledge faith. In other words, we believe God. We trust Him to manifest in our lives all He has promised us. To trust God is to rest in the assurance that He will bring it to pass. That gives us peace.

Peace is more than the absence of conflict. Peace is completeness, wholeness. *Peace* literally means "nothing missing, nothing broken." Once we are experiencing peace, we have joy. Joy is not happiness. Happiness can come and go. Joy is not a fleeting thing. It is a constant thing. It cannot be shaken by circumstances. It will see us through adverse circumstances.

Where is this righteousness, peace and joy? It is in the Holy Spirit. We must walk in the Spirit to dwell in the Kingdom. ✣

KINGDOM MANNA: Reading 73

KINGDOM PRINCIPLES 3

This is my commandment, That ye love one another, as I have loved you. Greater love hath no man than this, that a man lay down his life for his friends. Ye are my friends, if ye do whatsoever I command you.

Henceforth I call you not servants; for the servant knoweth not what his lord doeth: but I have called you friends; for all things that I have heard of my Father I have made known unto you.

Ye have not chosen me, but I have chosen you, and ordained you, that ye should go and bring forth fruit, and that your fruit should remain: that whatsoever ye shall ask of the Father in my name, he may give it you.

Jesus in John 15:12-16

Thou shalt love the Lord thy God with all thy heart, and with all thy soul, and with all thy mind. This is the first and great commandment. And the second is like unto it, Thou shalt love thy neighbour as thyself. On these two commandments hang all the law and the prophets.

Jesus in Matthew 22:37-40

The only law of the Kingdom is the law of love. If we love God and love each other, we fulfill the entire New Testament law.

To love God is to serve God. To love each other is to serve each other. We must have a servant's heart. A servant lays down his life for his friends. Jesus laid down His life for us, and we must lay down our lives for each other, thinking of others before we think of ourselves. This is contrary to the way most of the world thinks. Most people in the world (and even Christians) tend to be very self-centered, but this cannot be the case with servants of the Kingdom.

Ah, but what did Jesus say? If we lay down our lives for the Kingdom and for others, if we walk in love as servants, He no longer calls us servants. Now He calls us friends and reveals the hidden things of God to us, the things of the Spirit — righteousness, peace and joy, as we have already studied. When we understand these things and walk in or experience these things continually, everything else we need is added to us. Therefore, we lack nothing. We walk in fullness.

The degree of fullness we experience depends on how completely we walk in love toward God and toward each other. Life is about giving. Life is about loving. It is in giving and loving that we experience and receive the most in life. I've heard it said that you can't outgive God. Well, He gave it all when He became a man and went to the cross for us. We too, must give our all.

He that findeth his life shall lose it: and he that loseth his life for my sake shall find it. Jesus in Matthew 10:39

✠

KINGDOM PRINCIPLES 4

The wind bloweth where it listeth, and thou hearest the sound thereof, but canst not tell whence it cometh, and whither it goeth: so is every one that is born of the Spirit.   Jesus in John 3:8

Except a man be born again, he cannot see the kingdom of God.

                Jesus in John 3:3

We have already established, in previous KINGDOM MANNA teachings, that we must be born again to see, experience and enter into the Kingdom of God. If we are born again and experiencing the Kingdom, we are not like the world anymore. We are different (peculiar):

But ye are a chosen generation, a royal priesthood, an holy nation, a peculiar people; that ye should shew forth the praises of him who hath called you out of darkness into his marvellous light.   1 Peter 2:9

People in the world no longer understand us. They can't tell where we are coming from or where we are going because they don't think like we do. They don't reason like we do.

In the 16th chapter of Acts we are told about Paul and Silas being beaten, thrown into the most secure part of the prison, and put in chains. In that condition, at midnight, they began singing praises to God so loudly that the other prisoners heard them. Paul and Silas were either insane, or they were experiencing righteousness, peace and joy in the Holy Spirit (see Romans 14:17). As they were singing praises to God their chains fell off, and the prison doors swung open. They received the necessity of life they required at that moment, their freedom from prison.

The other prisoners probably didn't understand how or why these men would be praising God in their condition. They didn't know where Paul and Silas were coming from or where they were going with their praise songs. But when there was an earthquake and all the prison doors swung open, I expect all the prisoners realized that Paul and Silas knew something they didn't.

A few years ago I met a Jewish lady who claimed to be an atheist. Her son was a Christian. His wife had left him and was suing him for custody of his daughters. I shared with this lady about how God had fought a custody battle for me several years earlier, and I had won. Before her son went to court, the Jewish lady who claimed to be an atheist called me and asked me to pray that her son would gain custody of his daughters. She didn't understand me. She didn't know where I was coming from or where I was going, but she understood the results I got when I prayed.

The world is lost. They don't understand us. They don't know where we are coming from or where we are going. They don't know what it is to be born again or to see the Kingdom of God. But they recognize results when they see them. That is why we must bear fruit. That is why we must walk in love so that our way is prosperous. A poor, beaten down, sick man is not in a position to help anyone, but we are not poor, beaten down or sick. We are servants of a King who calls us friends and reveals to us the secrets of the Kingdom, secrets that will enable us to overcome and be victorious. Glory to God! Hallelujah! ✠

KINGDOM PRINCIPLES 5

And it came to pass after these things, that God did tempt Abraham, and said unto him, Abraham: and he said, Behold, here I am. And he said, take now thy son, thine only son Isaac, whom thou lovest, and get thee into the land of Moriah; and offer him there for a burnt offering upon one of the mountains which I will tell thee of.   Genesis 22:1-2

God made covenant with Abraham and promised to establish that covenant with Isaac, Abraham's heir by his wife, Sarah. Then, a few years later, He told Abraham to kill Isaac and sacrifice him as a burnt offering.

Put yourself in Abraham's place. Would you have obeyed God? Perhaps you or I might have questioned God in that situation. God had promised Abraham that he would be the father of many nations. Isaac was his heir who would carry on the lineage, bringing the promise of God to pass. If Abraham sacrificed Isaac, how would the promise of God ever come to pass?

But Abraham was a man of faith, and Romans 4:2-3 tells us that he was justified by faith. He obeyed God, believing that, if necessary, God would raise Isaac from the dead (see Hebrews 11:19). By this time in Abraham's life, it appears he trusted God completely.

The rest of the 22nd chapter of Genesis tells us that the angel of the Lord stopped Abraham from killing Isaac just in the nick of time. In this way, Abraham passed the test. He proved his obedience, and in doing so became a type and shadow of God's sacrifice of His only begotten Son, Jesus.

Like Abraham, we must be people of faith and obedience in order to live successfully in the Kingdom of God. God is not going to ask you to kill your child, but He may ask something of you that appears to be very difficult or makes no sense at all to you. Abraham's faith was proved by his obedience, even when it appeared that his obedience would cost him God's promise.

The place of total surrender to the plans and instructions of God produced in Abraham a complete trust in God, which was equal to the faith required to bring about the plans and purposes of God, not only in Abraham's life, but also for future generations in all the earth. Glory to God! ✢

KINGDOM MANNA: Reading 76

KINGDOM PRINCIPLES 6

I die daily. The Apostle Paul in 1 Corinthians 15:31

In a previous KINGDOM MANNA I shared with you how in 1999 God told me to get more involved in ministry. I joined Full Gospel Business Men's Fellowship International. I began to lead praise and worship at FGBMFI chapter meetings and other functions. I soon became President of the Southport, North Carolina Chapter and then a Field Representative in southeastern North Carolina. Through FGBMFI I met Miguel Escobar, a revivalist who has ministered in more than sixty nations. In 2002 I began to travel and minister with Miguel.

I expected God to prosper my business so I could continue to travel and minister, but just the opposite happened. I prayed and kept my confession in line with the Word of God. I sowed financial seed into other ministries, expecting a multiplied return. But nothing worked. I should have been successful, but I just couldn't make enough money to make ends meet. I kept going deeper and deeper in debt. It began to look like I was going bankrupt.

My financial situation began to put a strain on my marriage. At a time when it looked like I was going to lose everything, I told God that I would continue to obey Him, even if it cost me everything. It appeared that my hearing His voice and obeying Him was going to cost me everything. Then, just when the situation looked completely hopeless, God came through with a miracle.

In Luke 12:48 Jesus said, *"For unto whomsoever much is given, of him shall be much required."* God is looking for people He can trust. In Matthew 20:16 Jesus said, *"Many are called, but few are chosen."* In Greek, a stronger translation for the word *chosen* might be *trusted.* Many are called, but few are trusted. I thought I trusted God before I nearly lost everything, but I found a much deeper trust in Him when I became willing to lose everything. Because my trust in Him has deepened, He can now trust me with more.

To be at the forefront of this great move of God and harvest of souls that we are now entering into, we must completely trust God. The more we trust Him, the more He can trust us. And the more He trusts us, the more He can and will require of us. The result will be that we walk in more power and greater authority, seeing and experiencing greater success as we minister to others.

For those of us who are called and willing (and even perhaps some who are not so willing), God puts us through a process that brings maturity in our lives and prepares and positions us for greater ministry. This process not only brings us to the place that we trust Him more, so that He can trust us more, but it also perfects His love in us.

There is great freedom in trusting God completely. While the process of getting to that place of trusting Him is sometimes not so pleasant, the results are worth it. A life with no stress and the peace that passes all understanding is worth whatever it takes for us to get there (see Philippians 4:7). It would be nice if we could get there once and for always, and I believe there is a real possibility that will eventually be the case. But because our flesh wants to rule our spirits, at least for now, we must continue to die to self in order to walk in the Spirit and in that place of complete trust, the result of which is walking in love, power and authority.

As we mature, we will trust God more consistently, seeing and experiencing greater success in our lives and ministries. We will see, experience and know the Kingdom of God, which is within us. And we will see and experience the manifestation of the Sons of God on earth (see Romans 8:19). Glory to God! ✣

KINGDOM PRINCIPLES 7

*Them that walk after the flesh in the lust of uncleanness ... , presumptuous are they, **self-willed** ... .*　　　2 Peter 2:10, Emphasis added

Before Adam and Eve fell, they were not **self**-conscious people. They were God-conscious.

We know God communicated with Adam, for He gave him permission to eat of every tree in the garden except the tree of the knowledge of good and evil. God brought all the animals to Adam, and Adam named them. Obviously, Adam knew the voice of God. Hence he was God-conscious.

Before the fall Adam and Eve had not eaten of the tree of the knowledge of good and evil. They knew nothing of the battle going on between good and evil. Their thoughts and actions were not good or evil; they were pure and holy. They were clothed with God's glory, which is His goodness. It was all they knew, and it determined how they lived.

Then, on that fateful day, they ate of the tree that God had forbidden them to eat of. Suddenly they realized they were naked, not because they were not wearing clothes, but because they were no longer clothed in the glory of God. The glory had departed from them, and they became ashamed.

What did they do next? They tried to cover their shame themselves. **Self** had entered the picture, and **self** has been getting in the way ever since. In the natural, we are self-willed, self-conscious, self-made, self-righteous, selfish people. As children, most of us were not only taught to be this way; we were taught it is a good thing. We were taught to have pride in who we are, in our family name, in our religion and in our nationality.

Even if we didn't have a family, religion or nation we could be proud of, we became proud of ourselves and what we were determined to accomplish with our lives. For those that couldn't find anything to be proud of, shame took over. Pride and shame are closely related because the focus of both is **self**.

In Matthew 16:24-25 Jesus said, *"If any will come after me, let him deny himself, and take up his cross, and follow me. For whosoever will save his life shall lose it: and whosoever will lose his life for my sake shall find it"* (Emphasis added).

In order to see and experience the Kingdom of God, we must continually deny ourselves. We must cease being self-conscious and, like Adam before the fall, once again become God-conscious. We will never become righteous or holy by trying to be righteous or holy. Trying to become what we think we should be is just like Adam and Eve trying to hide their shame by making clothes of fig leaves.

When we die to self, once again we begin to live in and be clothed with the glory of God. We stop trying to be and simply become. We no longer are concerned with good and evil. Instead, we begin to realize that in the Kingdom we are in a process of being perfected. The more we move toward perfection, the less we have to continually die to self because self is less and less in the picture.

Chapter 5 of Matthew's account of the Gospel is mostly words spoken by Jesus. At the end of this discourse He says, *"Be ye therefore perfect, even as your Father which is in heaven is perfect."* There is only one path to perfection — dying to self.

Dying to self is not a pleasant thing for our flesh. Our flesh wants to rule us. Dying is not on the agenda of our flesh. Therefore, it is easy to think of dying to self in negative terms. But it is not a negative thing. In fact, it is a very positive thing. The more we die to self, the more we walk in love. The more we walk in love, the better our faith works. The better our faith works, the more successful we become. Dying to self is not a negative thing. It is a wonderful thing.

When Adam and Eve ate of the tree of the knowledge of good and evil, they were banished from the garden and prevented from eating of the Tree of Life. Today, because of the finished work of Jesus, we can once again eat of the Tree of Life. The way we eat of that tree is by dying to self and living in Him, for Jesus is the Tree of Life. ✞

KINGDOM MANNA: Reading 78

WE ARE NOT SCHIZOPHRENIC

I die daily.   The apostle Paul in 1 Corinthians 15:31

*Them that walk after the flesh in the lust of uncleanness ... , presumptuous are they, **self**-willed ... .*   2 Peter 2:10, Emphasis added

Therefore if any man be in Christ, he is a new creature: old things are passed away; behold, all things are become new. 2 Corinthians 5:17

As for me, I will behold thy face in righteousness: I shall be satisfied, when I awake, with thy likeness. Psalm 17:15

Lest we get the idea we are two people, flesh and spirit, constantly warring against each other, let's look a little deeper into the Word.

In previous KINGDOM MANNA teachings, I have said we are a spirit, we have a soul (mind) and we live in a body. While this makes it a little easier to understand who we are, we shouldn't get the idea that we are three individuals in one.

God is one. We know Him as God the Father, God the Son and God the Holy Spirit, but He is not three individuals. He is one, just as we are one. God is one triune being, and we are one triune being.

Not only is God one, and not only are we one, but we are one with Him, and He is one with us. Christ is the Head, and we are the Body, therefore we are an extension of Him. That is who we are, and who we are determines what we do (how we act). So, what is all this about dying to self? Who is this self we are to die to, if we are one with Christ, if we are a new creature because we are in Him?

You see, we are not just sinners saved by grace, as some teach. We were sinners, we got saved by grace and now we are new creatures in Christ. The apostle Peter said, in his second letter to the Church, *"Grace and peace be multiplied unto you through the knowledge of God, and of Jesus our Lord, according as his divine power hath given unto us all things that pertain unto life and godliness, through the knowledge of him that hath called us to glory and virtue: whereby are given unto us exceeding great and precious promises: that by these ye might be **partakers of the divine nature**, having escaped the corruption that is in the world through lust"* (2 Peter 1:2-4, Emphasis added).

196

"Partakers of the divine nature?" In his book, *Dawning of the Third Day,*[4] my friend Doug Fortune says that Jesus didn't merely die for us; He died *as* us. Glory to God! If Jesus died as us, dying the death we deserve, then guess what? We died with Him. It has been called the great exchange. But He didn't just die in my place; He died as me. God sent Him in the likeness of sinful flesh so we could become like Him (see Romans 8:3-4). That means the old me is dead, period. I am a new person (creature), and that new person is just like God! So why this battle between flesh and spirit? A good question. I think we should look deeper into this subject, which we will do in our next reading. ✛

KINGDOM MANNA: READING 79

WE ARE NOT SCHIZOPHRENIC 2

I die daily.   The apostle Paul in 1 Corinthians 15:31

*Them that walk after the flesh in the lust of uncleanness... Presumptuous are they, **self**-willed.*   2 Peter 2:10, Emphasis added

Therefore if any man be in Christ, he is a new creature: old things are passed away; behold, all things are become new.

2 Corinthians 5:17

4. Kernersville, NC, Doug Fortune Ministries, 2005, page 124

As for me, I will behold thy face in righteousness: I shall be satisfied, when I awake, with thy likeness.   Psalm 17:15

In 1 Peter 3:4, the apostle Peter is speaking to female saints specifically, but he says something interesting. He speaks of *"the hidden man of the heart,"* which lets me know the truth he is applying here is not only for women, but for all saints. He goes on to say that the hidden man of the heart is not corruptible and is of great price in the sight God. He is saying that who we are is not determined by what appears on the outside, but by what is in our hearts.

The apostle John said this: *"Hereby perceive we the love of God, because he laid down his life for us: and we ought to lay down our lives for the brethren. But whoso hath this world's good, and seeth his brother have need, and shutteth up his bowels of compassion from him, how dwelleth the love of God in him? My little children, let us not love in word, neither in tongue; but in deed and in truth. And hereby we know that we are of the truth, and shall assure our hearts before him. For if our heart condemn us, God is greater than our heart, and knoweth all things. Beloved, if our heart condemn us not, then have we confidence toward God"* (1 John 3:16-21).

Colossians 3:22 speaks of singleness of heart and Proverbs 23:7 says that a man is what he thinks in his heart.

The act of being born again is spiritual. While we literally become new creatures in Christ (see 2 Corinthians 5:17) our soul (mind) still remembers who we were before we were born again. Because our mind remembers, that memory remains a part of us. We are no longer that old person, but the memory of that old person wants to pull us back into a lifestyle that is more familiar to us than the new lifestyle we are now growing into because we are a new person. That is why we must renew our minds to the Word of God.

*And be not conformed to this world: but be ye transformed by the renewing of your mind, that ye may **prove** what is that good, and acceptable, and perfect will of God.*

Romans 12:2, Emphasis added

We are actually in a process of becoming what we have already become. The more we grow into this new person we have become, the less we will **prove** (do) only those things that are good and acceptable and the more we will **prove** (do) that which is perfect. Saints, we are being perfected because we have been perfected. The more we walk out this process, the more we will see ourselves as the finished product, having singleness of heart. This is not something we can accomplish by hard work or determination. Only God can accomplish this in us. God is greater than our heart; he knows all things (see 1 John 3:20). That is why we are in a process of dying to self, even though that *self* has already died. I know that to those who are not born again, all this sounds like double-talk. But to those of us who are walking it out in our lives, it makes perfect sense. Glory to God! ✛

KINGDOM MANNA: Reading 80

Satan Is Subtle

Be sober, be vigilant; because your adversary the devil, as a roaring lion, walketh about, seeking whom he may devour.   1 Peter 5:8

And Adam was not deceived, but the woman being deceived was in the transgression.   1 Timothy 2:14

Eve sinned because she was deceived, and the consequences affected the next six thousand years of mankind's existence on the earth. And it ain't over yet. Satan had no power over Eve or over mankind until Eve gave it to him.

Peter refers to Satan as the devil. He says he walks about as a roaring lion seeking someone to devour. Notice that Peter does not say that Satan *is* a roaring lion, but that he *masquerades* as a roaring lion.

The devil has no authority over us unless we give it to him. Perhaps the primary way he gains that authority over people, especially over believers, is by deceiving them. His methods are often very subtle, as was the case with Eve. That is why, as Peter said, we need to be sober and vigilant.

Webster's Dictionary says *sober* is, among other things: "seriousness, gravity, solemnity; free from exaggeration; sane or rational." *Webster's* definition of *vigilant* is: "keenly watchful to detect danger, wary; ever awake and alert; careless (meaning without care)."

The devil has many schemes to deceive or trick people into giving him authority over the circumstances of their lives. John tells us there are three primary ways he does this: by the lust of the flesh, the lust of the eyes and the pride of life (see 1 John 2:16).

Webster describes *lust* as: "to have a yearning or desire; to have a strong or excessive craving." In this context, another word we could use for *lust* is *pressure*. Our flesh wants to feel good (the lust of the flesh), our eyes desire that which looks good (the lust of the eyes), and in the process of gaining what our flesh and eyes desire, we want to look good in the sight of other people (the pride of life).

The devil is a master at putting pressure on us in these areas. How we deal with that pressure will determine if he is able to devour us, as a roaring lion, or if we will overcome him. He knows that the only real weakness believers have is their lack of understanding of who they are. The more we realize who we are, the less effective he will be at putting pressure on us.

Saints, the devil is defeated. He has no power or authority over us, unless we give it to him, and the primary reason believers give it to him is deception. He is a liar and the father of lies (see John 8:44). Unless he can convince you he has some power over you, he has none.

There is a popular mindset in the world today that says we are all victims. No one is actually responsible for their actions because they are a victim of what someone else or circumstances have done to them. This philosophy is prevalent among political liberals and socialists. Rather than equipping people to overcome their situations, this train of thought gives them excuses, which may make them feel good temporarily, but in the long run, keeps them enslaved to their situations.

We are only victims if we allow ourselves to be victimized. While we may not be able to control everything that comes our way, we can control the way we respond to the things that come our way. We can become and remain victims, or we can be overcomers. We are not victims to the wiles of the devil (see Ephesians 6:11). We are overcomers, and we have all the power and authority of Heaven at our disposal.

The devil is not our problem. It is how we see ourselves that either enables us to be overcomers or causes us to be victims. Let me say it again, "The devil is defeated!"

In the next few KINGDOM MANNA's, we are going to look at some of the ways the devil attempts to put pressure on us and at some of the ways we can overcome him. ✠

201

THE LUST OF THE FLESH

*For all that is in the world, the **lust of the flesh**, and the lust of the eyes, and the pride of life, is not of the Father, but is of the world.*

> 1 John 2:16, Emphasis added

Another word for *lust* is *pressure*. Many people understand *lust* as sexual desire. While sexual desire can be lust, lust applies to much more than sex. The lust of the flesh is any pressure put on our flesh.

Sexual desire (not addiction) is not necessarily evil. I desire my wife and that is as it should be. The lust of the flesh is actually pressure to operate in the flesh as opposed to operating in the Spirit or according to the Word of God.

Pressure to operate in the flesh can come from different places and concern different things. If I am unable to pay my bills, I may experience pressure to get out of faith and into fear. Fear is synonymous with worry, stress and anxiety. Operating in fear hinders a person from operating in the wisdom of God, hearing from the Spirit of God and making sound decisions.

Another area where people experience much pressure to operate in the flesh is concerning health. We may understand that God has made provision for us to be healthy and to overcome sickness or disease should it come knocking at our door. But should the manifestation of healing not come quickly when we pray and/or take authority over it in the name of Jesus, we may become tempted to once again get out of faith and into fear.

When the solution to financial problems or the manifestation of healing doesn't come quickly, a believer needs wisdom and guidance as to how to deal with the situation. It is essential that we operate in faith believing that God is our Provider and Healer and that He has made provision for both.

The facts may tell a person he/she has a financial or health problem, but the truth concerning those issues is found in the Word of God. The question becomes, are we going to believe the facts or the truth? Believing the truth will change the facts. However, if that change is not instantaneous or does not come quickly, we need wisdom and guidance to know how to deal with the facts.

To believe the facts is to give into the pressure or lust of the flesh. To believe the truth, even when we don't see the manifestation of it, is how we overcome the pressure or lust of the flesh.

I'm not going to tell you to never borrow money, go to the doctor or take medicine. While I don't think those solutions are God's best for us, my experience has been that sometimes they have been necessary. But I always put God first, applying His Word to the situation and then following the guidance of the Holy Spirit and operating in the wisdom God has given me.

If any of you lack wisdom, let him ask of God, that giveth to all men liberally, and upbraideth not; and it shall be given him. But let him ask in faith, nothing wavering. For he that wavereth is like a wave of the sea driven with the wind and tossed. For let not that man think that he shall receive any thing of the Lord. A double minded man is unstable in all his ways. James 1:5-8

✠

THE LUST OF THE FLESH 2

*For all that is in the world, the **lust of the flesh**, and the lust of the eyes, and the pride of life, is not of the Father, but is of the world.*

1 John 2:16, Emphasis added

Them that walk after the flesh in the lust of uncleanness ... , presumptuous are they, self-willed ...

2 Peter 2:10

As we have already studied, lust is pressure. We looked at two areas the devil uses to put pressure on our flesh: finances and health. There are other ways the devil uses our flesh to put pressure on us, but these two (finances and health) are something most of us have faced more than occasionally. Isn't it interesting that he uses our flesh to keep us operating in the flesh? He knows that if he can succeed in getting us to deal with the flesh by operating in the flesh, we will be of little or no good to the Kingdom of God? We will be defeated and in bondage rather than victorious overcomers. And we will be so focused on our problems that we won't have the strength or ability to help anyone else.

Don't allow the pressure of finances and/or health issues, or anything else for that matter, to get you focused on the problem rather than on the solution. The solution is always what God says. God's Word is truth.

While the facts you may be facing are real, believing and confessing the truth will change the facts.

Don't allow the lust of the flesh to keep you in bondage to the flesh. The flesh is no good. It cannot be rehabilitated or fixed. The only way to deal with the flesh is to crucify it. Even the apostle Paul said, *"I die daily"* (1 Corinthians 15:31). To operate in the flesh and/or give into the lust of the flesh is to be self-conscious rather than God-conscious.

As we die to self, the flesh and the lust or pressure of the flesh will have no power over us. We will be free from the bondage of sin and death, which includes bondage to the world's system. We will be able to walk in the Spirit according to the Word of God, enabling us to be overcomers. Glory to God! ✞

KINGDOM MANNA: Reading 83

The Lust of the Flesh 3

*For all that is in the world, the **lust of the flesh**, and the lust of the eyes, and the pride of life, is not of the Father, but is of the world.*

1 John 2:16, Emphasis added

We have looked at how the devil uses our flesh to put pressure on us to get in and stay in the flesh, rather than walking in the Spirit according to the Word of God. Perhaps we should note here that the devil doesn't necessarily seek out individuals and implement the principles we are studying here. Satan is not omnipresent, as God is. He can only be in one place at any given time, so he is probably not targeting you individually. These are simply principles he knew would work against us that he put in motion six thousand years ago in the Garden when he first tempted Eve.

Lust is pressure, and pressure is simply temptation. It is not sin to be tempted. If that were the case, Jesus would have sinned in the wilderness when He was tempted by the devil, and we know that Jesus never sinned.

People get into sin when they give in to temptation. We have made *sin* a very religious term but it simply means "missing the mark." People surrender to temptation when they accept the problem rather than the solution, which is the Word of God. By focusing on the problem instead of the solution, they miss the mark or they sin.

Sin produces death (see Romans 6:23). Death comes in many packages. It isn't always stopping to breathe and being put six feet under. People struggling with debt sometimes have heart attacks caused by the fear and worry (stress) that debt causes. Debt can put extreme pressure on a marriage, causing the death of that marriage. Sickness and disease rob people of happiness and make them ineffective in the roles they play in life. Often sickness and disease causes physical death.

Giving into other pressures or lusts of the flesh can also produce death in some form and to some degree. In Galatians Paul names several practices of the flesh people get into when they give into the lusts of the flesh:

Now the doings (practices) of the flesh are clear (obvious): they are immorality, impurity, indecency, idolatry, sorcery, enmity, strife, jealousy, anger (ill temper), selfishness, divisions (dissensions), party spirit (factions, sects with peculiar opinions, heresies), envy, drunkenness, carousing, and the like. Galatians 5:19-21, AMP

All of these are sin, and they all produce death. However, they are things the flesh likes. Because of our genetic makeup and our upbringing, we may not be tempted in all of these areas, but our weaknesses tend to surface and put pressure on us. We defeat our flesh by not giving into the pressure our flesh puts on us.

We must stay focused on the Word of God rather than on the pressure. That's why it is of utmost importance that we stay in the Word continually, feeding on it and confessing it until it becomes a part of us. That is also why it is imperative that we have an intimate relationship with God. Being one with Him gives us the power to focus on the solution and, by doing so, to overcome the problem.

As we mature in the Lord and realize who we are in the Lord, the flesh is no longer a problem for us. As we have established in earlier KINGDOM MANNA teachings, we are not schizophrenic. We are not two people. We do not have to continually choose between the flesh and the Spirit. We are new creatures in Christ, and as we renew our minds to that truth, the devil and/or the flesh will have no power over us. ✠

KINGDOM MANNA: Reading 84

The Lust of the Eyes

*For all that is in the world, the lust of the flesh, and the **lust of the eyes**, and the pride of life, is not of the Father, but is of the world.*

1 John 2:16, Emphasis added

I made a covenant with mine eyes; why then should I think upon a maid?   Job 31:1

Job is an extremely interesting book. It is probably one of the most misunderstood books of the Bible. Many have pondered and debated why Job suffered as he did. Ezekiel 14:14 tells us that God considered Job a righteous man, and yet Job allowed Satan to trip him up by applying pressure where he was the weakest. Somehow, Job knew that to desire a woman other than his wife was sin. He made an agreement with his eyes that he would not lustfully look at other women. Yet, it was his eyes that got him into trouble.

Job **saw** his sons and daughters partying and became concerned that they had possibly sinned and cursed God while in a drunken state. Job became fearful for his children's fate because of what he **saw** them doing, so he offered sacrifices, hoping to appease God's wrath (just in case God was angry with his children). Job **saw** something that disturbed him, and he allowed what he **saw** to pressure him into fear.

Like faith, fear is a force that produces results. This is the account of what happened when Satan next appeared before God:

Now there was a day when the sons of God came to present themselves before the LORD, and Satan came also among them. And the LORD said unto Satan, Whence comest thou?

Then Satan answered the LORD, and said, From going to and fro in the earth, and from walking up and down in it.

And the LORD said unto Satan, Hast thou considered my servant Job, that there is none like him in the earth, a perfect and an upright man, one that feareth God, and excheweth evil?

Then Satan answered the LORD, and said, Doth Job fear God for nought? Hast not thou made an hedge about him, and about his house, and about all that he hath on every side? Thou hast blessed the work of his hands, and his substance is increased in the land. But put forth thine hand now, and touch all that he hath, and he will curse thee to thy face.

*And the LORD said unto Satan, **Behold, all that he hath is in thy power**; only upon himself put not forth thine hand.*

So Satan went forth from the presence of the LORD. Job 1:6-12, Emphasis added

God considered Job to be a righteous man, but he knew Job was vulnerable in at least one area. Job had gotten into fear concerning his children, by giving in to the pressure or lust of his eyes (what he saw his children doing). Because of fear, Job was already in Satan's power, and Satan didn't know it until God pointed it out to him.

Evidently Job had no fear for his own life or for that of his wife. However, fear caused him to lose his children and all of his livestock (which caused him to become physically ill). In Job 3:25, Job says, *"For the thing which I greatly feared is come upon me, and that which I was afraid of is come unto me."*

My point is this: A person can walk uprightly and hate evil but still get out of faith and into fear. Satan often uses what people see to trip them up. Again, it comes back to where our focus is. Are we focused on the problem or on the solution?

Satan uses subtle ways to pressure people out of faith and into fear because their focus is in the wrong place. One cannot focus in two places at once.

James said it like this:

Blessed is the man that endureth temptation: for when he is tried, he shall receive the crown of life, which the Lord hath promised to them

*that love him. Let no man say when he is tempted, I am tempted of God: for God cannot be tempted with evil, neither tempteth he any man: but every man is tempted, when he is drawn away of **his own lust**, and enticed. Then when lust hath conceived, it bringeth forth sin: and sin, when it is finished, bringeth forth death.*

James 1:12-15, Emphasis added

KINGDOM MANNA: Reading 85

The Pride of Life

*For all that is in the world, the lust of the flesh, and the lust of the eyes, and the **pride of life**, is not of the Father, but is of the world.*

1 John 2:16, Emphasis added

*The fear of the Lord is to hate evil: **pride**, and arrogancy, and the evil way, and the froward mouth, do I hate.*

Proverbs 8:13, Emphasis added

*When **pride** cometh, then cometh shame: but with the lowly is wisdom.*

Proverbs 11:2, Emphasis added

*In the mouth of the foolish is a rod of **pride**: but the lips of the wise shall preserve them.*   Proverbs 14:3, Emphasis added

Pride goeth before destruction.   Proverbs 16:18, Emphasis added

A man's pride shall bring him low: but honour shall uphold the humble in spirit.   Proverbs 29:23, Emphasis added

For from within, out of the heart of men, proceed evil thoughts, adulteries, fornications, murders, thefts, covetousness, wickedness, deceit, lasciviousness, an evil eye, blasphemy, pride, foolishness: all these evil things come from within, and defile the man.

Jesus in Mark 7:21-23, Emphasis added

As a young boy I was taught there is good pride and bad pride. I was taught to be proud of myself when I did good, proud of my family name, proud of my nation and even proud of my religion. I was taught that bad pride was looking down on someone else because I thought I was better than them. Wrong! There is no good pride. Jesus listed pride right along with adultery, murder, wickedness, lying and so on. John said the pride of life is not of the Father but of the world.

The apostle Paul said, *"But by the grace of God I am what I am"* (1 Corinthians 15:10). Paul realized he could take no credit for anything good in his life. Anything good he had accomplished was only because of God's grace (empowerment).

A proud person is one who takes credit for accomplishments. Pride causes one to become puffed up, thinking more highly of himself/herself than he/she ought to.

Romans 10:9 says, *"If thou shalt confess with thy mouth the Lord Jesus, and shalt believe in thine heart that God hath raised him from the dead, thou shalt be saved."*

In the feudal system of the Middle Ages, a lord ruled over a certain geographical area and its people. He was their master, and they were expected to work for and obey him. However, he was also their provider. A good lord provided protection, shelter and food for those under him. As long as a serf lived in submission to his lord, he could expect to be protected and provided for.

When we confess Jesus as Lord, it is basically the same situation. We are recognizing Him as our Master, Protector and Provider. There is no room for pride in that. To get into pride is to get into rebellion against Him as Lord. It is to say, "I don't need Him; I can do it myself." It is to exalt ourselves above Him, which was the sin that the king of Babylon committed (see Isaiah 14:4) when he said, *"I will ascend into heaven, I will exalt my throne above the stars of God: I will sit also upon the mount of the congregation, in the sides of the north: I will ascend above the heights of the clouds; I will be like the most High"* (Isaiah 14:13-14).

Like all sin, pride produces death. It causes strife and division. It gives place to envy, unforgiveness and even fear. In Mark 7:21-23 Jesus listed pride along with several other sins. It is very possible that a little pride can grow and actually cause the other sins listed in these verses (see 1 Corinthians 5:1-6).

Pride is another subtle tactic of Satan. I think it is one of the most damaging and dangerous sins. It is what caused the king of Babylon to fall (see Isaiah 14:12) and sealed his fate (see verse 15).

To confess Jesus as Lord is to be saved from pride. The flesh wants to be proud and hang on to pride. But like any dying to self or crucifying our flesh, while it may be painful for awhile, it produces abundant life (see John 10:10 and Ephesians 3:20).

Humble yourselves therefore under the mighty hand of God, that he may exalt you in due time.   1 Peter 5:6

✤

Satan Is Subtle: The Solution

For all that is in the world, the lust of the flesh, and the lust of the eyes, and the pride of life, is not of the Father, but is of the world.

1 John 2:16

For as much then as Christ hath suffered for us in the flesh, arm your-selves likewise with the same mind: for he that hath suffered in the flesh hath ceased from sin; that he no longer should live the rest of his time in the flesh to the lusts of men, but to the will of God.

1 Peter 4:1-2

For if we would judge ourselves, we should not be judged, but when we are judged, we are chastened of the Lord, that we should not be condemned with the world. 1 Corinthians 11:31-32

The best way to die to self and not walk in the lust (pressure) of the flesh and of the eyes or in the pride of life, is to judge ourselves by the Word of God and simply do what the Word says.

Jesus suffered once and for all. When He said, *"It is finished"* (John 19:30), He meant, "It is finished." So you might ask, "Why does it still take suffering for us to die to self and walk in the Spirit?" The problem is the flesh doesn't understand any of the Word of God. Spiritual things must be spiritually discerned (see 1 Corinthians 2:14). False doctrines and even entire religions are in existence because of people interpreting the Word of God in the flesh. The Word of God can only be understood as it is spiritually discerned.

In order to spiritually discern something, we must die to self and walk in the Spirit. Satan applies pressure to the flesh in order to keep us in the flesh. If he can keep us in the flesh, we are unable to discern the things of the Spirit and overcome the flesh.

Paul tells us, in Romans 8:6-7, that to be carnally minded is death, but to be spiritually minded is life and peace. He goes on to say that the carnal mind is the enemy of God.

We must walk in the Spirit to overcome the flesh. However, we need to overcome the flesh to walk in the Spirit. This sounds like a definite *Catch 22*. What is the solution? Paul gives us the answer in Philippians 3:8-10:

I count all things but loss for the excellence of the knowledge of Christ Jesus my Lord: for whom I have suffered the loss of all things, and do count them but dung, that I may win Christ, and be found in him, not having mine own righteousness, which is of the law, but that which is through the faith of Christ, the righteousness which is of God by faith: that I may know him, and the power of his resurrection, and the fellowship of his sufferings, being made conformable unto his death.

If you have ever worked with or been an alcoholic or drug addict, you probably know that treatment programs teach that addicts must hit bottom before they are in a position to change. The same flesh that the devil uses to keep us in the flesh, God will use to deliver us from the flesh. In areas where we are unable to crucify our own flesh, God will use trials and tests to crucify it for us. James said that we are tried and tested when we are drawn away from the things of God by our own lusts (see James 1:14). Tests and trials are unpleasant, but the rewards far outweigh any suffering we must endure.

The apostle Paul, who suffered greatly for the Gospel, said this:

For our light affliction, which is but for a moment, worketh for us a far more exceeding and eternal weight of glory.

2 Corinthians 4:17

I can personally testify that this is true. While I don't want to repeat any of the trials I have suffered, I will be eternally grateful that God, in His grace and mercy, caused me to go through them.

Despise not the chastening of the LORD; neither be weary of his correction: for whom the LORD loveth he correcteth; even as a father the son in whom he delighteth.   Proverbs 3:11-12

✠

Denial

Then Jesus said unto his disciples, If any man will come after me, let him deny himself, and take up his cross, and follow me. For whosoever will save his life shall lose it: and whosoever will lose his life for my sake shall find it. Matthew 16:24-25

There is a psychological term *in denial*. To be *in denial* is considered to be a bad thing. Certainly, if denying the truth in a situation is being *in denial*, then it is a bad thing. But in the above scripture, Jesus instructs us to be *in denial* where the flesh is concerned. He tells us to deny ourselves (or the flesh), take up our cross and follow Him.

How do we do this? Paul tells us in Galatians 2:20,"*I am crucified with Christ: nevertheless I live; yet not I, but Christ liveth in me: and the life which I now live in the flesh I live by the faith of the Son of God, who loved me, and gave himself for me.*"

The Amplified Bible makes it a little clearer: "*I have been crucified with Christ [in Him I have shared His crucifixion]: it is no longer I who live, but Christ (the Messiah) lives in me; and the life I now live in the body I live by faith in (by adherence to and reliance on and complete trust in) the Son of God, who loved me and gave Himself up for me.*"

We have studied about Paul and Silas being in prison with open wounds on their backs, chained and with their feet in stocks. How did they react to this horrible situation? By praying and praising God. They were denying themselves and drawing strength from their inner man (see Ephesians 3:16).

In 1 Corinthians 15:31 Paul said, *"I die daily."* Paul considered himself crucified with Jesus. He was in a continual process of dying to self, his flesh nailed to the cross of Christ. It is impossible to hurt a dead person. Paul was not living in the natural, even though his mortal body was still alive. He was living in the Spirit. The life in his mortal body was being sustained by the Spirit and by faith in the finished work of Jesus on the cross:

> *For to me to live is Christ, and to die is gain. But if I live in the flesh* [in the mortal body], *this is the fruit of my labour: yet what I shall choose I wot not. For I am in a strait betwixt two, having a desire to depart, and to be with Christ; which is far better: Nevertheless to abide in the flesh is more needful for you.*   Philippians 1:21-24

Paul was so in love with Christ that it no longer mattered to him if he lived or died. In fact, he preferred to go on and be with the Lord in Heaven. But he was on a mission. He had a job to do, and he was also passionate about his job. Because his focus and his passion were on the right things and not on himself, he had reached a point in his life where he really didn't care about himself. Why should he? You can't hurt or kill a dead man, and Paul was in the habit of continually dying to self and living in Christ.

In the next couple of KINGDOM MANNA readings, I will be sharing with you some personal testimony along these lines. ✝

A TESTIMONY OF DYING TO SELF

[Yes] we have confident and hopeful courage and are pleased rather to be away from home out of the body and be at home with the Lord.

2 Corinthians 5:8, AMP

In the 1970s I wrote a rock musical about Jesus entitled, "Finally." In the early to mid 80s, I recorded it and then traveled and performed portions of it. My ultimate vision for "Finally" was to produce a major stage production with elaborate lighting and special effects. In the end, I couldn't seem to make that happen.

One day I thought to myself, "What if Jesus comes back before I get this stage production done?" Immediately I realized that I was in great error. The thing (ministry) God had given me to do had become more important to me than my relationship with Him.

I didn't know how to change the way I felt, so I asked the Lord to help me overcome my emotions. Several weeks later I was in High Point, North Carolina, staying with my mother. One afternoon, while my mother wasn't home, I went to the back bedroom of the house, turned on the radio and took a nap. I was awakened by the sound of footsteps coming down the hallway. I can't explain how, but somehow I knew my mother hadn't come home yet. I heard the DJ on the radio say it was twenty minutes before the hour.

As this *person* walked into the room, I was lying on my side facing the wall. Somehow I knew this person was an angel, and I became fearful. My past experiences with seeing and being aware of angels had not been fearful, and I'm not sure why I was afraid this time.

I continued lying on my side, with my eyes closed, as the angel placed his hand on my shoulder and turned me over in the bed, so that I was lying on my back. At that point, I opened my eyes to see this angel, but there was no one.

I realized I needed to use the bathroom. As I was standing in front of the toilet urinating, I felt water forming around my feet. For some reason, water was spraying everywhere, and the puddle around my feet was getting larger and deeper. At this point, I looked out the window that overlooks my mother's backyard and saw a river coming out from under my mother's house. The river was probably twenty feet wide and running very swiftly. On the banks of the river was very tall, lush green grass with tall trees beyond that. The river went on as far as I could see. I knew it went on forever. I also knew that this river was coming from the puddle that had formed around my feet. It was literally coming out of me.

In my mind's eye, I pictured myself out there walking beside the river, going away from my mother's house. Suddenly it was as if I was there, but, at the same time, I was still in the bathroom. By this time I realized I was out of my body and in eternity.

The thing that stands out most in my mind was the freedom I felt. There was no weight — emotional or physical. I was walking on the ground, but I could have just as easily walked in the air.

The next thing I remember I was back in my body and back in the bed, waking up again. I heard the DJ on the radio say that it was twenty minutes after the hour, so I know forty minutes had passed. I asked the Lord, "What was that about?" Immediately I thought of the scripture,

"He that believeth on me, as the scripture hath said, out of his belly shall flow rivers of living water" (Jesus in John 7:38).

While we live in mortal bodies, we are actually already in eternity. We crossed that line the day we were born again, and the life that is in us flows out of us and affects all we come in contact with. What I experienced that day was just a confirmation of that truth, causing an easy death to self, making the truth so real to me that nothing can come between me and my relationship with my Lord, not even the ministry He has called me to fulfill. ♱

KINGDOM MANNA: Reading 89

A Testimony of Dying to Self 2

Humble yourselves therefore under the mighty hand of God, that he may exalt you in due time: Casting all your care upon him; for he careth for you.   1 Peter 5:6-7

In the spring of 2000, I attended a Full Gospel Business Men's (FG-BMFI) Advance at Fort Caswell, North Carolina. It was a weekend of praise and worship, teaching and fellowship that I found extremely refreshing. On Saturday morning before breakfast, I was outside, walking and praying in the Spirit. The Lord spoke to me very clearly and said, "I am now anointing you to lead praise and worship."

I said, "Okay."

I have been a singer and a musician most of my life, but I had never had a desire to be a praise and worship leader. I very much enjoyed being involved in worship, but I preferred to be in the audience. Now, in an instant, one Word from the Lord changed all that. I began leading praise and worship at FGBMFI functions. About a year and a half later, I became praise and worship leader at Love of Christ Church in Bolivia, North Carolina. I also led praise and worship with various other ministries and at meetings that I began holding in various cities.

The same day the Lord told me He was anointing me to lead praise and worship, I met Miguel Escobar. Miguel is a revivalist who has ministered in more than sixty nations. Later that day the Lord told me I would travel with Miguel for a period of time, and I have.

During this time that I was becoming more and more involved in ministry, I also worked as a paint contractor. My business was successful, but suddenly it began to go downhill financially. I had plenty of work, but I couldn't seem to make enough money. Something was continually happening to steal my profit. I started out borrowing a little money here and a little there, planning to pay it back when I finished the next job. But something would always take that money, and I continued to go deeper into debt.

After several months of this, I had a conversation with God. I said, "God, I don't know what is going on. I know how to pray. I know how to operate in faith. I am keeping my confession in line with Your Word, but it isn't working. I know Your voice, and I know I am walking in obedience to You. I am going to obey You no matter what. If it costs me everything — my house, my wife, my dog (I love my dog, but I love my wife more) — I will obey You." For a little while things seemed to get better, and then went downhill faster.

Then, in 2003 I was in Portugal with Miguel. I was out walking in Lisbon one afternoon, praying in the Spirit. The Lord spoke to me and said, "It is time to get out of the painting business."

I said, "I'll do it, but you have to tell my wife."

Four months later He woke her up at 4:00 AM and told her. I gave the painting business to my sons and embarked on a career as a full-time minister a few weeks later.

I have shared this story with you in past KINGDOM MANNA readings, and I could go on with it and tell you more, but the point is this: When I told the Lord I would obey Him no matter what, I meant it. I don't care. I refuse to care. I am a dead man, and I have no cares. I will continue to pray in faith, walk in love and use my authority in the name of Jesus, but I don't care what happens to me. I trust God completely. What else can I do? I've tried to do it myself, and that didn't work. So do I keep trying what has not worked? Or do I obey God and trust Him? I think you know the answer to that.

Please don't misunderstand me. I'm not desperate. I'm not down. I'm not frustrated. I just don't care. There is so much freedom in that. I have that peace that passes all understanding (see Philippians 4:7). ✣

A Testimony: The Result of Dying to Self

Humble yourselves therefore under the mighty hand of God, that he may exalt you in due time.   1 Peter 5:6

I was leading praise and worship at a FGBMFI Fall Advance in South Carolina, and that year I had a room to myself. Usually there were two men to a room, but I guess there was an odd number of men, so I got the room by myself. On Friday night, I had stayed up late, talking with Dale Richardson, a former national director of Full Gospel from Lumberton, North Carolina. As I went to my room, I heard the Lord say to me, "Get up at 6:00 in the morning." I assumed He wanted me to get up and pray before breakfast.

The door to my room wouldn't lock, so I set a chair in front of it. I wasn't concerned about anyone breaking in on me, but I thought if someone came into my room by mistake, at least I would hear him and wake up. As I went to bed, I started to set my alarm clock. Again the Lord spoke and said, "Don't set a clock. I will get you up."

I said, "Okay" and went to bed.

On Saturday morning, I was awakened by footsteps coming into my room, but I didn't hear the door open. Immediately I realized that this person coming into my room was Jesus. I don't know how I knew. I just knew.

I was lying on my side facing the wall, and for some reason I didn't turn over and look at Him. I have found that when I am in the Spirit I sometimes do things that later don't make sense to me. Why would I not have looked at Jesus walking into my room in person?

He walked over to my bed and sat down on the side of it. I literally felt His weight on the mattress. I was still lying on my side facing away from Him. He leaned His weight into my back, and when He did, I leaned my weight into Him. He did it again, and I did it again. We did it a third time.

Again, I don't know why. Perhaps the three times has something to do with this being the third day of the Church. Maybe us leaning our weight into each other has something to do with us (the Lord and the

Church) being dependent on each other to fulfill the purposes and plans of God in this third day (He is the Head and we are His Body).

Then He began talking. Unlike when He spoke to me the night before, this time I heard Him in an audible voice, although He was speaking in a language that I couldn't understand. It was a strange-sounding tongue, unlike any unknown tongues I had ever heard. I don't know exactly how it was different, but I was very impressed by the difference.

As He continued to talk, I became frustrated that I couldn't understand Him. Finally, with a little bit of an attitude, I said, "Lord, I can't understand You! What are You saying?"

He stopped and, in English, said, "You've promoted Me."

I said, "Lord, how have I promoted You?"

Suddenly He was gone. Then I heard that inward voice that I know to be Him. He said, "Now I'm going to promote you." And He has.

Are there still challenges? Many. But I have stopped trying to make things happen myself. I simply listen to Him, obey Him and trust Him. The outcome is up to Him. I continue to promote Him — through praise and worship, prophetic words, teaching and the life I live in Him — and He continues to promote me. Glory to God!

I am no longer building a ministry. I simply promote Him and the outcome of anything I do is entirely up to Him. It doesn't matter if I am known or not. It doesn't matter if I appear to be successful or not, because being successful is not in any way about me. Being successful is about promoting and establishing the Kingdom of God in earth as in Heaven. ✠

A Testimony: The Easiest Job in the World

*Come unto me, all ye that labour and are heavy laden, and I will give you rest. Take my yoke upon you, and learn of me; for I am meek and lowly in heart: and ye shall find rest unto your souls. **For my yoke is easy, and my burden is light.***

Matthew 11:28-30, Emphasis added

When I was in Portugal with Miguel Escobar, we were at a conference in Lisbon at a church that was very large by European standards. There aren't many large churches in Europe.

There were about two hundred church workers who had been serving the thirteen or fourteen hundred people attending the conference. Since they had been busy during the conference, some of them asked if we would come back the day after the conference ended and minister to them. We didn't have anywhere to be that day, so we agreed. It was a holiday in Portugal, and we were told that not many would show up, but the two hundred church workers came, plus about another hundred people.

As Miguel began to minister that night, it was as if his words were hitting an invisible wall and bouncing back at him. I have discovered that ministers can be the hardest to minister to. Perhaps that's the reason he was getting no response from the audience. Finally he just stopped, looked at me and told me to come up and share something. I stood up, having no idea what to say. I heard the Holy Spirit say, "Tell them to turn to the person beside them and pray for that person." So I told them what to do and they did it. The presence of God manifested in that place in a powerful way. People were hugging each other and crying, as they prayed for one another.

At one point, Miguel and I were over to the side, leaning against the wall. We were just observing what the Holy Spirit was doing. I said to Miguel, "This is the easiest job in the world." Miguel laughed.

Later many came forward to receive prayer from us. Most fell out in the Spirit when they were prayed for. I personally prophesied to many through interpreters. We later learned that there had been many problems and some fighting among the church workers. There were even marriages in trouble among them. That night God restored relationships and marriages.

All I did was obey the Lord, and He made us look real good. But it wasn't us. It was entirely by the Spirit. All glory to God!

How does this apply to what we have been studying? We walk in the Spirit when we stay dead to self and listen to Him. In case you haven't noticed, it is not about us. It is all about Him. After all, we are not our own; we belong to Him.

I haven't asked him, but I suspect Miguel was led of the Spirit when he told me to come up and share that night. All I did was say what the Spirit told me to say, and the Lord did the rest. Amazing!

For ye are bought with a price: therefore glorify God in your body, and in your spirit, which are God's.   1 Corinthians 6:20

✠

BE ENCOURAGED

Hearken to me, ye that follow after righteousness, ye that seek the LORD: look unto the rock whence ye are hewn, and the hole of the pit whence ye are digged.

Awake, awake, put on strength, O arm of the LORD; awake, as in the ancient days, in the generations of old.   Isaiah 51:1 and 9

We know there is a physical and a spiritual Zion. God has preserved a remnant of the nation of Israel through the centuries. The Jews have been scattered throughout the earth, persecuted and killed, and yet they remain today. No other people group has been dispersed like the Jews and still kept their identity. Not only have they kept their identity; God has preserved their original language. Ancient Hebrew is being taught and spoken in the nation of Israel today.

The rebirth of the nation of Israel in the twentieth century is one of the greatest fulfillments of biblical prophecy and one of the greatest proofs of the existence of the almighty and sovereign God. God's plan for planet earth and the Kingdom of God is right on schedule, and no one can stop it or slow it down.

Isaiah 51:1, 9 and the verses in between are for physical Zion, but many scriptures, especially prophecy, have more than one application. I believe this scripture is also for spiritual Zion.

Out of the remnant of the Jews, God birthed another remnant. On the Day of Pentecost, as recorded in the second chapter of Acts, the apostolic Church was born. The Kingdom of God began to come in earth as it is in Heaven.

Revelation of the New Covenant began to build upon and complete the things God had revealed and established under the Old Covenant. Types and shadows in the Old Testament began to become reality in the New Testament. Early on, God revealed that salvation was not for the Jews only, but for the entire world. He sent Peter to a Gentile named Cornelius and then raised up Paul to take the Gospel to the nations.

Out of the remnant of the Jews came another remnant. They were first called Christians at Antioch (see Acts 11:26), and they were made up of both Jews and Gentiles. Then, when the Roman emperor, Constantine, made Christianity the state religion in the fourth century, the Holy Spirit departed from the Church, for the most part. Christianity went from being a living organism to a dead organization, and the Dark Ages followed. Still, down through the centuries, God has had a remnant.

Foxe's Book of Martyrs[5] historically records this fact. The remnants down through the centuries were people seeking more of God. Each remnant walked in a little more revelation than the *status quo,* and all were persecuted for the stand they took.

In the sixteenth century, Martin Luther received revelation concerning salvation by grace rather than works. The Catholic Church considered this heresy, but Luther spread his revelation at the risk of his life. Luther's revelation brought about great strides toward the restoration of the apostolic Church.

In the nineteenth and twentieth centuries, great moves of God such as the Welsh Revivals, the Azusa Street Revival and the Charismatic Movement made tremendous strides in restoring the baptism with the Holy Spirit, bringing with this experience signs, wonders, miracles, the

5. Reading, England, Spire Books, 2002

operation of the gifts of the Spirit (see 1 Corinthians 12:3-11) and the manifestation of the fruit of the Spirit (see Galatians 5:22-23).

Today God continues to build upon that which He has reestablished in recent years. People are experiencing His presence in very real and powerful ways. Corporate worship is bringing an intimacy between God and His people that is awesome and indescribable. The level of faith in the Body of Christ is rising, to believe God for the *greater things* that Jesus spoke of in John 14:12.

Like the Jews, this remnant has suffered much, as God has been preparing and positioning us for that which is now emerging. Many have suffered to the point of despair, as God has refined us, separating the dross from the pure gold in us, so we will remain dead to self, enabling us to walk in the Spirit. We are being transformed into His likeness (see Romans 12:2 and 1 John 3:2), prepared and positioned for that which He has called us and chosen us to be and to do (see 2 Corinthians 11:15). Glory to God! ✠

KINGDOM MANNA: Reading 93

Be Encouraged 2

Hearken to me, ye that follow after righteousness, ye that seek the LORD: look unto the rock whence ye are hewn, and the hole of the pit whence ye are digged. Look unto Abraham your father, and unto Sarah that bare you: for I called him alone, and blessed him, and increased him. For the LORD shall comfort Zion: he will comfort all her waste places; and he will make her wilderness like Eden, and her desert like the garden of the LORD; joy and gladness shall be found therein, thanksgiving, and the voice of melody.

Hearken unto me, my people; and give ear unto me, O my nation: for a law shall proceed from me, and I will make my judgment to rest for a light of the people. My righteousness is near; my salvation is gone forth, and mine arms shall judge the people; the isles shall wait upon me, and on mine arm shall they trust. Lift up your eyes to the heavens, and look upon the earth beneath: for the heavens shall vanish away like smoke, and the earth shall wax old like a garment, and they that dwell therein shall die in like manner: but my salvation shall be for ever, and my righteousness shall not be abolished.

Hearken unto me, ye that know righteousness, the people in whose heart is my law; fear ye not the reproach of men, neither be ye afraid of their revilings. For the moth shall eat them up like a garment, and the worm shall eat them like wool: but my righteousness shall be for ever, and my salvation from generation to generation.

Awake, awake, put on strength, O arm of the LORD; awake, as in the ancient days, in the generations of old.   Isaiah 51:1-9

As for me, I will behold thy face in righteousness: I shall be satisfied, when I awake, with thy likeness.   Psalm 17:15

We are pregnant with the glory of God. Like a women travailing in childbirth, we are travailing, about to give birth to awesome and wonderful things, as we move closer and closer to the Kingdom of God in earth as it is in Heaven. And, like a woman who has given birth, we will soon forget the suffering.

For now, we must find our peace and joy, not in our circumstances, but in our relationship with our Lord and Savior and in His promises to us. However, as we walk out this process, becoming more and more like our God who is love, we don't have to find peace and joy at all. Peace and joy will find us. They will **overtake** us.

Peace and joy are the by-products of perfection. As we move into perfection, the circumstances around us will have no ability to rob us of that peace that passes all understanding or the joy that goes far beyond mere happiness. We will realize and possess the promise that God made to Abraham (which Abraham did not enter into in his lifetime). The blessing of Abraham will continuously **overtake** us. Is this any less than the plowman **overtaking** the reaper and the treader of grapes him that sows seed, spoken of by the prophet Amos (see Amos 9:13)?

Back up to verse 11 in the 9th chapter of Amos, and you will see those three words spoken over and over in prophetic scripture: *in that day.* Saints, I believe this is referring to the day in which we live, the third day (millennium) of the Church and the seventh day (millennium) since the creation recorded in Genesis.

Some reading the above scripture from Isaiah might assume from verse 6 that the earth is going to be completely destroyed and possibly cease to exist, but that assumption is not consistent with the other verses in this passage or in other scripture passages. Verse 7 speaks of a people that know righteousness and have God's law written in their hearts. In verse 8 God says His righteousness shall be forever and His salvation from generation to generation.

We were created for this day and for the ages to come. We were not created for some great escape. We were created to behold His face in righteousness, being awakened with His likeness (character) (Psalm 17:15). We were created to be overcomers or "overtakers," as we are overtaken by God's nature and character. Surely we were born for such a time as this! ✞

BE ENCOURAGED 3

Hearken to me, ye that follow after righteousness, ye that seek the LORD: look unto the rock whence ye are hewn, and the hole of the pit whence ye are digged. Awake, awake, put on strength, O arm of the LORD; awake, as in the ancient days, in the generations of old.

Isaiah 51:1, 9

As for me, I will behold thy face in righteousness: I shall be satisfied, when I awake, with thy likeness.   Psalm 17:15

The above scriptures speak of a people transformed (think of a caterpillar that transforms into a butterfly) into the likeness of God, a righteous people possessing the nature and character of God.

Richard Stearns, president of World Vision, in his book, *The Hole in our Gospel*[6] (page 74) made this statement: *"It takes transformed people to transform the world."* The transformation that takes place when we are born again and baptized with the Holy Spirit is not the transformation that will transform the world. Those experiences are but the door into the process that births in us the nature and character of God, and it is that transformation that will transform the world.

---

6. Nashville, TN, Thomas Nelson, 2010

There is a remnant that is now emerging as we enter into this third day (millennium) of the Church. We have been severely tested and tried, being refined in the fires of adversity, to come forth as pure gold. As we submit to this process, not only are we experiencing the transformation Stearns spoke of in his book; we are actually beginning to get a glimpse of the ages to come, spoken of by the apostle Paul (see Ephesians 2:7, 3:21 and Colossians 1:26).

The first two days (millennia) of the Church were the Church Age. The day (millennium) we are now entering into, commonly referred to as the third day of the Church, is the Kingdom Age. As we enter into the Kingdom Age, some of us are getting a glimpse of the ages to come. We don't yet know what to call what we are barely seeing, and we certainly are not yet there experientially. We must first walk out what we are now experiencing, but just getting a glimpse of what lies beyond is encouragement enough to keep us pressing ahead into a glorious future. The present troubles do not, in any way, compare to the glory that lies ahead. Hallelujah!

Whereof I am made a minister, according to the dispensation of God which is given to me for you, to fulfil the word of God; even the mystery which hath been hid from ages and from generations, but now is made manifest to his saints: to whom God would make known what is the riches of the glory of this mystery among the Gentiles; which is Christ in you, the hope of glory: whom we preach, warning every man, and teaching every man in all wisdom; that we may present every man perfect in Christ Jesus: whereunto I also labour, striving according to his working, which worketh in me mightily. Colossians 1:25-29

Never before has there been a time like this time! Never before has there been a day like this day! Surely we were born for such a time as this!

For the earnest expectation of the creature waiteth for the manifesta-
tion of the sons of God. Romans 8:19

The time we are now entering into has been labeled such things as *The Third Day, Kingdom* and *The Manifested Sons of God,* but saints, labels are not important. What is important is that we realize God is building on that which has already come and giving us a glimpse of that which is to come and that He has chosen us to walk out this process that will bring the restitution of all things. We must stay the course. We must finish the race, resting in Him and realizing that He is the Author and the Finisher of our faith.

All glory to God! Bless His name forever! Hallelujah! ✠

KINGDOM MANNA: Reading 95

The Promise

For the promise, that he should be the heir of the world, was not to Abraham, or to his seed, through the law, but through the righteous-ness of faith.

Therefore it is of faith, that it might be by grace; to the end the promise might be sure to all the seed; not to that only which is of the law, but that also which is of the faith of Abraham; who is the father of us all.

Romans 4:13, 16

Now to Abraham and his seed were the promises made. He saith not, And to seeds, as of many; but as of one, And to thy seed, which is Christ.

Galatians 3:16

For God made promise to Abraham, because he could swear by no greater, he sware by himself, saying, Surely blessing I will bless thee, and multiplying I will multiply thee.

Wherein God, willing more abundantly to shew unto the heirs of promise the immutability of his counsel, confirmed it by an oath: That by two immutable things, in which it was impossible for God to lie, we might have a strong consolation, who have fled for refuge to lay hold upon the hope set before us: Which hope we have as an anchor of the soul, both sure and stedfast, and which entereth into that within the veil; whither the forerunner is for us entered, even Jesus, made an high priest for ever after the order of Melchisedec.

Hebrews 6:13-14, 17-20

Whereof I am made a minister, according to the dispensation of God which is given to me for you, to fulfil the word of God; even the mystery which hath been hid from ages and from generations, but now is made manifest to his saints: to whom God would make known what is the riches of the glory of this mystery among the Gentiles; which is Christ in you, the hope of glory.

Colossians 1:25-27

And these all, having obtained a good report through faith, received not the promise: God having provided some better thing for us, that they without us should not be made perfect.   Hebrews 11:40

Much of the Old Testament gives us a picture of the New Testament. We sometimes call these pictures types and shadows. The promise God gave to Abraham, to bless and multiply him, was manifested in wealth and descendants, and yet the revelation of the Spirit makes it obvious there is a greater and eternal application of this promise. The apostle Paul saw this, and a thread of this truth runs through his letters to the churches. Like Abraham, who died without receiving much of what he was promised, Paul, too, died without receiving much of what he saw as the greater and eternal manifestation of the promise God made to Abraham:

And if ye be Christ's, then are ye Abraham's seed, and heirs according to the promise.   Galatians 3:29

The promise was not to Abraham only or to Paul, who saw the greater application of it; it is to all who belong to Christ. We are all heirs of the promise.

Many have focused on the natural blessing that came on Abraham, but to focus on that alone and not on the greater application of that promise is to fall short of the manifestation of the promise. While the manifestation of the promise that God made to Abraham made him a much wealthier man than he already was and gave him a son when he and Sarah were too old to have children, the promise had a more far-reaching effect than what Abraham saw and experienced. Actually, the manifestation of the promise in Abraham's lifetime was only the door through which God could then begin to bring about a process that would one day bring the greater manifestation of that promise.

As we continue on, let's look a little deeper into that promise and all it entails. ✠

The Promise 2

For the promise, that he should be the heir of the world, was not to Abraham, or to his seed, through the law, but through the righteousness of faith.

Therefore it is of faith, that it might be by grace; to the end the promise might be sure to all the seed; not to that only which is of the law, but that also which is of the faith of Abraham; who is the father of us all.

Romans 4:13 and 16

Now to Abraham and his seed were the promises made. He saith not, And to seeds, as of many; but as of one, And to thy seed, which is Christ.

Galatians 3:16

And if ye be Christ's, then are ye Abraham's seed, and heirs according to the promise.

Galatians 3:29

The promise God made to Abraham was not for him only or for the apostle Paul, who saw the greater application of it. It is to all who belong to Christ. We are all heirs of the promise.

When Jesus came in the flesh, most were clueless about who He was and why He was here. The Jews of that day were looking for someone to deliver them from Rome, not for someone to deliver them from sin. For the most part, they didn't even know they needed deliverance from sin, but every day they were faced with and felt the oppression of Rome.

The Word/faith movement of the mid-twentieth century has brought many in the Body of Christ to the same place today. The Word/faith teachers have taught us much about faith and how to bring about the manifestation of the things we all need to survive and succeed in the natural, but most of us have stopped there. In fact, many of us have not even gotten there. While many are not yet or are still getting the Word/faith message as it has been taught for the last fifty or sixty years, there is a greater application of that message that a few are now beginning to see.

The problem lies with our focus. Because of Sarah's age, Abraham was focused on the deadness of her womb. He couldn't see how God could make him the father of many nations, so he decided to help God out a little and got into a lot of trouble (that has had far-reaching effects, still felt in our world today). The reason Abraham was focused on the impossibility of the fulfillment of the promise God had made to him was because he was focused on the natural manifestation of the promise, rather than the greater and eternal application of that promise.

When Jesus came in the flesh, the Jews were focused on the Roman occupation of their homeland, which made it impossible for them to see who Jesus was and why He was among them. The result was that they crucified Him, not realizing they were actually bringing about His reason for being here. However, they brought much pain and suffering on themselves in the process.

The problem with the Word/faith movement, for the most part, has not been the message or the way it has been taught. It is the way it has been received. And that has to do with where people's focus is. Self-centered believers who focused on their own problems and/or dreams have missed the point. Perhaps some of the teachers have also missed the point. Perhaps that is why we have witnessed so much manipulation going on when offerings are received. Perhaps that is why so many give expecting an almost magical return on their giving, rather than the kind of increase the Scriptures speak of.

So what is the promise? And how do we receive it? In the lessons ahead, we will dig deeper into this subject that I believe is the very core of the Gospel. ✠

The Promise: In His Likeness

And God said, Let us make man in our image, after our likeness.

Genesis 1:26

As for me, I will behold thy face in righteousness: I shall be satisfied, when I awake, with thy likeness. Psalm 17:15

God spoke creation into existence. When God said it, it was a done deal. When He said, *"Let us make man in our image, after our likeness,"* it had to happen. I have often read this scripture, thinking of *image* and *likeness* as the same thing, but a study of the Hebrew words that translate as *image* and *likeness* show they are two related but different things.

The Hebrew word for *image* is *tselm*. Among other things it means "to be a representative of." The Hebrew word for *likeness* is *demuwth*.

It has to do with character. So to be made in God's *image* is to be His representative. When He created Adam in His image, Adam became God's representative on earth. However, to be made in His likeness is to take on the character or nature of God. One can be a representative of someone without being like that person. It was God's original intent that we be, not only His representatives, but that we also become like Him, having His character.

Genesis 1:27 says:

So God created man in his own image, in the image of God created he him; male and female created he them.

What happened to *likeness?* We see that God created Adam and Eve in His image, to be His representatives on earth, but nowhere in verse 27 is *likeness* mentioned. So Adam and Eve were created in His image, but not in His likeness. However, in verse 26, God spoke of both *image* and *likeness,* and once God said it, it had to come to pass.

I asked the Lord, "Why did You make man in Your image, but not in Your likeness?" Suddenly the answer became very clear to me. Image can be created. Advertising agencies do it all the time. But character cannot be created. Character has to be developed.

We know from the Genesis account of Creation about two trees that were planted in the Garden of Eden. One was the Tree of Life, and the other was the tree of the knowledge of good and evil. We also know that Adam and Eve were forbidden to eat of the tree of the knowledge of good and evil:

And the Lord God took the man, and put him into the Garden of Eden to dress it and to keep it. And the Lord God commanded the man, saying, Of every tree of the garden thou mayest freely eat: but of the tree of the knowledge of good and evil, thou shalt not eat of it: for in the day that thou eatest thereof thou shalt surely die.

Genesis 2:15-17

We all know the story of how Satan came as a serpent and tempted Eve to eat of the forbidden fruit:

And the serpent said unto the woman, Ye shall not surely die: for God doth know that in the day ye eat thereof, then your eyes shall be opened, and ye shall be as gods, knowing good and evil.   Genesis 3:4-5

Eve ate of the forbidden fruit and gave some to her husband, Adam, who also ate of it. However, they did not immediately die.

As we continue our study, we will consider how God began a process to develop His character in man. ✣

KINGDOM MANNA: Reading 98

THE PROMISE: IN HIS LIKENESS 2

And God said, Let us make man in our image, after our likeness.

Genesis 1:26

And the LORD God took the man, and put him into the Garden of Eden to dress it and to keep it. And the LORD God commanded the man, saying, Of every tree of the garden thou mayest freely eat: but of the tree of the knowledge of good and evil, thou shalt not eat of it: for in the day that thou eatest thereof thou shalt surely die.

Genesis 2:15-17

In 2 Peter 3:8 we are told that one day is with the Lord as a thousand years and a thousand years as one day. Peter is giving us insight as to how God looks at history on planet Earth. He created the Earth in six days and rested from His labor on the seventh day. Biblical history is recorded as seven one-thousand-year days. From Adam to Abraham was two thousand years or two days. From Abraham to Jesus was two thousand years or two days, and from Jesus until now has been two thousand years or six days total. We are now entering into the seventh thousand-year day. Like the seventh day of Creation, this millennium will be a Sabbath or a day of rest, when the finished work of Jesus, which He accomplished on the cross, will come into full and complete manifestation in us. This will coincide with the corporate Body of Christ coming into fullness and completion bringing about the fullness and completion of the apostolic Church born on the Day of Pentecost, as recorded in Acts 2.

God told Adam that if he ate of the forbidden fruit, he would die in that day. Adam lived nine hundred and thirty years (see Genesis 5:5), dying in the first thousand-year day of mankind on Earth.

Satan convinced Eve to eat of the forbidden fruit by telling her a partial truth. He lied when he told her that she would not die, but he told the truth when he said that her eyes would be opened and that she and Adam would become like gods, knowing good and evil. In Genesis 3:22, God said, *"Behold, the man is become as one of us, to know good and evil."* In eating of the forbidden fruit, man had become like God, knowing good and evil, which was the first step toward becoming the full likeness of God.

Even though man had become like God, knowing good and evil, he still was not like God in character. In fact, it seems that just the opposite was true. Instead of moving toward becoming the likeness of God, Adam moved away from the likeness or character of God.

In 1 John 4:8 and 16 we are told that God is love. Love is the character of God. It is not only the main attribute of God; it is who God is. He is love. I used to wonder why a God who is love would create man, knowing that man would disobey Him and, in doing so, bring sin and death into the world. Wouldn't it have been more loving to never have created man at all? Creating man, knowing that he would fall and cause much suffering for generations to come, looked very selfish to me.

We must realize that God sees the bigger picture. He could create man in His image, but character cannot be created; it has to be developed. Developing character is a process. In order for His character to be developed in man, man had to first become aware of good and evil. Before the fall, Adam had no knowledge of good or evil, so he had to first become like God in that respect.

It appears that God set him up. God forbade him to eat of the fruit of that particular tree, knowing he was going to eat of it anyway. Man's disobedience started him on a journey that would one day develop in him the character of God. However, that couldn't happen until God first became a man Himself, succeeding where Adam had failed:

And so it is written, The first man Adam was made a living soul; the last Adam [Jesus] was made a quickening spirit. Howbeit that was not first which is spiritual, but that which is natural; and afterward that which is spiritual. 1 Corinthians 15:45-46

✣

The Promise: In His Likeness 3

And God said, Let us make man in our image, after our likeness. So God created man in his own image, in the image of God created he him; male and female created he them. Genesis 1:26-27

As for me, I will behold thy face in righteousness: I shall be satisfied, when I awake, with thy likeness. Psalm 17:15

And so it is written, The first man Adam was made a living soul; the last Adam was made a quickening spirit. Howbeit that was not first which is spiritual, but that which is natural; and afterward that which is spiritual. 1 Corinthians 15:45-46

Now to Abraham and his seed were the promises made. He saith not, And to seeds, as of many; but as of one, And to thy seed, which is Christ.
Galatians 3:16

And if ye be Christ's, then are ye Abraham's seed, and heirs according to the promise. Galatians 3:29

God led Abraham to the land of Canaan, promising him descendants that would one day become a great nation (while sojourning in

Egypt) and then return to Canaan, a land flowing with milk and honey. Is Canaan any less than a type and shadow of where the Lord is leading His followers today?

Canaan was the perfect place for the nation of Israel to be established in a homeland. The only problem was there were already people living there who would have to be conquered in order for Israel to possess the land. Isn't there also much in us that must be conquered in order for us to reach perfection, possessing God's nature and character?

The Promised Land we are being led to today is not a physical place, but a spiritual place, where we possess the nature and character of God. Then, we will not only be created in His image; we will become His likeness. Is this not why Jesus went to the cross, so the blessing of Abraham could come on the Gentiles (see Galatians 3:14)? Saints, that's us. The greater application of the promise God made Abraham was that He would bring Abraham's descendants (and we are his spiritual descendants) to a perfect place, a place where they would possess the nature and character of God, a place of perfection. Glory to God!

Christ hath redeemed us from the curse of the law, being made a curse for us: for it is written, cursed is every one that hangeth on a tree: that the blessing of Abraham might come on the Gentiles through Jesus Christ; that we might receive the promise of the Spirit through faith.

Galatians 3:13-14

But the path of the just is as the shining light, that shineth more and more unto the perfect day. Proverbs 4:18

We are pilgrims on a journey toward perfection, which is our destiny. God must have a people that actually, experientially, reach perfection, in order for all that have gone before to reach perfection:

And these all [the great men and women of faith mentioned in this chapter], *having obtained a good report through faith, received not the promise: God having provided some better thing for us, that they without us should not be made perfect.*   Hebrews 11:39-40

Today there is a Remnant Bride the Lord is calling out of the Body of Christ to be the firstfruits of this glorious truth. Those of us He has chosen to be a part of this Remnant Bride have been severely tested and tried, as He has prepared and positioned us to walk into our destiny, and the end result will be glorious! Surely we were born for such a time as this! ⚜

KINGDOM MANNA: Reading 100

The Promise: In His Likeness 4

And so it is written, The first man Adam was made a living soul; the last Adam was made a quickening spirit. Howbeit that was not first which is spiritual, but that which is natural; and afterward that which is spiritual.   1 Corinthians 15:45-46

This verse is talking about Adam and Jesus, but is it not a picture of us? We are born naturally first, born with knowledge of good and evil, but unable to overcome evil with good. No matter how hard we have tried, we have always fallen short.

Just as Adam and Eve tried to cover their own shame with fig leaves (see Genesis 3:7), we try to become righteous by changing our behavior. Just as it took the shedding of blood to cover Adam and Eve's shame, only the shedding of blood can cleanse us of sin and shame. God killed animals and made coats of skin to cover Adam and Eve. Under the laws of Moses the shed blood of animal sacrifices covered the sins of the people of Israel. But under the New Testament, glory to God, Jesus' shed blood has not just covered our sin, but, rather, has done away with it, clothing us in righteousness and in the glory of God. Hallelujah!

In man's original state, without knowledge of good or evil, he was clothed in the glory of God (see Psalm 8:5). When he became aware of good and evil, because he didn't yet have the character of God, he was unable to overcome evil with good. Thus, he lost the glory and realized he was naked. He tried to cover his own nakedness, but his efforts were futile. God had to shed blood in order for man's sin to be covered. Like the animal sacrifices that Moses instituted, this was a type and shadow of the shed blood of Jesus that has done away with our sin.

When Jesus said, *"It is finished,"* He meant it is finished. There is nothing else for us to do. There is nothing else we *can* do. The only way to salvation is to accept that Jesus has done everything that can be done to assure our salvation.

Peter tells us, in his second epistle, that we have been given everything that pertains to life and godliness through the knowledge of the One who has called us to glory and virtue, and that He has made us partakers of the divine nature (character of God) by His exceeding great and precious promises. It is by faith that we have been made the righteousness of God (see 2 Corinthians 5:21), just as Abraham's faith was counted unto him for righteousness (see Romans 4:3).

We do not become righteous by changing our behavior. We must realize that we are already righteous. When we begin to see ourselves as righteous, we will lose that sin-consciousness and, instead, become

God-conscious. The more God-conscious we become, the more we advance on our pilgrimage into fullness, completion, perfection. Glory to God! ✠

THE PROMISE: IN HIS LIKENESS 5

And so it is written, The first man Adam was made a living soul; the last Adam was made a quickening spirit. Howbeit that was not first which is spiritual, but that which is natural; and afterward that which is spiritual.   1 Corinthians 15:45-46

In man's original state, without knowledge of good or evil, he was clothed in the glory of God (see Psalm 8:5). When he became aware of good and evil, because he didn't yet have the character of God, he was unable to overcome evil with good. Thus, he lost the glory and realized he was naked. He tried to cover his own nakedness, but his efforts were futile. God had to shed blood in order for man's sin to be covered. Like the animal sacrifices that Moses instituted, this was a type and shadow of the shed blood of Jesus that has done away with our sin.

Sin is sin, and I don't think one sin is any greater than another sin. But if sins could be somehow ranked, I think pride would be very near the top, if not at the top. To think that somehow we can assure our own salvation by changing our behavior is nothing but pride and arrogance. It is the same as saying that Jesus didn't need to go to the cross.

We can't overcome the sin in our lives by trying to obey the Law. Trying to obey the Law will only produce a sin-consciousness, which is sin in and of itself. Until we realize that we are completely dependent on God, not only for our righteousness but also for our provision and protection, we are going to have a hard row to hoe. We will go through trial after trial and test after test, until we finally completely surrender to God and admit that we are helpless to save ourselves, provide for ourselves or protect ourselves.

Saints, sin is not going to keep us out of Heaven or stop the glory of God. If it could, none of us would make it, and God's glory would never manifest. Perhaps the only thing that can stop us from walking out our salvation and walking in His glory is a sin-consciousness, which is the product of fear and not faith. Without faith it is impossible to please Him (see Hebrews 11:6), and it is our faith in the finished work of Jesus that makes us righteous (see 2 Corinthians 5:21).

An even more beautiful thing is that when we totally surrender to Him, completely trusting Him (which causes us to become who He has already made us), we begin to take on His character. We become love, as He is love, which brings about the manifestation of what He spoke in the beginning about making man after His likeness.

It took Adam's disobedience and Jesus' sacrifice to enable us to become completely like God. We are not there yet, but we are on our way.

Positionally, we are already there. Jesus accomplished that. Experientially, however, we are on our way (see Philippians 3:13-16). That's good news! That's the Gospel of the Kingdom! ✜

The Promise: In His Likeness 6

And so it is written, The first man Adam was made a living soul; the last Adam was made a quickening spirit. Howbeit that was not first which is spiritual, but that which is natural; and afterward that which is spiritual. 1 Corinthians 15:45-46

As we have already studied, man in his original state was without knowledge of good or evil. He was clothed in the glory of God (see Psalm 8:5). When he became aware of good and evil, because he didn't yet have the character of God, he was unable to overcome evil with good. Thus, he lost the glory and realized he was naked. He tried to cover his own nakedness, but his efforts were futile. God had to shed blood in order for man's sin to be covered. Like the animal sacrifices that Moses instituted, this was a type and shadow of the shed blood of Jesus that has done away with our sin.

We know that Jesus is going to present the Church to Himself, and it will be a glorious Church (see Ephesians 5:27). This tells me that the character of God is going to have to manifest in us in fullness. Romans 8:19 tells us that all creation is in earnest expectation of the manifestation of the mature sons of God. Amos tells us that God will do nothing unless He first reveals it to His prophets (Amos 3:7). We are a prophetic Church, and I believe the Kingdom of God is going to be revealed in us corporately as His character is established in us, paving the way for His

Kingdom to come in earth as in Heaven (see Matthew 6:10 and Luke 11:2).

How long will this take? I don't know. I believe we are just beginning to see the firstfruits of it. This remnant that God is calling out and raising up is just the beginning. I believe we are about to see a great harvest, bringing many into the Kingdom and many saints to maturity, having not only the image of God, but also His character. While many are focusing on a catching away of believers and a great tribulation, I am focused on this exciting time in which we live. What did Jesus say?

> *Take therefore no thought for the morrow: for the morrow shall take thought for the things of itself. Sufficient unto the day is the evil thereof?*
>
> Matthew 6:34

There is plenty of tribulation to deal with today without focusing on a great tribulation somewhere off in the future. Today is when we need to be overcomers. Overcoming today will prepare us for whatever comes tomorrow. As we take on His character, we will become overcomers in a way that is far beyond anything we can ask or think (see Ephesians 3:20). Not only will we overcome in our circumstances, but we will overcome the Adamic nature that focuses on good and evil, enabling us to receive the riches of the glory of the mystery, which is Christ in us, the hope of glory (see Colossians 1:27). All glory to God! ✞

THE PROMISE: THE HOPE OF GLORY

For God made promise to Abraham, because he could swear by no greater, he sware by himself, saying, Surely blessing I will bless thee, and multiplying I will multiply thee.

*Wherein God, willing more abundantly to shew unto the heirs of promise the immutability of his counsel, confirmed it by an oath: That by two immutable things, in which it was impossible for God to lie, we might have a strong consolation, **who have fled for refuge to lay hold upon the hope set before us: Which hope we have as an anchor of the soul, both sure and stedfast, and which entereth into that within the veil;** whither the forerunner is for us entered, even Jesus, made an high priest for ever after the order of Melchisedec.*

Hebrews 6:13-14 and 17-20, Emphasis added

*Whereof I am made a minister, according to the dispensation of God which is given to me for you, to fulfil the word of God; even the mystery which hath been hid from ages and from generations, but now is made manifest to his saints: to whom God would make known what is the riches of the glory of this mystery among the Gentiles; **which is Christ in you, the hope of glory.***

Colossians 1:25-27, Emphasis added

Webster defines *refuge* as "a place of shelter, protection or safety; anything to which one has recourse for aid, relief or escape." Is this any less than the spiritual Promised Land we are in route to or even now entering into? When God swore by Himself that He would bless Abraham and multiply him, it became a done deal. Nothing could change or stop it from coming to pass, not even Abraham himself. **Just as God set Adam up to fail, He set Abraham up to succeed.** As the heirs of promise, has he done any less with us?

It is not by our own choice that we have fled the past in order to lay hold of the hope set before us. To think you were even capable of making that choice on your own is pride and arrogance. It was only the Father drawing us (see John 6:44) that enabled us to choose God's salvation, and that choice was only made because He first chose us (see John 15:16).

Because we are chosen, we cannot fail. Because of the promise, we cannot fail. Because of God, we cannot fail. You see, it is not about us. It is all about Him. Glory to God!

It is not about your problems or your dreams. It is about the Kingdom of God coming in earth as it is in Heaven. It is not about you being successful or failing. It is about Him being successful, and He cannot fail because love never fails (see 1 Corinthians 13:8). If He cannot fail, then we cannot fail because we are in Him, and He is in us, the hope of glory (see Colossians 1:27).

What did Jesus pray?

Neither pray I for these alone, but for them also which shall believe on me through their word; that they all may be one; as thou, Father, art in me, and I in thee, that they also may be one in us: that the world may believe that thou hast sent me. And the glory which thou gavest me I have given them; that they may be one, even as we are one: I in them, and thou in me, that they may be made perfect in one; and that the world may know that thou hast sent me, and hast loved them, as thou hast loved me. Father, I will that they also, whom thou hast given me, be with me where I am; that they may behold my glory, which thou hast given me: for thou lovedst me before the foundation of the world.

Jesus in John 17:20-24

If we are in Him and He is in us, and we are one with each other, then it is no longer our life that we are living. It is His life being lived in and through us. Is this any less than the Gospel of the Kingdom? I think not! Bless the name of the Lord forever! ⚜

KINGDOM MANNA: READING 104

THE PROMISE: THE HOPE OF GLORY 2

For God made promise to Abraham, because he could swear by no greater, he sware by himself, saying, Surely blessing I will bless thee, and multiplying I will multiply thee.

*Wherein God, willing more abundantly to shew unto the heirs of promise the immutability of his counsel, confirmed it by an oath: That by two immutable things, in which it was impossible for God to lie, we might have a strong consolation, **who have fled for refuge to lay hold upon the hope set before us: Which hope we have as an anchor of the soul, both sure and stedfast, and which entereth into that within the veil;** whither the forerunner is for us entered, even Jesus, made an high priest for ever after the order of Melchisedec.*

Hebrews 6:13-14, 17-20, Emphasis added

254

*Whereof I am made a minister, according to the dispensation of God which is given to me for you, to fulfil the word of God; even the mystery which hath been hid from ages and from generations, but now is made manifest to his saints: to whom God would make known what is the riches of the glory of this mystery among the Gentiles; **which is Christ in you, the hope of glory**.*   Colossians 1:25-27, Emphasis added

Neither pray I for these alone, but for them also which shall believe on me through their word; that they all may be one; as thou, Father, art in me, and I in thee, that they also may be one in us: that the world may believe that thou hast sent me. And the glory which thou gavest me I have given them; that they may be one, even as we are one: I in them, and thou in me, that they may be made perfect in one; and that the world may know that thou hast sent me, and hast loved them, as thou hast loved me. Father, I will that they also, whom thou hast given me, be with me where I am; that they may behold my glory, which thou hast given me: for thou lovedst me before the foundation of the world.

Jesus in John 17:20-24

If we are in Him and He is in us, it is no longer our life that we are living. He is living His life in and through us, not just individually, but corporately.

*I am crucified with Christ: nevertheless I live; yet not I, but Christ liveth in me: and the life which I now live in the flesh I live by **the faith of the Son of God**, who loved me, and gave himself for me.*

Galatians 2:20, Emphasis added

Are you getting this? It is not even our faith that saves us. It is the faith of the Son of God, It is His faith! Saints, it ain't about us. It is all about Him.

So, if this is true (and it is), what is all this dying-to-self business about? If He is living His life in us and through us, then we literally are new creatures in Christ, causing all the old things (old nature/old man) to be gone (passed away/dead) and all things (our nature and character) have become new (see 2 Corinthians 5:17). So why do we experience this dying-to-self process?

Could it be that we don't fully understand and/or believe the finished work of Jesus? Could it be that our minds have not yet been fully renewed to the Word of God (see Romans 12:2)? Saints, we are not a combination of old and new. We are not schizophrenic. We may appear to be, but, in truth, we are not.

Therefore if any man be in Christ, he is a new creature: old things are passed away; behold, all things are become new. And all things are of God, who hath reconciled us to himself by Jesus Christ, and hath given to us the ministry of reconciliation; to wit, that God was in Christ, reconciling the world unto himself, not imputing their trespasses unto them; and hath committed unto us the word of reconciliation. Now then we are ambassadors for Christ, as though God did beseech you by us: we pray you in Christ's stead, be ye reconciled to God. For he hath made him to be sin for us, who knew no sin; that we might be made the righteousness of God in him. 2 Corinthians 5:17-21

✦

THE PROMISE: THE MANIFESTATION OF GLORY

Therefore if any man be in Christ, he is a new creature: old things are passed away; behold, all things are become new. **And all things are of God, who hath reconciled us to himself by Jesus Christ, and hath given to us the ministry of reconciliation;** *to wit, that God was in Christ, reconciling the world unto himself, not imputing their trespasses unto them; and hath committed unto us the word of reconciliation. Now then we are ambassadors for Christ, as though God did beseech you by us: we pray you in Christ's stead, be ye reconciled to God. For he hath made him to be sin for us, who knew no sin; that we might be made the righteousness of God in him.*

2 Corinthians 5:17-21, Emphasis added

Whereof I am made a minister, according to the dispensation of God which is given to me for you, to fulfil the word of God; even the mystery which hath been hid from ages and from generations, but now is made manifest to his saints: to whom God would make known what is the riches of the glory of this mystery among the Gentiles; **which is Christ in you, the hope of glory.** Colossians 1:25-27, Emphasis added

If we are in Christ (and we are), we are new people. All the old is gone, vanished, and everything is new (*all things*). What part of *"all things*" don't we understand? All means all. Now go back and re-read 2 Corinthians 5:17-18 above.

"All things are of God." If all things are of God, then why do we struggle with sin in our lives? Why do we beat ourselves up and determine over and over to change our behavior? Even worse, why do we beat others over the head and try to get them to change? We can't fix ourselves, and we can't fix anyone else. Only God can fix His creation, and He has already done everything that needs to be done in order to make that a reality.

When He promised Abraham a place flowing with milk and honey, He was promising us a place where we can live a perfect or perfected life. Hebrews 11:40 makes this clear:

> *And these all, having obtained a good report through faith, received not the **promise**: God having provided some better thing for us, that they without us should not be made **perfect**.*
>
> Hebrews 11:40, Emphasis added

God opened the door to this perfection when He chose a man named Abram and changed his name to Abraham, causing him to become the father of many nations, all potential carriers of the blessing of Abraham, which is actually the blessing of God or the promise God made to Abraham. This promise will culminate in a people whom the apostle Paul speaks of in his letter to the Church at Ephesus as the glorious Church.

Our job is to preach (proclaim) this truth. It is the Gospel of the Kingdom that Jesus spoke so frequently about. Our job is not to scare the hell out of people by preaching fire and brimstone. Our job is not to beat people over the head with the sin we perceive to be in their lives. Our job is to preach the Gospel of the Kingdom, which is the ministry of reconciliation; which is *"that God was in Christ, reconciling the world unto himself, not imputing their trespasses unto them"* (2 Corinthians 5:19).

Is preaching the Gospel of the Kingdom any less than preaching the blessing of Abraham, which is that God has reconciled and is in the process of reconciling everything to Himself? God will have a perfect (perfected) people, and every generation since Abraham has brought us a little closer to this truth. While we have experienced this truth positionally by faith and in part, no generation has yet experienced it in fullness. But Saints, we are now entering the seventh day (millennium) since Creation, a Sabbath day of rest, when a generation of believers will experience that perfection. A generation reaching that perfection experientially will enable all those who have died without experiencing it completely to also come to completion (perfection). Then and only then can Jesus present the Church to Himself without spot, wrinkle or any such thing, holy and without blemish (see Ephesians 5:27). Then and only then can all things be reconciled to God (see 2 Corinthians 5:18-19). What an awesome plan! ✤

KINGDOM MANNA: READING 106

MELCHISEDEC

For God made promise to Abraham, because he could swear by no greater, he sware by himself, saying, Surely blessing I will bless thee, and multiplying I will multiply thee.

Wherein God, willing more abundantly to shew unto the heirs of promise the immutability of his counsel, confirmed it by an oath: That by two immutable things, in which it was impossible for God to lie, we might have a strong consolation, who have fled for refuge to lay hold upon the hope set before us: which hope we have as an anchor of the soul, both sure and stedfast, and which entereth into that within the veil; whither the forerunner is for us entered, even Jesus, made an high priest for ever after the order of Melchisedec.

Hebrews 6:13-14, 17-20

Melchisedec, also spelled Melchizedek, is only mentioned in two places in the Old Testament.

And the king of Sodom went out to meet him [Abram] *after his return from the slaughter of Chedorlaomer, and of the kings that were with him, at the valley of Shaveh, which is the king's dale. And Melchizedek king of Salem brought forth bread and wine: and he was the priest of the most high God. And he blessed him, and said, Blessed be Abram of the most high God, possessor of heaven and earth: and blessed be the most high God, which hath delivered thine enemies into thy hand. And he* [Abram] *gave him* [Melchizedek] *tithes of all.*

Genesis 14:17-20

David, in Psalm 110, speaking prophetically of Jesus, said:

The LORD hath sworn, and will not repent, Thou art a priest for ever after the order of Melchizedek.   Psalm 110:4

The writer of Hebrews quotes this psalm in Hebrews 5:6 and 6:20. Then in chapter 7 we are given a glimpse of who Melchisedec was and is.

For this Melchisedec, king of Salem, priest of the most high God, who met Abraham returning from the slaughter of the kings, and blessed him; to whom also Abraham gave a tenth part of all; first being by interpretation King of righteousness, and after that also King of Salem, which is, King of peace; without father, without mother, without descent, having neither beginning of days, nor end of life; but made like unto the Son of God; abideth a priest continually.

Hebrews 7:1-3

The writer then goes on to speak of the greatness of Melchisedec and contrasts the difference between the Levitical priesthood and the Melchisedec priesthood (see Hebrews 7:4-28). The primary issue used to contrast the difference between the two priesthoods is tithing, perhaps because Abraham tithed to Melchisedec, and tithing was commanded under the Levitical Law.

Let's delve a little deeper into the contrast between the two priesthoods, utilizing this issue of tithing. ✣

MELCHISEDEC 2

For this Melchisedec, king of Salem, priest of the most high God, who met Abraham returning from the slaughter of the kings, and blessed him; to whom also Abraham gave a tenth part of all; first being by interpretation King of righteousness, and after that also King of Salem, which is, King of peace; without father, without mother, without descent, having neither beginning of days, nor end of life; but made like unto the Son of God; abideth a priest continually.

Hebrews 7:1-3

As we have already noted, the writer of Hebrews goes on to speak of the greatness of Melchisedec and contrasts the differences between the Levitical priesthood and the Melchisedec priesthood (see Hebrews 7:4-28).

Under the Levitical priesthood (which came many years after Abraham lived), Israel was compelled by the Law to tithe, but Abraham tithed to Melchisedec simply because he wanted to. It seems clear to me that this is why tithing is not taught in the New Testament. I realize this goes against what many in the Church teach today concerning tithing, but we must realize the issue here is not so much tithing, as it is the difference between the Law and faith. Old Testament Israel was justified by the Law, but New Testament saints are justified by faith. We know that being justified by faith does not do away with the Law (see Matthew 5:17-18), but it is our faith that actually enables us to obey the Law and, in the course of time, will bring about the fulfillment of the Law:

Forasmuch as ye are manifestly declared to be the epistle of Christ ministered by us, written not with ink, but with the spirit of the living God; not in tables of stone, but in fleshy tables of the heart. And such trust have we through Christ to God-ward: not that we are sufficient of ourselves to think any thing as of ourselves; but our sufficiency is of God; who also hath made us able ministers of the new testament; not of the letter [of the Law] *but of the spirit: for the letter killeth, but the spirit giveth life.*   2 Corinthians 3:3-6

We also know that when we walk in the Spirit, being led by the Spirit, we become the mature sons of God, not fulfilling the lusts or pressure of the flesh. We know that lust or pressure of the flesh is what causes believers to break the Law. The way we overcome the flesh is by walking in the Spirit.

For as many as are led by the Spirit of God, they are the sons [mature children] *of God.*   Romans 8:14

This I say then, Walk in the Spirit, and ye shall not fulfil the lust [pressure] *of the flesh. For the flesh lusteth* [pushes] *against the Spirit, and the Spirit* [lusteth or pushes] *against the flesh: and these are contrary the one to the other: so that ye cannot do the things that ye would. But if ye be led of the Spirit, ye are not under the law.*

                    Galatians 5:16-18

Being led by the Spirit keeps us on our pilgrimage toward perfection. Nothing less will bring us to the fulfillment of the promise, which is fullness, completion and perfection.

Much damage is being done to the Church today by the way tithing is taught. The writer of Hebrews used tithing to contrast the difference between the Law and faith, but many teachers today use the Abrahamic tithe to say that believers are obligated to tithe because Abraham tithed without being under the Law. What they fail to realize is that Abraham's gift to Melchisedec wasn't about the amount (tenth/tithe), but it was what he purposed in his heart to do.

What did the apostle Paul say?

Every man according as he purposeth in his heart, so let him give; not grudgingly, or of necessity: for God loveth a cheerful giver.

2 Corinthians 9:7

To teach anything else actually puts believers under the Law, causing lack, not only in their finances, but also in other areas of their lives. ✠

KINGDOM MANNA: READING **108**

MELCHISEDEC 3

For this Melchisedec, king of Salem, priest of the most high God, who met Abraham returning from the slaughter of the kings, and blessed him; to whom also Abraham gave a tenth part of all; first being by interpretation King of righteousness, and after that also King of Salem, which is, King of peace; without father, without mother, without descent, having neither beginning of days, nor end of life; but made like unto the Son of God; abideth a priest continually.

Hebrews 7:1-3

David, in Psalm 110, speaking prophetically of Jesus, said:

The LORD hath sworn, and will not repent, Thou art a priest for ever after the order of Melchizedek.   Psalm 110:4

For the priesthood being changed, there is made of necessity a change also of the law.   Hebrews 7:12

The priesthood has changed, and with the change in the priesthood, the Law has changed. Not that it has been done away with, but it has been fulfilled (see Matthew 5:17). The Law is no longer something to be obeyed. It is now written in our hearts and minds:

I will put my laws into their mind, and write them in their hearts: and I will be to them a God, and they shall be to me a people.

Hebrews 8:10

(For not the hearers of the law are just before God, but the doers of the law shall be justified. For when the Gentiles, which have not the law, do by nature the things contained in the law, these, having not the law, are a law unto themselves: which shew the work of the law

written in their hearts, their conscience also bearing witness, and their
thoughts the mean while accusing or else excusing one another;) in the
day when God shall judge the secrets of men by Jesus Christ according
to my gospel.   Romans 2:13-16

What was Paul's Gospel? It was the proclaiming of the blessing of Abraham coming on the nations. It was the Gospel of the Kingdom, proclaiming Christ in us, the hope of glory, becoming the manifestation of glory. Is this any less than the second coming of Christ that so many are focused on today? Many think this will happen when Jesus touches down on the Mount of Olives, physically returning to earth, but, saints, if that is your focus, you may miss His second coming. The actual physical return of Jesus to earth would be His third, or perhaps fourth, (or even some other number) coming.

If I read my Bible correctly, Jesus made an appearance on earth before He came as a baby born of a virgin in Bethlehem. Perhaps His first coming was as Melchizedek, *"King of righteousness, and after that also King of Salem, which is, King of peace; without father, without mother, without descent, having neither beginning of days, nor end of life; but made like unto the Son of God"* (Hebrews 7:2-3).

Some think Melchizedek was Shem, Noah's son, but we know Shem's ancestors and descendents, which disqualifies Shem as being Melchizedek. Who else but Jesus could have appeared on earth as a priest, with no earthly father or mother, with no beginning and no end, and served what we commonly refer to as "communion" to Abraham, and all of this long before the first Passover lamb was slain? Who else could it be but the Lamb who was slain from the foundation of the world (see Revelation 13:8)? Who else could have a continual priesthood (see Hebrews 7:3)? How else can we have eternal life except by being a part of His priesthood?

Now of the things which we have spoken this is the sum: we have such an high priest, who is set on the right hand of the throne of the Majesty in the heavens; a minister of the sanctuary, and of the true tabernacle, which the Lord pitched, and not man. Hebrews 8:1-2

Now hath he obtained a more excellent ministry, by how much also he is the mediator of a better covenant, which was established upon better promises. Hebrews 8:6

Christ hath redeemed us from the curse of the law, being made a curse for us: for it is written, cursed is every one that hangeth on a tree: that the blessing of Abraham might come on the Gentiles [nations] *through Jesus Christ, that we might receive the promise of the Spirit through faith.* Galatians 3:13-14

Hallelujah! ✣

KINGDOM MANNA: Reading 109

My Gospel

(For not the hearers of the law are just before God, but the doers of the law shall be justified. For when the Gentiles, which have not the law, do by nature the things contained in the law, these, having not the law, are a law unto themselves: which shew the work of the law

*written in their hearts, their conscience also bearing witness, and their thoughts the mean while accusing or else excusing one another;) in the day when God shall judge the secrets of men by Jesus Christ according to **my gospel**.* Romans 2:13-16, Emphasis added

Many times, in Paul's letters to the churches, he speaks of the mystery. In the 1st chapter of Colossians he tells us what the mystery is:

*Whereof I am made a minister, according to the dispensation of God which is given to me for you, to fulfil the word of God; even the mystery which hath been hid from ages and from generations, but now is made manifest to his saints: to whom God would make known what is the riches of the glory of this mystery among the Gentiles; **which is Christ in you, the hope of glory**.* Colossians 1:25-27, Emphasis added

He goes on to say, "*Whom we preach, warning every man, and teaching every man in all wisdom; that we may present every man perfect in Christ Jesus: whereunto I also labour, striving according to his working, which worketh in me mightily*" (Colossians 1:28-29). Paul considered this mystery (which is Christ in us, the hope of glory), to be such a personal revelation to him that he called it "*my Gospel*" and said that he was made a minister to deliver this message (Gospel) to the nations (Gentiles). Paul saw what the third-day Church is just now beginning to experience. To him, it was the hope of glory. To us, it is becoming the manifestation of glory. It is the blessing of Abraham being revealed in the sons of God, made possible by the finished work of Jesus.

Saints, we could not have been born into a more exciting time in the history of planet Earth! Perhaps in the future there will be something more exciting, but this is certainly more exciting than anything up until now. Surely we were born for such a time as this!

The Gentiles Paul is speaking of in Romans 2:13-16 are the Gentiles living *"in the day when God shall judge the secrets of men by Jesus Christ according to my gospel."* What day is that? Can it be any other than the third day (millennium) of the Church?

And what is God going to judge? It is the secrets of men. But how is He going to judge the secrets of men? Will it be by our thoughts or our deeds? No! It will be by Jesus Christ according to the Gospel that Paul preached. It will be according to the finished work of Jesus, not according to our own righteousness or lack thereof. Thank God! You see, saints, this third-day judgment is not about condemning anyone. Rather, it is about perfecting a people, to be, not only God's representatives on earth, but to have His very nature and character, with His laws written in their minds and hearts. This is what will cause the earth to be filled with the knowledge of the glory of the Lord, as the waters cover the sea (see Habakkuk 2:14). This is what will bring the Kingdom of God in earth as it is in Heaven. This is what will usher in the Kingdom Age. Hallelujah!

This is who we are and why we are here. Surely you are seeing that it is not about us getting more "stuff" or living the American dream. Surely you are seeing that it is not about some great escape while our enemy takes over the world. No, saints, it is about the plans and purposes of God coming to completion/fullness/perfection. It is about the restitution of all things. It is about the Kingdom of God coming in earth as it is in Heaven. And it is glorious. Praise the Lord! Bless His name forever! ⚜

SIGNS OF THE TIMES

Many shall run to and fro, and knowledge shall be increased.

Daniel 12:4

Some very significant historical advancements in the Kingdom of God have been marked by very significant historical advancements in the natural realm. Jesus was born in Bethlehem at a time when Judea was under Roman occupation. The Roman government built a vast highway and sea route system to move goods and troops throughout the Roman Empire. It was these same routes of travel that the early Christians used to take the Gospel to the nations, obeying what is commonly referred to as the Great Commission of Jesus (see Matthew 28:18-20 and Mark 16:15-18).

In the sixteenth century, when Martin Luther was instrumental in starting what became known as the Protestant Reformation, two significant things occurred. Johannes Gutenberg invented the printing press. Until that time the leadership of the Catholic Church had been successful in keeping the Bible out of the hands of the common people, enabling them to interpret the Scriptures for the people. With the invention of the printing press, the Bible and other writings became available to the masses.

Up until that time, copies of the Bible had been written only in Hebrew, Greek and Latin, none of which could be understood by the common people living in countries where those languages were not spoken or understood. Martin Luther began translating the Bible into his native German, enabling the people to read and interpret the Scriptures for themselves.

Around the mid-twentieth century the Charismatic Movement was marked by the invention of the cassette tape, making messages by anointed preachers/teachers available, to be listened to anytime, anywhere. The message of the baptism with the Holy Spirit, the faith message, messages about healing, prosperity and other biblical subjects were circulated worldwide on cassette tapes. Personally, I have listened to many hours of anointed messages while working, driving or just quietly listening and taking notes. I have also listened to the Bible being read on cassette tape.

Today, with the Internet and many other new inventions, information is instantly available anywhere in the civilized world. I can write teachings, prophecies or meeting announcements and send them instantly to everyone in my address books. Then the recipients can forward my writings to others, with the potential of an audience greater than radio or television. With the Internet, cell phones and even newer devices, I can continually stay in touch with those I am connected to for fellowship, encouragement and ministry.

I believe the Internet and other inventions of today signify that we are entering the time when the apostolic Church is coming into fullness or coming to completion. This is the most exciting time in all of history so far. As I often say, surely we were born for such a time as this! Surely we were born for this time! Glory to God! ✠

A PROPHETIC DREAM

Brethren, if a man be overtaken in a fault, ye which are spiritual, restore such an one in the spirit of meekness; considering thyself, lest thou also be tempted. Galatians 6:1

Jim Behringer is a stone mason, a businessman and a prophet of God. He is also a friend of mine. He lives near Raleigh, North Carolina. The following is a prophetic dream Jim had:

In this dream Jim saw pastors, one at a time, standing behind a podium or in a pulpit in front of their congregations. Some of these pastors were going through severe trials and tests without knowing why. Some were receiving revelation from God that would take their congregations in new directions other than the religious traditions and ideas they were accustomed to. Their congregations were not being receptive and, in many cases, were coming against the pastors. Some of the pastors were even being questioned and attacked by their spouses and families. These pastor's lives had reached a point of desperation. They could no longer deal with the circumstances they found themselves in.

In the dream, there was a large table to the left of the pulpit on the stage. Jim said he couldn't see it in the dream, but he knew it was there. On this table was a pile of firearms. Each pastor was exiting his pulpit to the left, going to the table, picking out a gun, putting it to his head and pulling the trigger.

Jim awoke from this dream very troubled and asked the Lord what it meant. He was told that these pastors were caught in the crosshairs of a separation that is in progress, a process of separating that which is of God from that which is not of God — in individual lives and in churches. These pastors were totally unprepared for and unable to deal with the circumstances they found themselves in. Then the Lord told Jim that He is raising up a remnant of tried and tested believers to rescue these pastors from hurting or destroying themselves.

We have entered into a time that Jesus referred to as *the harvest,* when there will be a separating of the wheat from the tares (see Matthew 13:24-30). Another word for this separation is *judgment.* All things must be judged so that only what is of God will remain.

Some of us have been going through a time of severe judgment, preparing and positioning us to minister to others who are going through it or are yet to go through it. If you know you are a part of this remnant, you also need to know that you are very important to the Kingdom of God. You have a job to do, and many lives depend on you doing that job. This is not a time to shrink back, and it certainly is not the time to give up. We must persevere. We must finish the race:

Wherefore seeing we also are compassed about with so great a cloud of witnesses, let us lay aside every weight, and the sin which doth so easily beset us, and let us run with patience the race that is set before us, looking unto Jesus, the author and finisher of our faith; who for the joy that was set before him endured the cross, despising the shame, and is set down at the right hand of the throne of God. For consider him that endured such contradiction of sinners against himself, lest ye be wearied and faint in your minds. Hebrews 12:1-3

We Have a Job to Do

For ye see your calling, brethren, how that not many wise men after the flesh, not many mighty, not many noble, are called: for God hath chosen the foolish things of the world to confound the wise; and God hath chosen the weak things of the world to confound the things which are mighty; and base things of the world, and things which are despised, hath God chosen, yea, and things which are not, to bring to nought things that are: that no flesh should glory in his presence.

1 Corinthians 1:26-29

It doesn't matter who you are or what your background is. You may not think you qualify for the things God has chosen you to do. Guess what? You probably don't. That's a good thing. Your inadequacy will cause you to depend on and trust in God.

Two things that probably have greater influence than anything over the minds of people are government and religion. Government is humanism at its best. It is people looking to people to solve their problems. It is man-centered. Religion is God-centered, to some degree, but denies the power of God, so, in reality, religion also tends to be man-centered. When God does something new in the earth, where does He go to find a person or people He can count on to bring it to pass? Does He go to government or a religious system? In Luke's account of the Gospel, the 3rd chapter, we find the answer to these questions:

Now in the fifteenth year of the reign of Tiberius Caesar, Pontius Pilate being governor of Judaea, and Herod being tetrarch of Galilee, and his brother Philip tetrarch of Ituraea and of the region of Trachonitis and Lysanias the tetrarch of Abilene, Annas and Caiaphas being the high priests, the Word of God came unto John the son of Zacharias in the wilderness. Luke 3:1-2

Verse 1 names the political leaders of that day, and verse 2 names the religious leaders of that day. Did God ordain political leaders or religious leaders to announce the coming of Jesus? No. The end of verse 2 says, *"The Word of God came unto John, the son of Zacharias in the wilderness."* John was a man unconventionally dressed, living on a diet of big grasshoppers and honey, and hanging out, not in a great metropolitan area or on a university campus, but in the wilderness. Jesus said of John, *"Truly I say to you, among those born of women, there has not risen a greater than John the Baptist"* (Matthew 11:11).

To many people, government is the central focus of their lives. To others, religion is. God has a way of bypassing what people think is the center and creating a new center. Mark 1:5 tells us that all the citizens of Judea and Jerusalem went out into the wilderness to be baptized of John.

I think it is significant that Jerusalem is mentioned here. The Temple was in Jerusalem, and Jerusalem was the religious center of Judaism. One might think God would have chosen Jerusalem as the place to announce the greatest event in all of history up until that time. But he didn't. He chose the wilderness.

God has a history of choosing seemingly insignificant people to lead great moves of the Holy Spirit and to impact society and nations. Often these people are found in insignificant places.

275

God has always had a remnant. Usually that remnant was outside the political arena and the religious system. Often they were persecuted by one or both. In reality, they were ahead of both, on the cutting edge of history. They were who they were and did what they did, not because they had the credentials or great intelligence, but because they were chosen by God and equipped by Him.

The previous KINGDOM MANNA conveyed a dream that my friend, Jim Behringer, had. The remnant that God spoke to Jim about concerning the prophetic dream he had is consistent with the kind of people God usually chooses to accomplish His purposes. We may not be the most educated, the most successful or the most qualified for the job, but if we will humbly submit ourselves to God's call on our lives, He will equip and enable us to do great exploits that will advance the Kingdom of God on earth.

I can do all things through Christ which strengtheneth me.

Philippians 4:13

KINGDOM MANNA: Reading 113

Prophetic Word 5

Have I not known you? Did I not know you before I formed you in the womb, and did I not foreknow the purposes and plans I have for you? Is it not I who has brought you through the tests and trials of your life to this moment in history?

For, you see, the tests and trials were not only implemented in the hard times. Even during the good times I was watching, testing and trying you to see where you would take your stand, what decisions you would make and which way you would go. Not that I needed an answer, for I know the end from the beginning. The tests and trials are not to prove yourself to Me. The tests and trials are to prove yourself to yourself, for you need confidence in the trust that you have toward Me and in the faith you have in My Word. You need to know that you know that you know where you stand, standing on the promises of My Word and standing in complete trust of My good intentions for you, as you walk the path I have prepared for you. You are standing on the threshold of a vast expanse.

VISION: *I am seeing myself standing on a threshold, on the edge of a cliff. Behind me is a mountain-top plain, and before me is a vast expanse that goes as far as I can see. I see an endless sky above a terrain of rolling hills, dotted with towns and villages and farms. I am aware that it is an area prepared by God for the overcomers, for the remnant that has stood through the tests and trials that have prepared us for the Promised Land. I see myself leaping off this cliff and soaring through the clouds like an eagle. My heart feels completely free, and I have great anticipation of the glory that will fill up the days ahead.*

Is it not I who have orchestrated your steps? Is it not I who have brought you to where you are and made you what you are? I know: you look back, and you think, "If only I had done this differently or done that differently." Do you not know that I am the Author and the Finisher of your faith? Why do you take responsibility for your successes or for your failures? You are what you are, and you are who you are by the grace and the mercy of the living God. There is no other like Me, and there is no other who will succeed in building My people into a habitation of God through the Spirit, the manifested sons of God in the earth.

There is no turning back. There is no going back to the old way. As you enter into this new day (the third day since I finished My work and sat down at the right hand of the Father, the seventh day since my Father finished His creative work and rested), much has changed. You can no longer mix the traditions of men and the ways of the Babylonian system with your assignment in the Kingdom of God. You are entering a time of total trust and completed faith. Contamination of trust and faith will result in failure. But pure trust and faith will cause you to soar like eagles to new heights of success and glory, beyond anything you have ever known before.

Do not grow weary in well doing. Never fear. Allow fear no place in your life. The world's system, the Babylonian system, must fail, but the Kingdom has no end. ✠

KINGDOM MANNA: Reading 114

Righteousness Exposes Unrighteousness

And Enoch also, the seventh from Adam, prophesied of these, saying, Behold, the Lord cometh with ten thousands of his saints, to execute judgment upon all, and to convince all that are ungodly among them of all their ungodly deeds which they have ungodly committed, and of all their hard speeches which ungodly sinners have spoken against him. These are murmurers, complainers, walking after their own lusts; and their mouth speaketh great swelling words, having men's persons in admiration because of advantage.

But, beloved, remember ye the words which were spoken before of the apostles of our Lord Jesus Christ; how that they told you there should be mockers in the last time, who should walk after their own ungodly lusts. These be they who separate themselves, sensual, having not the Spirit.

But ye, beloved, building up yourselves on your most holy faith, praying in the Holy Ghost, keep yourselves in the love of God, looking for the mercy of our Lord Jesus Christ unto eternal life.

And of some have compassion, making a difference: and others save with fear, pulling them out of the fire; hating even the garment spotted by the flesh.   Jude 14-23

The book of Enoch was considered to be sacred Scripture by first-century Christians. It is a very interesting book, and from it we can learn much about Enoch. While Enoch was given credit for the content of most of the book, it wasn't actually written down until the second and first centuries before Christ.

If you isolate the Enoch prophecy found in verses 14 and 15 above, it might seem that Jude is talking about a physical return of Jesus to the earth. However, when read in context with the remaining verses, it becomes evident he is talking about something that occurs during the last time or last days (Jesus coming with ten thousands of His saints).

In 2 Peter 3:8 we are given an important key to understanding the significance of where we are prophetically on the timeline of history. Peter informs us that a day is with the Lord as a thousand years and a thousand years as a day. There are seven days in a week, and the Bible clearly speaks of seven millennia of the history of mankind on earth. So, the last days would be toward the end of the week.

On the Day of Pentecost, as recorded in Acts 2:16-17, Peter let us know that the events of that day were taking place in the last days. The apostolic Church that was birthed on the Day of Pentecost has been in existence during the fifth and sixth days (millennia). We are now entering the seventh day (millennium). So, we are in the last days of the week the Bible focuses on, and, glory to God, this day (millennium) is only the beginning. Enoch, in his book, speaks of ten thousand years. We can hardly imagine what is yet to come.

Paul tells us, in his letter to the Romans, that all creation is waiting for the manifestation of the sons (mature believers) of God. The remnant I often speak of has and continues to be in an intense process of becoming those mature believers.

We, the remnant, may be small at the present time, but we are about to bring the greatest harvest into the Kingdom that history has ever witnessed (ten thousands of saints). Glory to God!

As we manifest the glory of God throughout the earth (see Habakkuk 2:14), the evil and wicked will be exposed, simply because of the contrast between us and them. As this happens, many outside the camp will come in, realizing that our righteousness is much more desirable than their wickedness.

Peter has admonished us to always be ready to give an answer to everyone who asks us about the hope that is in us (see 1 Peter 3:15). We must respond to everyone in love, saving those who will be saved. We are the firstfruits of this great harvest, and while we don't ignore and are not ignorant of evil and wickedness, we must always see the potential for everyone to come to a saving knowledge of the truth (see 1 Timothy 2:4).

Saints of God, Jesus is going to have a glorious Church (see Ephesians 5:27), and I believe it will be a very large Church. All glory to God!
✢

THE END

And Jesus went out, and departed from the temple: and his disciples came to him for to shew him the buildings of the temple. And Jesus said unto them, See ye not all these things? Verily I say unto you, there shall not be left here one stone upon another, that shall not be thrown down.

And as he sat upon the mount of Olives, the disciples came unto him privately, saying, Tell us, when shall these things be and what shall be the sign of thy coming, and of the end of the world?

And Jesus answered and said unto them, Take heed that no man deceive you. For many shall come in my name, saying, I am Christ; and shall deceive many. And ye shall hear of wars and rumours of wars; see that ye be not troubled: for all these things must come to pass, but the end is not yet. For nation shall rise against nation, and kingdom against kingdom: and there shall be famines, and pestilences, and earthquakes, in divers places. And these are the beginning of sorrows.

Then shall they deliver you up to be afflicted, and shall kill you: and ye shall be hated of all nations for my name's sake. And then shall many be offended, and shall betray one another, and shall hate one another. And many false prophets shall rise, and shall deceive many. And because iniquity shall abound, the love of many shall wax cold. But he that shall endure unto the end, the same shall be saved. And this gospel of the kingdom shall be preached in all the world for a witness unto all nations; and then shall the end come. Matthew 24:1-14

Have you ever noticed that Jesus seemed to have a habit of interrupting a question or conversation by interjecting something completely different from the subject being discussed? In the above scripture the disciples were taking notice of the Temple buildings. Suddenly Jesus makes what must have been a startling statement to them. He prophesies the destruction of the Temple (which took place in AD 70).

This must have still been on their minds as they asked Him when this would occur, thinking it had something to do with the end of the world or end of the age. However, the rest of this passage is about things that would happen before the end of the age. Actually, all of these prophetic words of Jesus took place in the disciples' lifetimes, except the Gospel of the Kingdom being preached in all the world, and they were working on that.

I think there are two key verses in this passage of scripture. In verse 13, Jesus speaks of enduring to the end. Then in verse 14, He talks of the Gospel of the Kingdom being preached in the entire world for a witness to all nations. I frequently speak of the tests and trials that believers endure. Endurance requires and produces overcoming. It is in overcoming that we find salvation.

Salvation, in this passage of scripture, is not talking about the initial born-again experience. It is talking about the ongoing process of being saved. Saved from what? Saved from tests and trials. Saved how? Saved by being saved from ourselves or dying to self, becoming like God in character, which enables us to walk in love and experience peace and joy, regardless of our circumstances. When we walk in this place of enduring and overcoming, our main focus becomes the Gospel of the Kingdom.

Jesus knew the world's system was on a collision course with disaster and that the Kingdom would suffer attack. He made a point of encouraging His disciples (which includes us) to be strong, enduring to the end and preaching the Gospel as we march toward victory.

Far too many today are focused on a great escape (rapture), which they equate with victory, rather than enduring and overcoming. Many are just hanging on, hoping that soon they will be taken out of here. I've got news for them. Jesus is not coming for a beat-up, beaten-down, barely-getting-by Church. He is going to present to Himself a glorious Church (see Ephesians 5:27). We need to be about becoming glorious.

Take therefore no thought for the morrow: for the morrow shall take thought for the things of itself. Sufficient unto the day is the evil thereof.

Jesus in Matthew 6:34

✠

KINGDOM MANNA: Reading 116

Being Ready

Then shall the kingdom of heaven be likened unto ten virgins, which took their lamps, and went forth to meet the bridegroom. And five of them were wise, and five were foolish. They that were foolish took their lamps, and took no oil with them: but the wise took oil in their vessels with their lamps. While the bridegroom tarried, they all slumbered and slept.

And at midnight there was a cry made, Behold, the bridegroom cometh; go ye out to meet him. Then all those virgins arose, and trimmed their lamps. And the foolish said unto the wise, Give us of your oil; for our lamps are gone out.

But the wise answered, saying, Not so; lest there be not enough for us and you: but go ye rather to them that sell, and buy for yourselves.

And while they went to buy, the bridegroom came; and they that were ready went in with him to the marriage: and the door was shut.

Afterward came also the other virgins, saying, Lord, Lord, open to us.

But he answered and said, Verily I say unto you, I know you not. Watch therefore, for ye know neither the day nor the hour wherein the Son of man cometh. Jesus in Matthew 25:1-13

In those days came John the Baptist, preaching in the wilderness of Judaea, and saying, Repent ye: for the kingdom of heaven is at hand.

Matthew 3:1-2

From that time Jesus began to preach, and to say, Repent: for the kingdom of heaven is at hand. Matthew 4:17

There has been much teaching that applies Matthew 25:1-13 to the catching away or what is commonly referred to as the rapture of the church. However, Jesus is talking about the Kingdom of Heaven in this passage of scripture, and He and John the Baptist both clearly said that the Kingdom of Heaven is at hand. This passage of scripture is not about a catching away of believers. It is talking about how we should conduct ourselves daily as citizens of the Kingdom.

We must continually be ready (with our lamps full of oil and our wicks trimmed) for whatever the Lord brings across our paths and into our lives. We don't know when certain opportunities will come or when certain tests and trials will come.

Not only must we be ever ready ourselves for whatever comes our way; we need to continually encourage other believers to be ready.

284

Let us hold fast the profession of our faith without wavering; (for he is faithful that promised;) and let us consider one another to provoke unto love and to good works: not forsaking the assembling of ourselves together, as the manner of some is; but exhorting one another: and so much the more, as ye see the day approaching. Hebrews 10:23-25

KINGDOM MANNA: Reading 117

Perfect Peace

Thou shalt keep him in perfect peace, whose mind is stayed on thee: because he trusteth in thee. Isaiah 26:3

For to be carnally minded is death; but to be spiritually minded is life and peace. Romans 8:6

Be careful for nothing; but in every thing by prayer and supplication with thanksgiving let your requests be made known unto God. And the peace of God, which passeth all understanding, shall keep your hearts and minds through Christ Jesus. Philippians 4:6-7

In times of peace, free societies flourish. Freedom from the sacrifices and devastation of war enables people to build and prosper. And personal peace works in much the same way. Adverse circumstances will rob a person of inner peace, if allowed to do so. When we are at peace within ourselves, our soul (mind) prospers. And in the prosperity of our soul lies the ability to change our circumstances.

In the 2nd verse of John's 3rd epistle, he says, *"Beloved, I wish above all things that thou mayest prosper and be in health, even as thy soul prospereth."* How does our soul prosper? By keeping our mind on the things of God, by living our lives in relationship with Him and by renewing our minds continually to His Word (Romans 12:2). In other words, where we focus determines if we have peace or not. If our focus is on the things of God and our relationship with Him, rather than on our circumstances, we will experience peace in our souls. Our souls will prosper. Peace produces tranquility, contentment, completeness and wholeness. We can have the peace of God in the most adverse circumstances, but only when we live our lives completely surrendered to and totally trusting Him.

Adverse circumstances are nothing more than a test. Adverse circumstances will prove whether or not we are completely surrendered to and totally trusting God. In Romans 8:28, Paul tells us that all things work together for the good of those who love God and are the called according to His purpose. However, the manifestation of this promise is dependent on our being completely surrendered to and totally trusting Him.

In Philippians 4:11-13, Paul said this:

I have learned, in whatsoever state I am, therewith to be content. I know both how to be abased, and I know how to abound: every where and in all things I am instructed both to be full and to be hungry, both to abound and to suffer need. I can do all things through Christ which strengtheneth me.

In other words, our peace is not dependent upon what we have or what we don't have. It is not dependent upon good circumstances or bad circumstances. It is not dependent upon what we see in the natural realm or what we don't see. It is dependent upon our faith, which believes God, regardless.

Now faith is the substance of things hoped for, the evidence of things not seen.   Hebrews 11:1

Does being content mean we accept lack or adversity as the will of God for us? I think not. It means we believe God, simply because He said it and not because we see it. If it is impossible for God to lie (and it is, see Hebrews 6:18), then we can believe Him and totally trust Him, no matter what. However, there is a dying to self, a preparation process, a maturing that must take place in us, enabling us to prosper and causing all things to work for our good.

In order to handle success, we must be equipped to handle success. It is God's desire that we be successful in every area of our lives. The trials and tests of life are not there to cause us problems. They are there to equip us for success. When we realize this truth, it becomes easier to focus on the things of God in all circumstances, completely surrendered to His plan for our lives and totally trusting Him. In total surrender and trust is great peace. In total surrender and trust is perfect peace.

Now the Lord of peace himself give you peace always by all means.
                                                              2 Thessalonians 3:16

✠

GOOD, ACCEPTABLE, PERFECT

And be not conformed to this world: but be ye transformed by the renewing of your mind, that ye may prove what is that good, and acceptable, and perfect, will of God. Romans 12:2

So the last shall be first, and the first last: for many be called, but few chosen. Matthew 20:16

When people are truly born again and begin a relationship with God, the natural thing is to want to do something for Him. Is this not the way it is with all close, personal relationships?

When I was first married, I wanted to give gifts to my wife. I didn't know her well enough to know the kinds of gifts she wanted, so I gave her things based on what I thought she might like. I quickly learned not to give my wife things like vacuum cleaners or kitchen utensils. Women appreciate flowers and jewelry much more. A vacuum cleaner is a good gift and would probably be accepted. It is useful and needed in a household that has carpets, but jewelry ... , now that's a perfect gift for a woman, especially when that woman is the love of your life.

So is our relationship with God. We want to do something for Him and please Him. The problem is, until our relationship with Him has developed, we don't really know what He wants or what He requires of us. Romans 8:14 says:

For as many as are led by the Spirit of God, they are the sons [mature children] *of God.*

We can do good things and even acceptable things without being led by the Spirit. However, in order to know what the perfect will of God is for our lives, we must be led by the Spirit of God. Being led by the Spirit of God brings maturity to our lives, enabling us to know the perfect will of God.

In the spring of 2000, the Lord told me He was anointing me to lead praise and worship. Leading praise and worship is a good and acceptable thing. I had tried to do it a couple of times before I was anointed to do it, but somehow it just wasn't me. During corporate worship, I preferred being in the audience. I have been a singer and musician most of my life, but I wasn't a praise and worship leader until God anointed me for that job.

I have seen musicians and singers more talented than me, leading praise and worship, when it was obvious they were not anointed to do so. They were just performing songs. Was what they were doing good? Yes. Was it acceptable? Maybe. Was it the perfect will of God for them? No.

Maturing in the Lord requires putting aside our own agenda. You may have many talents. You may see many needs, but without the calling and anointing of God you will not accomplish much. However, being in the perfect will of God insures success.

Many that are called settle for doing good and acceptable things. While the called may get by only doing good and acceptable things, there are those who have been chosen for perfect things.

God does not allow the chosen to settle for good or acceptable. That's why some of us have been through a severe process of trials and tests. To be chosen means you didn't volunteer. You were drafted. Those of us who were drafted have been through boot camp, which has prepared us for battle and to be overcomers, building character in us and positioning us for the job we have to do (which, by the way, we don't get to choose either). Our assignment was handed to us by our Commander in Chief.

Because of His preparation, positioning and bringing us to maturity, He knows He can trust us. The word that translates from the Greek as *chosen* also translates as *trusted*. Matthew 20:16 and 22:14 could read, "Many are called, but few are trusted."

The tests and trials we go through build a two way trust in us. As we trust Him more, He can trust us more.

While we may be walking in things we would not have chosen, my experience has been that being in His perfect will brings joy and great peace to my life. I am in awe of the things He does in and through me, when I stay surrendered to Him and simply trust Him. I wouldn't have it any other way. ✠

A Hard Place

And he went into the synagogue, and spake boldly for the space of three months, disputing and persuading the things concerning the Kingdom of God. But when divers were hardened, and believed not, but spake evil of that way before the multitude, he departed from them, and separated the disciples, disputing daily in the school of one Tyrannus.

Acts 19:8-9

This is from the account of Paul's ministry in Ephesus. Paul had wanted to go to Ephesus earlier, but was not allowed by the Spirit to do so. He had then briefly visited while on his way to Jerusalem. Now he was back.

Upon his arrival, he found some disciples among the citizens (see Acts 19). He asked them if they had received the Holy Spirit since they believed. Their response was that they hadn't heard anything about the Holy Spirit.

He then asked them what they were baptized into. Their response was, "John's baptism." These folks were not even born again. All they knew was John's baptism of repentance. Then Paul preached Jesus to them, baptized them in the name of Jesus and got them baptized with the Holy Spirit, after which, they spoke with tongues and prophesied. There were only about twelve of them, but Paul had a church started in Ephesus. Thank God he did! Without the Church at Ephesus there would be no Book of Ephesians.

Paul then went into the synagogue and preached Jesus to the Jews in Ephesus, but the majority of the Jews didn't believe Paul's Gospel. When they began to speak evil of him and his Gospel, he separated the disciples he had from them and started holding meetings in the lecture hall of Tyrannus.

Despite a small beginning and opposition, Paul continued preaching every day from about 10:00 AM until 2:00 PM (according to the Amplified Bible). These meetings continued for two years. Acts 19:10 tells us that everyone in Asia, both Jews and Greeks, heard the Word of the Lord Jesus because of Paul's success in Ephesus. Evidently many came to Ephesus to hear Paul in Tyrannus' school. For those that couldn't come, God wrought special miracles by the hands of Paul (see Acts 19:11-12). While he preached, he wore cloths on his body. These cloths were then taken to the sick and demon possessed. When they touched the cloths, the diseases and evil spirits departed from them.

My point is this: Ephesus was a hard place, with plenty of opposition. Many there worshipped false gods and were into sorcery. The religious community (Jews) wanted nothing to do with Paul's Gospel. He started with only a few believers who didn't even know they needed to be born again. But Paul was led by the Spirit to be there. He was on assignment, on a mission for God.

Perhaps some work had been done in the spiritual realm between the time Paul had first wanted to go to Ephesus and when the Spirit actually sent him. Even though there were adverse circumstances, Paul knew the time was right and that he was supposed to be there. I suspect he took the first twelve people he had connected with as a great encouragement to continue on, and his perseverance paid off. Without television, radio or the Internet, the Gospel was heard by everyone living in Asia. Now that's amazing!

There is a lesson of encouragement here for us. Small beginnings, difficulties and adverse circumstances are not a gauge of whether or not we are in the will of God. We are His sheep, and we know His voice (see John 10:27). We simply listen to His voice and walk in obedience. The outcome is up to Him. It is His responsibility. Our responsibility is to obey. His responsibility is to prosper our obedience. Glory to God! ✞

Times of Refreshing

Repent ye therefore, and be converted, that your sins may be blotted out, when the times of refreshing shall come from the presence of the Lord.

Peter in Acts 3:19

Prior to some recent meetings I facilitated, a group of believers were meeting weekly to pray for the meetings. Several prophetic words came forth as we met. There was one thing the Spirit said to us more than once. He said, "God is doing a new thing." He specified that it was not new to God, but that it would be new to us.

As we held these meetings, it became evident that the structure of the meetings wasn't much different than other meetings most of us had been in. There was worship, ministry and preaching/teaching. Most were inspired and encouraged, as we spent time in the presence of God, but these things were not really new to those of us who have been holding and attending meetings like this for several years now.

So what is the new thing the Spirit of God was speaking about? While some individuals present experienced a new thing in their lives as we were taught, ministered to and enjoyed the manifested presence of God that filled the room, I was expecting something more. Yes, I left each meeting refreshed, but it seemed to me we were missing the new thing the Spirit had spoken about.

Could this new thing be directly related to the new day (millennium) we are now entering into, this third day (millennium) of the Church and seventh day (millennium) since Creation? In Peter's second letter to the churches he said this:

Beloved, be not ignorant of this one thing, that one day is with the Lord as a thousand years and a thousand years as one day.

2 Peter 3:8

Peter wrote to the churches of many things, but here he said to be not ignorant of this **one thing**. He placed great importance on the comparison of a day being equal to a thousand years. I have discovered that understanding many prophetic scriptures, as they relate to the history of planet Earth, hinge on this truth. Because most of the Church has not understood this truth, much of the recent teaching on the end times has, at best, been a mixture of intellectual and revealed knowledge.

In the Greek language, there are two very different words for *time*. One is *chronos*, which means time as usual, as in the chronological order of days on a calendar. The other is *kairos*, which means an appointed time or a moment in time pregnant with destiny. The word that Peter used in Acts 3:19 is *kairos*. At least a few who were present in the meetings we held experienced a *kairos* moment during the meetings, but the new thing the Spirit was speaking of is much more than the experience of a meeting. It is the experience of a new day, the third day of the Church and the seventh day of Creation. It is more than a *kairos* moment. It is a *kairos* day!

Jesus said, *"Behold, I cast out devils, and I do cures to day and to morrow, and the third day I shall be perfected"* (Luke 13:32). While He may have been speaking of His immediate, impending crucifixion and resurrection, He was also prophetically speaking of the third day of the Church when He will be perfected in a people.

The writer of Hebrews said, *"There remaineth therefore a rest to the people of God"* (Hebrews 4:9). God ordained the seventh day of Creation to be a day of rest, and, saints, we are now entering into that day.

As Jesus is perfected in us, we partake of His perfection, not just positionally, but also experientially, causing us to rest in His finished work, bringing us (the apostolic Church/the Bride of Christ) to completion. This is the new thing the Spirit was speaking to us about. Surely we were born for such a time as this! All glory to God!

Let us hold fast the profession of our faith without wavering; (for he is faithful that promised;) and let us consider one another to provoke unto love and to good works: not forsaking the assembling of ourselves together, as the manner of some is; but exhorting one another; and so much the more, as ye see the day [third day/seventh day] *approaching.*

Hebrews 10:23-25

✣

SIX DAYS SHALL YOU LABOR

Six days shalt thou labour, and do all thy work: but the seventh day is the sabbath of the LORD thy God: in it thou shalt not do any work. For in six days the LORD made heaven and earth, the sea, and all that in them is, and rested the seventh day: wherefore the LORD blessed the sabbath day, and hallowed it. Exodus 20:9-11

There remaineth therefore a rest to the people of God. For he that is entered into his rest, he also hath ceased from his own works, as God did from his. Let us labour therefore to enter into that rest, lest any man fall after the same example of unbelief. For the word of God is quick, and powerful, and sharper than any twoedged sword, piercing even to the dividing asunder of soul and spirit, and of the joints and marrow, and is a discerner of the thoughts and intents of the heart. Hebrews 4:9-12

Beloved, be not ignorant of this one thing, that one day is with the Lord as a thousand years and a thousand years as one day.

2 Peter 3:8

God created the world as we know it in six days and rested on the seventh. Then He commanded Israel to rest one day each week. The writer of Hebrews takes this example and commandment and gives it a new meaning in Hebrews 4:9-12, seeming to have an understanding of 2 Peter 3:8.

In our last KINGDOM MANNA reading we looked at the new thing God is doing, and I asked this question: Could this new thing be directly related to the new day (millennium) we are now entering into, this third day (millennium) of the Church and seventh day (millennium) since Creation? The answer is a very emphatic *Yes*!

This third day of the Church is the seventh day of Creation. It is the Sabbath rest the writer of Hebrews is talking about. The Old Testament sabbaths were but types and shadows of the New Testament rest spoken of in Hebrews. God didn't rest on the seventh day of Creation because He was tired. He rested because He was finished. He looked at all He had created and commented that it was *"very good"* (Genesis 1:32 and 2:1-3). Yet, after the fall of man in the Garden of Eden, we see God laboring to keep mankind on track, moving toward the time when He could introduce salvation that would reverse the curse man had brought on himself and all creation.

Four thousand years (four days) after Creation and the fall of man, God the Son, Jesus, hung on the cross and said, *"It is finished."* God had done all He could do to save mankind and His creation, but once again, we see the Church laboring for the next two thousand years (two days) trying to enter into that rest. Hence, the contradiction of Hebrews 4:9-12.

It is impossible to *labor* to enter into *rest*. Rest is "a ceasing from labor." God labored six days over Creation before ceasing from His work and entering into the Sabbath rest. Man has labored for six thousand years trying to enter into rest, initially under the Law and the last two millennia trying to enter into the salvation Jesus completed on the cross. This is why the Church, for the most part, has had salvation backward, remaining under the Law. We have tried to become holy by changing our behavior, by laboring. What some are beginning to realize in this third day of the Church and seventh day of Creation is that the finished work of Jesus on the cross has made us holy. When we grasp that truth by the dividing asunder of our soul and spirit (dying to self), our behavior will change. We will be holy, not only positionally, because of what Jesus accomplished, but also experientially, because we have entered into the rest that remains for the people of God. Bless His name forever! ✛

KINGDOM MANNA: READING 122

A NEW THING

Now therefore ye are no more strangers and foreigners, but fellowcitizens with the saints, and of the household of God; and are built upon the foundation of the apostles and prophets.   Ephesians 2:19-20

And he gave some, apostles; and some, prophets; and some, evangelists; and some, pastors and teachers; for the perfecting of the saints, for the work of the ministry, for the edifying of the body of Christ: till we all come in the unity of the faith, and of the knowledge of the Son of God, unto a perfect man, unto the measure of the stature of the fulness of Christ.   Ephesians 4:11-13

We are on a journey. We are trailblazers. We are going to a new place, and in order to get there, we are going to have to do a new thing. New to God? No. He knows the end from the beginning (see Isaiah 46:10). He already sees where we are going. We must begin to see what He is seeing.

The more we see what God is seeing, the clearer our path and destination will become. Does that mean we forsake everything we know? I don't think so. Does it mean we no longer do any of the things we have been doing? I don't think so. But it does mean we discern what is of God and what is not.

Matthew 15:6 and Mark 7:13 both speak of traditions causing the Word of God to have no effect. It is time we lay down traditions, habits, ideas, doctrines, behaviors and anything else that may appear to be holy, but, in reality, is only religious. How do we do this? By the revealed Word of God.

For the word of God is quick, and powerful, and sharper than any twoedged sword, piercing even to the dividing asunder of soul and spirit, and of the joints and marrow, and is a discerner of the thoughts and intents of the heart.   Hebrews 4:12

We must allow the Scriptures to come alive to us and in us, dividing that which is of the Spirit from that which is of the soul (us/our minds). We must let that living Word reveal the source of our thoughts and the intentions of our hearts. We must forget those things that are behind and reach for those things that are ahead, pressing toward the mark (prize) of the high calling of God in the anointed Jesus (see Philippians 3:13-14).

The apostolic Church that was birthed on the Day of Pentecost, as recorded in the 2nd chapter of Acts, will only come to fullness and completion when we get our focus off of doing church and onto being the Church. It is time to grow up. It is time to start looking and acting like Jesus, doing the things He did and even greater things (see John 14:12).

There is a pattern of the New Testament Church in the Book of Acts. I know of people today who have tried to reproduce that pattern, but I don't believe God wants to reproduce that pattern today. I believe He wants to build on that pattern and bring the New Testament Church to completion.

The completed Church is not going to look like the early Church, and it is certainly not going to look like what came after the early Church. It is going to be a new thing, and it will be glorious (see Ephesians 5:27). Glory to God! ⚜

KINGDOM MANNA: Reading 123

A New Song

Praise ye the LORD. Sing unto the LORD a new song, and his praise in the congregation of saints.   Psalm 149:1

This is one of several psalms that speak of a new song (see Psalm 33:3, 40:3, 96:1, 98:1 and 144:9).

In the spring of 1970, Scott Ross introduced Jesus to me and I was born again. Scott was a DJ who had worked in the New York City broadcast market prior to being born again himself. He had emceed the Beatles at Shea Stadium and partied with the likes of Bob Dylan and the Rolling Stones.

In the early 1970s Scott produced a four-hour syndicated radio program. The show consisted of the pop hits of the day, with Scott making comments between songs. He would always use his comments to somehow preach the Gospel. On one of Scott's programs, he read from the Psalms and then asked his listeners to begin praying that God would bring forth a new song in them. He even prayed that God would reach and save people in the pop music world and that they would then begin to write and record this new song. Within months God had answered Scott's prayer, and new albums were available.

Long before the name *Contemporary Christian Music* was coined, people like Larry Norman of the rock group People, Phil Keaggy of Glass Harp, Paul Stooky of Peter, Paul and Mary, and Chuck Girard of the Hondels were recording a new kind of Christian music. Soon there were others: Keith Green, The Second Chapter of Acts, Honeytree, Barry McGuire and on and on.

Today we have many different styles of Christian music by many different artists. I believe the prayer Scott Ross prayed on his syndicated radio program was prophetic and spoke of things to come. I think God put Scott in that position to announce publicly the coming forth of a new song. But I believe the new song that has and is coming forth is much more than music or musical style. The new song itself is an announcement or proclamation of a new thing.

In ancient Israel, when a new king was crowned, there was always a new song written for that king and sung at his coronation. I believe the new music that is coming forth today, much of which is praise and worship music, is preparing a people for this third day of the Church and the fulfillment of the Feast of Tabernacles. God is bringing forth a new song and doing a new thing today. We should be exuberantly excited about it and determining where we fit into it. But we should be even more exuberantly excited that the restitution of all things is at hand. All glory to God!

Let us hold fast the profession of our faith without wavering; (for he is faithful that promised;) and let us consider one another to provoke unto love and to good works: not forsaking the assembling of ourselves together, as the manner of some is; but exhorting one another; and so much the more, as ye see the day approaching.   Hebrews 10:23-25

PROPHETIC WORD 6

I am sending you forth as expressions of My love, into the darkness, into the deep darkness of planet Earth, where many fear to go and some refuse to go. Fear not. Light overcomes darkness, and you are of the Light, if you abide and walk in the Light.

I am the Light of the world. I dwell in you, and if you abide in Me, the darkness cannot hurt you or overcome you. Darkness always flees from light. When you turn on a light switch, the darkness always goes. The only way the darkness can return is when the light switch is turned off, when the light is removed. Everywhere you go, you will shine the light of My glory, if you abide in Me continually. My light will manifest in you without measure, and the world will know that I am God Almighty.

I am sending you forth as expressions of My love, as sheep among wolves and lambs for the slaughter. But know this: I am with you. My protection is all around you. They cannot hurt you. They cannot harm you. You, who have died to self and are walking with Me. Do not fear them. I am your Shield and your Buckler. If I am for you, who can be against you?

I am sending you forth as expressions of My love, to those who don't want to hear the truth, to those who want to go their own way, to those who hate and despise you. But know this: You must be a witness before them and to them. The very life you live will expose them for what they are. Some will fall down and repent, but others will go to their destruction.

I don't desire that any perish. My love, the love that I am, dwells in you. You will go to great lengths, as I send you, and all who are willing shall come into the Kingdom and find rest for their souls. Be not dismayed that some will continue to reject you, but know that many will come. This is the hour of My visitation. This is the hour of My revelation. This is the hour when the sons of God have begun to manifest in the earth.

I am sending you forth as expressions of My love, to those who are hungry, to those who desire the truth, to those who are seeking Me, seeking My Kingdom, seeking My righteousness. And they are many, many more than you know. I have prepared a people like none other in the history of the planet. The sons of God are coming into the time when I will manifest in and through them to a desperate world that has lost hope.

I am sending you forth as expressions of My love, apostles, prophets, evangelists, overseers and teachers, operating in the gifts of the Holy Spirit, equipping all the saints for the work of the ministry, to be expressions of My love. This is not about you; it is all about Me, for I am the Way, the Truth and the Life. I am the Door through which all must pass to enter into My rest, to find the peace that passes all understanding, to inherit eternity, to live forever.

I am sending you forth as expressions of My glory, of My goodness, of My mercy, of My grace, of My power, of My character, of My love.

Go! Do not count the cost. Do not consider things suffered. Keep your eyes on Me, and listen only to Me. A great harvest must be brought in. We have a great job to do.

I have prepared you. I have positioned you. You will bear much fruit because I have declared it. I have decreed it. You will do great exploits and bring in a great harvest.

Listen to Me. Obey Me. I am sending you forth as expressions of My love. And Love never fails! ✝

PROPHETIC WORD 7

My glory is being revealed to My chosen ones, to My trusted ones. Know this: the time is at hand when you, My chosen ones, My trusted ones, must demonstrate My glory, My goodness before a wicked and perverse generation. Many are wicked and perverse because they have fallen into deception and not because of their choosing. They have become prey to wrong understanding, to wrong information. Who will set them straight, unless you go as I send you? Who will set them straight, unless you demonstrate My power and My glory, My goodness? Who will set them straight, unless you preach, declaring My gospel, My good news that I have come to heal the brokenhearted, to cast out devils, to restore sight to the blind, to bring deliverance to the captives, to set free those who are beaten down, to proclaim, to preach, to declare Jubilee.

I am coming in great glory. My glory must be known as a witness to those in darkness. My glory must be seen by those who have rejected Me in the past, but are unknowingly seeking Me. They are seeking peace, deliverance, truth. How will they know that I am peace, deliverance and truth unless you tell them, unless you demonstrate My power, My glory, My goodness to them? They are like sheep without a shepherd, and I am sending you forth to bring them into the fold.

Stop focusing on the tests and the trials I have put you through. I have prepared you. I have positioned you. While that process continues for many of you, you must focus on the job at hand. You must focus on the work we have to do. And you must focus on Me. Without intimacy with Me you will not survive the attacks of the enemy. You will not have the peace that passes all understanding. Yes, you must know My Word. Yes, you must understand the covenant we have with each other. But you must know Me intimately, to experience My glory in its fullness.

This is what I desire for you: that you experience My glory in its fullness. The covenant we have is without measure, and the glory I desire that you experience is without measure. There is no limit and no end to our relationship. We are one, and we are destined to go from glory to glory. ✢

KINGDOM MANNA: READING 126

PROPHETIC WORD 8

"Not this time! Not this time," says the Lord. "In the past you have fallen when the pressure of persecution, the pressure of temptation, the pressure of trials and tests has come against you. But not this time! You must stand strong. You must stand immovable. You must stand focused on Me, full of My Word, full of My power, full of My grace.

"Do not look at yourself based on what you appear to be in your own eyes. Look at yourself based on My Word, on who My Word says you are, on what My Word says you are. You must begin to see yourself as I see you, for I don't see you in the process you are going through. I see you completed as a manifested son of the living God.

"Like Me, you must see the end from the beginning. You must focus on the finished work, on the fullness that I desire for you. As you walk with Me, more and more you will relate to eternity rather than time. Time has limitations, and while you do live temporarily in a capsule of time, you are no longer subject to time, as you once were. You are eternal, you who have crossed over from death to life, you who are born anew by the eternal life that I am.

"In eternity, the end is as real as the present. In eternity, there is no beginning and no end, only eternity. You must not allow the limitations of this physical world to hold you back, for we are in the business of taking this present physical world, with its limitations to fullness, to perfection.

"This is not spiritual *'pie in the sky.'* This is not *'in the sweet by and by.'* This is present. This is now. This is My Kingdom coming on earth as it is in Heaven.

"You are the forerunners. You are the Elijahs. You are the John the Baptists. You are the prophetic voice to bring it to pass, to speak it into existence. You are My trumpet call, announcing that which is about to be.

"Know who you are. See yourself as I see you, you who are chosen, you whom I trust, you in whom I have great confidence, you in whom I have invested Myself without measure, without limitation." ✠

Prophetic Word 9

As surely as the seasons change, I am calling you higher. As surely as the seasons change, I am saying to you, "Come up here." Just as I said to John, "Come up here, and I will show you things to come." Know this: those *things to come* are upon you. I have spoken a word to you. I have shown my prophets what I am about to do.

What I am about to do has already begun. What I am about to do has already been set in motion. Some have seen it and have tasted of it. Some have seen it and are already doing it. Some have seen it and are about to move into it. But know this: none have seen it in its fullness. None have seen it completely. But you will.

As surely as the seasons change, the thing I have spoken to you is nigh. You are at the door. You are crossing the threshold. You will never be the same again. You cannot go back now. Forget the former things and press on into the fullness of My glory. Forget the former things and press on into the fullness of My power. Forget the former things and press on into the fullness of My authority.

Forget not that which I have revealed, but forget the traditions of men, the religious thinking, the ways of doing things that have kept you from moving into My fullness, for a great work must be accomplished in this day. Never before has there been a time like this time. Never before has there been a day like this day. Never before have I had a people like those I have been preparing, positioning and maturing for those things which are now coming on the earth. For the manifestation of the sons of God is now in motion. My glorious Church is being built.

As surely as the seasons change, the knowledge of the glory of the Lord will cover the earth as the waters cover the sea. As surely as the seasons change, you were created for this time. I have My chosen ones. I have My called-out ones. Now you choose others. Now you call out others. "How," you ask, "can we choose and call out when the Word clearly says that no one can come unless the Father draws him." Have I not given you My authority? Have I not given you My name? You declare it. You prophesy it. You call it into existence. You make it so.

The time to wait for what I am about to do is past. It is time to pass from prophetic intercession to prophetic declaration. You call it to pass. You speak it into existence. It is time for those of you who can receive My fullness to walk with Me. Say what I am saying. Do what I am doing. You are of the firstfruits company that will be instrumental in bringing about the greatest move of God the world has ever witnessed. Use your authority to bring in those who cannot yet receive My fullness.

I cannot fail, and you will not fail. You have not chosen Me, but I have chosen you. The work I have begun in you I will complete, and you will come into My fullness.

Not all can receive this word, but to those who can, I say, "Come up here. Sit with Me in heavenly places, for you are the overcomers. You are the kings and priests who will rule with Me in My Kingdom. It is in you that I have placed My authority and My power. Nothing can stop you now. Nothing can hold you back. I created you for this time. Creation is crying out for the manifested sons of God, and I will bring it to pass.

"Walk with me. Do what I do. Say what I say. See what I see. I am giving you revealed knowledge that will cause you to see through My eyes, to see as I see, to see what I see. Speak it. Declare it. For I have given you the power to bring it into existence.

"No longer listen to the prophets of doom. No longer let your conversation agree with the enemy's campaign against My creation. Speak the end from the beginning. I assure you, the end is glorious. Will I not complete what I have begun?" ✠

REVIVAL

*I have found favor with you here in eastern North Carolina. **I will personally visit you.** There will be a revival greater than that of the great Wales Revival at the turn of the century* [the twentieth century]. *There will be kings and leaders who will come from north and south and east and west to study the Eastern North Carolina phenomenon.*

A prophetic word by Derek Prince

delivered in Jacksonville, North Carolina

April 6, 1975

(Emphasis added)

And what will ye do in the day of visitation?   Isaiah 10:3

The day of thy watchmen and thy visitation cometh.   Micah 7:4

Glorify God in the day of visitation.   1 Peter 2:12

Now therefore ye are no more strangers and foreigners, but fellowcitizens with the saints, and of the household of God; and are built upon the foundation of the apostles and prophets, Jesus Christ himself being the chief corner stone; in whom all the building fitly framed together groweth unto an holy temple in the Lord: in whom ye also are builded together for an habitation of God through the Spirit.

Ephesians 2:19-22

God is up to something! He is on the move! Get ready!

The above prophecy was given years ago. It was given in eastern North Carolina for eastern North Carolina. However, the same day there was a prophecy given in the Tidewater area of Virginia that was the same message as the eastern North Carolina prophecy. The only difference was that the Virginia prophecy said the revival would come out of Virginia.

In November of 1620, a group of pilgrims sailed to the shores of Virginia on the Mayflower. They had fled England because of religious persecution. They had spent twelve hard years in Holland before sailing on to the New World. Before ever setting foot on the North American continent, they made a written covenant with Almighty God. Part of that covenant stated:

Having undertaken for the Glory of God, and the Advancement of the Christian Faith… a voyage to plant the first colony in the northern parts of Virginia…

Those pilgrims were not just fleeing religious persecution; they were on a mission orchestrated by God to establish a nation where people would be free to worship God and free to sow the seeds of that freedom around the world. And the American church has done just that for many years. These seeds of freedom are not political freedom, but, in many cases, they produce political freedom. The freedom that has been sown around the world is freedom from the sin and death that Adam opened the door to when he fell in the Garden six thousand years ago.

As President George W. Bush stated many times during his administration, "Freedom is not our right. It is a gift from Almighty God." I believe God is moving and about to move simultaneously in many places in the United States and around the world. The revival that has started in the United States has been going on for many years in other parts of the world.

But this is not just another revival. It is not just another move of God. It is a pivotal move of God that will bring the apostolic Church that was birthed on the Day of Pentecost, as recorded in the 2nd chapter of Acts, to completion. Glory to God!

God is about to visit us as never before, but He is not coming as a tourist. He is coming to take up residence with us. He has a people, a remnant that He has been preparing for a long time. This group of believers has been severely tested and tried, as He has been preparing, positioning and maturing us for this historical moment in time.

Surely we were born for such a time as this! ✝

An Effectual, Open Door

But I will tarry at Ephesus until Pentecost. For a great door and effectual is opened unto me, and there are many adversaries.

1 Corinthians 16:8-9

The effectual fervent prayer of a righteous man availeth much.

James 5:16

When something is effectual, it works. It produces the desired result. A great, effectual door is a major, working door that enables one to enter where one desires to enter. An effectual, fervent prayer is a working, intensely enthusiastic prayer, prayed by someone who has been made the righteousness of God by the finished work of Jesus (see Romans 3:20-22). Could it be that great and effectual doors are opened by effectual, fervent prayer? I think so.

Paul had wanted to go to Ephesus long before the Spirit sent him there. Perhaps something happened in the Spirit realm between the time Paul wanted to go and the time the Spirit sent him. Even when he finally was able to start a work in Ephesus, there were many adversaries. Yet, Paul somehow (probably by the Spirit) knew a great, working door was open there. In the 19th chapter of Acts we are told that everyone in Asia heard the Gospel because of Paul's two-year stay in Ephesus, where he ministered five hours a day (according to the Amplified Bible) in the lecture hall of Tyrannus.

There was a great revival in Wales in 1859. Then, in 1904, many people were praying for another visitation of God, like the one in 1859. Their prayers were answered when God raised up a twenty-six-year-old coal miner named Evan Roberts. Roberts preached three times a day, seven days a week, for about two years, spearheading a revival that not only changed the church in Wales, but also impacted society at large.

In 1906 William Seymour, a black man, was preaching in Los Angeles, California. One night the Lord led him to go to a part of town where black people were not allowed after dark. He obeyed and was led to a certain apartment where he knocked on the door. There were some white ladies inside praying that God would send someone to start a revival in Los Angeles. Seymour said, "I'm the man." Within a short period of time the Azusa Street Mission was open, and revival was happening. For over two years the visible glory cloud didn't leave the building, and on several occasions the fire department was called to the building because flames were seen coming out the roof. Many miracles took place in that old building that had previously been a stable.

Numerous people in the United States and around the world are praying for revival today, but the revival we need today is more than the revivals of the past. I believe the revivals of the past (including recent ones) were but stepping stones to what God is about to do. I believe we are about to see the apostolic Church (that was birthed on the Day of Pentecost, after Jesus ascended into Heaven) come to fullness. I believe that in the time just ahead we will see the completion of the apostolic Church. ✛

An Effectual, Open Door 2

But I will tarry at Ephesus until Pentecost. For a great door and effectual is opened unto me, and there are many adversaries.

1 Corinthians 16:8-9

The effectual fervent prayer of a righteous man availeth much.

James 5:16

In the last KINGDOM MANNA, we looked at how Paul had wanted to go to Ephesus, but was prevented by the Spirit to do so until the appointed time. At the appointed time, a great move of God took place in Ephesus and in all of Asia, because of Paul's obedience. We also took a very brief look at the Welsh and Azusa Street revivals of the nineteenth and twentieth centuries. Today many are looking for another revival to sweep the world, bringing many into the Kingdom and impacting society and governments.

Many people think of revival as signs, wonders and miracles. While signs, wonders and miracles should be the norm for the Church, we are not to run after or seek after them. Signs, wonders and miracles should be following us. As we walk in love and in obedience to the leading of the Holy Spirit, as mature believers, signs, wonders and miracles will follow us, as we go and proclaim the Gospel, baptizing, casting out devils and healing the sick (see Mark 16:17-18), doing the things Jesus did and greater things (see John 14:12-14).

We must be a people of prayer, but we must also be a people of action. James told us to be doers of the Word and not hearers only (see James 1:22) and to prove our faith by our actions (see James 2:14).

We shouldn't pray for another outpouring. The Holy Spirit was poured out on the Day of Pentecost (see Acts 2), and He hasn't gone anywhere. He is still here indwelling us. But we do need to pray that God will prepare the way for us so we will be successful as we go forth putting our faith into action.

In order to grow a crop, a farmer plants in good soil. The same seed planted in bad soil will die and rot, producing nothing. As we pray for God to prepare the way for us, we are asking Him to prepare the soil. We need to go where there is a working door, open to the Gospel of the Kingdom. This occurs when we first determine where God wants to work, and then we pray (come into agreement with God) about that area. Then we must go when the Spirit leads us to go, just as the apostle Paul, Evan Roberts and William Seymour did.

A study of past revivals usually points to one person that spearheaded the revival. I believe the next great revival will be spearheaded by many at the same time. It is the Lord's desire to work through His Body, rather than through a single individual. There is a remnant of the Body of Christ today that God has been preparing for this work. As we discover our individual callings and anointings, determining where we fit in the whole (see Ephesians 2:21) and then using those callings and anointings to build up the Body and reach the world, revival will come.

I live in eastern North Carolina, where revival has been prophesied for many years. God has been positioning, preparing and maturing a people to spearhead this coming revival. Many have been severely tested and tried during that process. Much prayer has been going on for a long time, but prayer alone won't bring revival. We are going to have to put action to our prayers. The revival is not coming down from Heaven; it is coming out of us. (I need to note here that as I have traveled, I have met believers in other areas of the United States and in other countries who believe revival is coming out of *their* areas, and I believe they, too, are hearing from God.)

While it is obvious that God marks certain areas for His purposes, such as He did in Ephesus during Paul's time, His desire is to reach all mankind (see Habakkuk 2:14). Paul reached all of Asia because of what God did with him in Ephesus. As we determine where the great, working doors are opening, because we have been led to pray for those areas, and then put action to our prayers, we will see a revival of the apostolic Church that will take that Church to a glorious completion (see Ephesians 5:27), impacting the whole world. ✠

KINGDOM MANNA: READING 131

PRAYER, WORD AND ACTION

This book of the law shall not depart out of thy mouth; but thou shalt meditate therein day and night, that thou mayest observe to do according to all that is written therein: for then thou shalt make thy way prosperous, and then thou shalt have good success.　　Joshua 1:8

Blessed is the man that walketh not in the counsel of the ungodly, nor standeth in the way of sinners, nor sitteth in the seat of the scornful. But his delight is in the law of the LORD; and in his law doth he medi-

tate day and night. And he shall be like a tree planted by the rivers of water, that bringeth forth his fruit in his season; his leaf also shall not wither; and whatsoever he doeth shall prosper.   Psalm 1:1-3

Prayer is more than making a request to God. Prayer is coming into agreement with God. Prayer is speaking the Word of God, which will bring His promises to pass.

When God spoke the above scripture to Joshua, the only written Word of God that Joshua had was the *Torah*, or what is today the first five books of the Bible. God told Joshua to keep that Word in his mouth or, in other words, to speak it continually. He was to meditate or think about it and contemplate it day and night (that's all the time). He said then Joshua would observe to do it or, in other words, he would see himself doing it.

God said, "Joshua, speak My Word continually, think about it and contemplate it continually, because when you do, you will see yourself doing everything My Word says you can do and being everything My Word says you are. Then, you will be prosperous and successful" (My paraphrase). Psalm 1:1-3 is a confirmation to us of the same thing God said to Joshua.

How would Joshua see himself doing the Word? He would see it with the eye of his mind. He would visualize himself being and doing what the Word said he could be and do. In other words, he would get it on the inside, and then it would materialize on the outside.

In order to increase individually and corporately as the Body of Christ, we must abide in His Word and cause His Word to abide in us. Jesus said it this way: *"If ye abide in me, and my words abide in you, ye shall ask what ye will, and it shall be done unto you. Herein is my Father glorified that ye bear much fruit; so shall ye be my disciples"* (John 15:7-8).

We must feed on the Word of God continually, thinking about it and speaking it continually until we see ourselves fulfilling our purpose and calling. This is not a formula to get rich. It is a formula that will cause the Kingdom of God to manifest inside us, so we can then do our part to bring the Kingdom of God on earth as it is in Heaven. Financial wealth may come in the process, but prosperity and success are much more than finances. Jesus told us to seek first the Kingdom of God and His righteousness, and everything else we need will come (see Matthew 6:33 and Luke 12:31).

We are on this earth to establish God's Kingdom. The process of establishing the Kingdom will bring the apostolic Church to fullness and completion. We can pray for revival for a long, long time, but unless we abide in the Word, and the Word abides in us, and unless we put action to the faith that the Word will cause to manifest in us, we will not see revival.

It will take all of the above working together to bring revival. And we must realize that the revival we are now entering into is much more than the revivals of the past. What we are about to experience is much more than revival. The Lord is bringing His Church to maturity/completion/perfection. Never before has there been a time like this. Surely we were born for such a time as this! Surely we were born for this time! ✠

KINGDOM MANNA: Reading 132

Preparing the Way

Comfort ye, comfort ye my people, saith your God. The voice of him that crieth in the wilderness, Prepare ye the way of the LORD, make straight in the desert a highway for our God, every valley shall be exalted, and every mountain and hill shall be made low; and the crooked shall be made straight, and the rough places plain: and the glory of the LORD shall be revealed, and all flesh shall see it together: for the mouth of the LORD hath spoken it. Isaiah 40:1 and 3-5

And it shall come to pass, that whosoever shall call on the name of the LORD shall be delivered: for in mount Zion and in Jerusalem shall be deliverance, as the LORD hath said, and in the remnant whom the LORD shall call. Joel 2:32

Beloved, think it not strange concerning the fiery trial which is to try you, as though some strange thing happened unto you: but rejoice, inasmuch as ye are partakers of Christ's sufferings; that, when his glory shall be revealed, ye may be glad also with exceeding joy.

Yet if any man suffer as a Christian, let him not be ashamed; but let him glorify God on this behalf. For the time is come that judgment must begin at the house of God. 1 Peter 4:12-13, 16-17

Judgment that begins at the house of God is not condemnation. It is a judgment of the flesh, to rid us of fleshly desires, ambitions, habits, pressure, etc. I should note that fleshly things do not always, and maybe not even usually, appear as the things most people think of as sins. In many cases, the sins of the flesh manifest as religious ideas and traditions, even wrong thinking concerning moral issues. As we abide in His Word, and His Word abides in us, that Word will divide soul (flesh) and spirit (see Hebrews 4:12). We will begin to see the contrast between the two and become better able to identify the difference. This is not a pleasant experience, but the more we recognize it and submit to it, the easier it becomes.

The process (judgment) we go through during this surgery brings down the high places in our lives that exalt themselves against the Word of God. It also brings up the low places that are designed to keep us down. It makes the rough ways smooth and the crooked ways straight. Ultimately, it manifests the glory of God in us, on us and around us, making that glory visible for others to see (see Isaiah 40:1-5). The result is deliverance (see Joel 2:32) from our flesh that enables us to bring deliverance to others.

In order for the Kingdom of God to manifest on earth as it is in Heaven, it must first manifest in a people, bringing a fallen world closer to its destination, which is restitution. We are trailblazers, building a highway.

If you've ever ridden an interstate highway through the mountains, you've seen where hills were cut down and low places filled in to make the highway as level as possible. Jesus said, *"Come unto me, all ye that labour and are heavy laden, and I will give you rest. Take my yoke upon you, and learn of me; for I am meek and lowly in heart: and ye shall find rest unto your souls. **For my yoke is easy, and my burden is light**"* (Matthew 11:28-30, Emphasis added). His yoke becomes easy as the highway we are on gets leveled out, made smooth and straight. Those of us whom God has chosen to be at the forefront of this process are trailblazers. We are going into territory that, at times, may seem uncharted to us, but we can rest in the knowledge that our Lord has prepared the way. Our determination and willingness to continue on regardless of the cost will make the way easier for others who will follow.

We are the remnant that has been chosen for the task at hand. We are up to the task, not because of our qualifications, but because He has qualified us and is continuing to qualify us. We did not do the choosing. We were chosen. All the glory goes to our Creator, the Almighty God, to our Savior and Lord, Jesus, and to our Comforter and Teacher, Holy Spirit. ✠

KINGDOM MANNA: Reading 133

Doers of the Word

But be ye doers of the word, and not hearers only, deceiving your own selves. For if any be a hearer of the word, and not a doer, he is like unto a man beholding his natural face in a glass: for he beholdeth himself, and goeth his way, and straightway forgetteth what manner of man he was. But whoso looketh into the perfect law of liberty, and continueth therein, he being not a forgetful hearer, but a doer of the work, this man shall be blessed in his deed. If any man among you seem to be religious, and bridleth not his tongue, but deceiveth his own heart, this man's religion is vain. James 1:21-26

O generation of vipers, how can ye, being evil, speak good things? For out of the abundance of the heart the mouth speaketh. A good man out of the good treasure of the heart bringeth forth good things: and an evil man out of the evil treasure bringeth forth evil things. But I say unto you, That every idle word that men shall speak, they shall give account thereof in the day of judgment. For by thy words thou shalt be justified, and by thy words thou shalt be condemned.

Jesus in Matthew 12:34-37

In the first scripture above, in verses 22 and 23, James is talking about being doers of the Word. But then, in verse 25, he talks of being doers of the work. As citizens of the Kingdom of God, we all have a job to do. As the Church of Jesus Christ, we are all ministers and all have ministries. We are all doers of the work. In order to be successful doers of the work, we must be doers of the Word.

We become doers of the Word by abiding (living) in the Word and, as a result, having the Word abide (live) in us (see John 15:7). We must feed on it continually. We must speak it, meditate on it, see ourselves as the Word says we are and do it (see Joshua 1:8). As we live our lives in the Word and the living Word becomes a part of us, the words that come out of our mouths will line up with the Word, activating the blessing and producing success and prosperity in our lives.

To be a doer of the Word and a doer of the work (our assignment) is to walk in love, in faith and in the Spirit. The opposite is walking in the flesh. When we operate in the Spirit, the words that come out of our mouths are faith-filled words that produce success and prosperity. When we operate in the flesh, the words that come out of our mouths are idle words (see Matthew 12:36) that bring judgment on us.

God created us in His image and is making us to be in His likeness (see Genesis 1:26-27). He created the world we live in by speaking words. The same creative power that God used to create the universe is in our mouths. That's why Jesus said, *"By thy words thou shalt be justified, and by thy words thou shalt be condemned"* (Matthew 12:37).

As children, many of us learned the saying, "Sticks and stones may break my bones but words can never hurt me." That's simply not true. Words are powerful. They have the power to control our destiny. Proverbs 18:20-21 says, *"A man's belly shall be satisfied with the fruit of his mouth; and with the increase of his lips shall he be filled. Death and life are in the power of the tongue: and they that love it shall eat the fruit thereof."*

Jesus said that what is abundant in our hearts will come out of our mouths (Matthew 12:34 and Luke 6:45). It is of the utmost importance that our hearts be filled with the living and powerful Word of God. There is no other way to accomplish what He has called and chosen us to do. There is no other way to live an abundant life (see John 10:10). ✝

KINGDOM MANNA: Reading 134

Coming into Agreement with God's Plan

And I say unto thee, That thou art Peter, and upon this rock I will build my church; and the gates of hell shall not prevail against it. And I will give unto thee the keys of the kingdom of heaven: and whatsoever thou shalt bind on earth shall be bound in heaven: and whatsoever thou shalt loose on earth shall be loosed in heaven.

Jesus in Matthew 16:18-19

Verily I say unto you, Whatsoever ye shall bind on earth shall be bound in heaven: and whatsoever ye shall loose on earth shall be loosed in heaven. Again I say unto you, That if two of you shall agree on earth as touching any thing that they shall ask; it shall be done for them of my Father which is in heaven. For where two or three are gathered together in my name, there am I in the midst of them.

Jesus in Matthew 18:18-20

When two or more of us are gathered together in the name of Jesus (see Matthew 18:20), He takes up residence with us. This scripture is not just referring to when we come together to have church. It is referring to us *being* the Church. The Amplified Bible puts it this way: "*For wherever two or three are gathered (drawn together as my followers) in (into) my name, there I AM* [Exodus 3:14] *in the midst of them.*" This is a picture of the Church built on the proper foundation, with each of us doing our part.

In Ephesians 2:19-22 Paul said it this way: "*Now therefore ye are no more strangers and foreigners, but fellowcitizens with the saints, and of the household of God.*" In other words, we know one another. We are fellow citizens, and we are family. We look alike and act alike because we think alike. No, we are not all the same, but we are of like mind, each doing our part to complete the whole. "*And are built upon the foundation of the apostles and prophets, Jesus Christ himself being the chief corner stone; in whom all the building fitly framed together groweth unto an holy temple in the Lord. In whom ye also are builded together for an habitation of God through the Spirit.*" This could never happen in the natural, and it will not happen for those who are trying to build it themselves. It can only come about **by and through the Spirit**.

Except the LORD build the house, they labour in vain that build it.

Psalm 127:1

As we become the Church, the dwelling place of God on earth, in unity with Him and with each other, all of Heaven's resources and authority are available to us. The gates of Hades (Hell) cannot stop us from invading the devil's territory and taking everything that belongs to us. If we bind it on earth, it is bound in Heaven. If we loose it on earth, it is loosed in Heaven. We can have what we say because our thoughts line up with His thoughts, and our words line up with His words. Why would He not give us the desires of our hearts (see Psalm 37:4) when those desires are His desires?

His desire is to bring the Kingdom of God in earth and on earth as it is in Heaven (see Matthew 6:10 and Luke 11:2). As that becomes the priority in our lives, all else pales in comparison. Therefore, as that becomes the priority in our lives, there is nothing He will withhold from us.

But seek ye first the kingdom of God, and his righteousness; and all these things shall be added unto you. Jesus in Matthew 6:33

If ye abide in me, and my words abide in you, ye shall ask what ye will, and it shall be done unto you. Herein is my Father glorified, that ye bear much fruit; so shall ye be my disciples.

Jesus in John 15:7-8

The Proper Foundation

Now therefore ye are no more strangers and foreigners, but fellowcitizens with the saints, and of the household of God; and are built upon the foundation of the apostles and prophets, Jesus Christ himself being the chief corner stone.   Ephesians 2:19-20

And I say unto thee, That thou art Peter, and upon this rock I will build my church; and the gates of hell shall not prevail against it. And I will give unto thee the keys of the kingdom of heaven: and whatsoever thou shalt bind on earth shall be bound in heaven: and whatsoever thou shalt loose on earth shall be loosed in heaven.

Jesus in Matthew 16:18-19

Today we have churches built on all kinds of foundations, denominational foundations, doctrinal foundations, pastoral foundations, evangelical foundations and others. The two scriptures above make it clear that the proper foundation for the Church is apostles and prophets.

Some would argue that the apostles and prophets mentioned by Paul in Ephesians 2:19-20 are referring to the original apostles and prophets recorded in the book of Acts. I have no argument with that position, but I believe Paul was referring to future contemporary apostles and prophets as well.

In Matthew 16:18, Jesus called Simon *Peter*, meaning a small stone or small boulder in Greek. Then he said, *"Upon this rock* [meaning a huge boulder or a massive rock in Greek], *I will build my church."* Jesus is the Apostle (foundation) of the Church (see Hebrews 1), and He is also the High Priest (see Hebrews 3:1) and Chief Corner Stone (see Ephesians 2:20). Peter, also an apostle, is part of that rock foundation the Church is built upon.

As you know, for centuries apostles and prophets were, for the most part, nonexistent or ignored. Today there is an unprecedented prophetic move going on in the Church. Still, I think we are just beginning to understand and recognize the importance of the operation of the prophetic in the Church.

A prophet is basically one who speaks for God or speaks the Word of the Lord. It may be a general word or a specific word. It may be for an individual or for a group. It can even be for the entire Body of Christ or for nations. It may apply to time in general or to a specific time.

The Bible is a prophetic book that can only be understood as the Holy Spirit reveals it to us:

All scripture is given by inspiration of God, and is profitable for doctrine, for reproof, for correction, for instruction in righteousness: that the man of God may be perfect, thoroughly furnished unto all good works. 2 Timothy 3:16-17

We have also a more sure word of prophecy; where unto ye do well that ye take heed, as unto a light that shineth in a dark place, until the day dawn, and the day star arise in your hearts: knowing this first, that no prophecy of the scripture is of any private interpretation. For the prophecy came not in old time by the will of man: but holy men of God spake as they were moved by the Holy Ghost. 2 Peter 1:19-21

Whether prophecy from the Scriptures or a word of prophecy spoken through the mouth of a fellow believer, the purpose of prophecy is so we can learn and be comforted (see 1 Corinthians 14:31). Without the prophetic scriptures and words of prophecy I have received from other believers, I probably would have abandoned the call of God on my life long ago. We need to hear from God on a regular basis.

Part of the proper foundation of the Church is prophecy. In a sense, all believers are prophets (see 1 Corinthians 14:31). However, there are those called to prophetic ministries who must be recognized and allowed to operate in the Church. There is also the function of apostle, which we will look at in our next reading. ☩

THE PROPER FOUNDATION 2

Now therefore ye are no more strangers and foreigners, but fellowcitizens with the saints, and of the household of God; and are built upon the foundation of the apostles and prophets, Jesus Christ himself being the chief corner stone. Ephesians 2:19-20

Apostles and prophets, both past and contemporary, are the foundation of the Church. We have briefly looked at the function of prophets and prophecy in the Church. Now let's look at the function of apostles and the apostolic in the Church.

An apostle is many things. Paul considered the function of apostle to be the highest in the Church (see 1 Corinthians 12:28). Paul refers to the people who make up the Church as God's building (see 1 Corinthians 3:9). Then he refers to himself as a wise master builder (see 1 Corinthians 3:10). The Greek for master builder is one word, *architekton*, from which comes the English word *architect*.

Architekton is actually two Greek words put together. *Arche* means "first, beginning or chief." *Tekton* means "craftsmen or seed-bearer, implying to produce from a seed or travail in birth." An architect builds from a plan upon the proper foundation. The Spirit of God gave Paul the plan to establish the Church among the Gentiles. Paul, as he was led by the Holy Spirit, traveled to the Gentile nations, establishing the Church among the Gentiles, so that he and others could then build upon that foundation.

I believe God is raising up apostles today with a clear picture of what the true Church should look like and act like. I don't see these contemporary apostles as being over pastors or over local churches, as much as I see them being in relationship with pastors and local churches.

The so-called offices in the Church today are not so much positions of authority, as they are ministries of service. Apostles, prophets, evangelists, pastors and teachers are all servants given to the Body of Christ for the perfecting of the saints, to build us up and equip us for ministry (see Ephesians 4:11-12).

Till we all come in the unity of the faith, and of the knowledge of the Son of God, unto a perfect man, unto the measure of the stature of the fulness of Christ: that we henceforth be no more children, tossed to and fro, and carried about with every wind of doctrine, by the sleight of men, and cunning craftiness, whereby they lie in wait to deceive; but speaking the truth in love, may grow up into him in all things, which is the head, even Christ: from whom the whole body fitly joined together and compacted by that which every joint supplieth, according to the effectual working in the measure of every part, maketh increase of the body unto the edifying of itself in love.   Ephesians 4:13-16

While it is interesting that Paul considered the ministry of apostle to be the highest in the Church, he also considered apostles and prophets to be the foundation of the Church. The foundation is the lowest part of a building, that which the building rests upon. I think this denotes the servant leadership of the apostle.

After centuries of men trying to build the Church on the wrong foundations, Jesus is laying the proper foundation through the ministry of apostles and prophets, and the end result is going to be glorious (see Ephesians 5:26-27). Hallelujah! ✠

KINGDOM MANNA: Reading 137

Prophetic Word 10

"I have separated you unto Myself," says the Lord. "I have called you. I have anointed you. I have separated you unto Myself because I have chosen you.

"Why do you think you have suffered as you have suffered? Why do you think you have been tested and tried as you have been tested and tried? It was to build My character in you and put My love in your heart of hearts. It was to bring you to the place that you completely trust Me and to a place that I can completely trust you. You see, you are Mine. You belong to Me.

"Is there anything I will withhold from you? No. Is there anything you cannot do? No. For we are one, and you can do all things through the anointing. The anointing you have is My anointing. You have My mind, and you have My authority.

"So your light affliction has been but for a little while. It has prepared you to carry the weight of My glory. Yes, you are carriers of My glory, for, you see, My glory must be known throughout the earth.

"I will send some of you here and some of you there. I have called some of you to stay where you are. You each have a job. You each have a purpose. No one is called to do it all. Find where you fit. Pieces jointly fitted together becoming a habitation for the Spirit of the Almighty God.

"The time is now. The day has come. Arise and go forth in the spirit of Elijah. Go forth in the power of the Holy Spirit. Go forth in the authority of the name that is above all names.

"It is not about your nation. It is not about the systems of the world. It is about the Kingdom of God coming on earth as it is in Heaven. You are here to establish My Kingdom. You are here to proclaim it and build it until it fills the earth.

"Will I not walk with you? Will I not go before you and come behind you? The battle is not yours. The battle is Mine, but the victory, oh, the victory is ours. Focus on the victory, for I have decreed it. Nothing can stop us now." ✝

PROPHETIC WORD 11

"I am hovering. I am hovering," says the Lord. "As I hovered over the waters when I called forth the dry land, I am hovering. I am hovering over you, over your family, over your ministry, over your business, over your job, over your area and over your nation.

"As I called forth the dry land out of the water, I am calling forth My purposes out of you, out of your family, out of your ministry, out of your business, out of your job, out of your area and out of your nation. Come into agreement with Me and declare it. Come into agreement with Me and speak it into existence. Prophesy it.

"Do not let your confession down. Do not go by what you see, feel or think. Do not listen to the voice of your conscience or to the thoughts that bombard you from the world or from the enemy's camp. Listen to the voice of My Spirit, and speak the words I give you.

"Focus on Me. Focus on My Word. Plant My Word in your heart and in your mind, and when you speak, My Word is what you will hear coming out of your mouth. And then you will have what you say. Prophesy it, prophesy it, prophesy it until it comes to pass.

"You can have it your way ... when your way is My way. And My way is that you walk in the blessing. I paid a terrible, terrible price for you to walk in the blessing. What makes you think I would have you walk below the blessing? What makes you think I would have you walk in a mixture of blessing and curse? Did I not pay the price for you? What part of the blessing did I not buy for you? If I paid the price in full (and I did), why would you walk in any less than the entire blessing?

"Your light affliction is but for a little while. It is not My plan and purpose for you. The only purpose of the trial and test that has overtaken you is so that you can become the overcomer I have created you to be. My plan and purpose is for you to walk in victory, reaping the spoils of battle, ruling and reigning with Me in My Kingdom.

"I need you to be strong this day. I need you to be determined and focused, with your face to the plow, never looking back, guiding your destiny with the reins of My Word and My Spirit.

"As the mule wears blinds to keep it on the straight and narrow furrow, I admonish you to put blinds on your destiny, the blinds of My Word and My Spirit, so your destiny can look neither to the right nor to the left and never back, but always where you guide it. As the farmer guides the mule from behind, you must continually steer your destiny with My Word and by My Spirit.

"I am trusting you. I am believing in you. I am counting on you. I am empowering you. I am rising up big in you. Is there anything we cannot do? Is there anything we cannot accomplish? I will have My way, and I have chosen you to be a part of My plan. I will restore all things to Myself, beginning with you." ✣

BLINDS ON YOUR DESTINY

No man, having put his hand to the plough, and looking back, is fit for the kingdom of God.   Jesus in Luke 9:62

In our last KINGDOM MANNA, which was a prophetic word, I wrote this:

As the mule wears blinds to keep it on the straight and narrow furrow, I admonish you to put blinds on your destiny, the blinds of My Word and My Spirit, so your destiny can look neither to the right nor to the left, and never back, but always where you guide it. As the farmer guides the mule from behind, you must continually steer your destiny with My Word and by My Spirit.

As I endeavor to teach the Word, I frequently speak of focus. Where we focus our attention has much to do with the outcome of the situations we find ourselves faced with. If we focus on the problems we face, we will continually be dealing with those problems. However, if our focus is on the Lord, on His Kingdom, on His Word and on the guidance and revelation we are getting from the Holy Spirit, we will overcome the problems we are presented with. We will actually begin to see problems as opportunities rather than challenges.

We are destined for greatness:

Thou, which hast shewed me great and sore troubles, shalt quicken me again, and shalt bring me up again from the depths of the earth. Thou shalt increase my greatness, and comfort me on every side.

Psalm 71:20-21

In his book, *Chosen for Greatness*,[7] Kelley Varner said that somewhere in the eons of eternity, the Father, Son and Holy Spirit held a meeting. The minutes of that meeting became *"the volume of the book"*:

Wherefore when he cometh into the world, he saith, Sacrifice and offering thou wouldest not, but a body hast thou prepared me: in burnt offerings and sacrifices for sin thou hast had no pleasure.

Then said I, Lo, I come (in the volume of the book it is written of me,) to do thy will, O God. Hebrews 10:5-7 (Also see Psalm 40:7)

This meeting, Kelley said, which the Father, Son and Holy Spirit held, was a one and only meeting. There never has and never will be a reason or need for another such as this one. Everything that has happened, is happening or ever will happen in a time/space world happened in that meeting. All of Creation, all the plans, purposes and works of God were accomplished/finished in that meeting. The Lamb of God (Jesus) was slain in that meeting. And guess what? You and I were present at that meeting. I agree with Kelley. Paul wrote:

Blessed be the God and Father of our Lord Jesus Christ, who hath blessed us with all spiritual blessings in heavenly places in Christ:

7. Shippensburg, PA, Destiny Image Publishers: 2003, page 20

*according as he hath chosen us in him **before the foundation of the world**, that we should be holy and without blame before him in love: having predestinated us unto the adoption of children by Jesus Christ to himself, according to the good pleasure of his will, to the praise of the glory of his grace, wherein he hath made us accepted in the beloved.*

Ephesians 1:3-6, Emphasis added

Our destiny was sealed in that meeting, and, saints, we are destined for greatness. That is why we must stay focused, not on problems or even on our dreams and desires, but on the Lord, on His Kingdom, on His Word and on the guidance and revelation we are getting from the Holy Spirit.

So how do we stay focused? By resting (see Hebrews 4:9-10) in the truth that our destiny is sealed in the finished work of Jesus and in the knowledge that it is all about Him and not about us, therefore the outcome is His concern, not ours. After all, He is the Author and Finisher of our faith (see Hebrews 12:2). If our names are written in the Lamb's Book of Life, in the volume of the book, He will see to it that we arrive at our destination.

He knew us before we were formed in the womb (see Jeremiah 1:5), and He chose us before the foundation of the world (see Ephesians 1:4). That knowledge should take the pressure off of us to perform and free us to become our destiny.

⚜

BUSINESS AS USUAL IS OVER

But seek ye first the Kingdom of God, and his righteousness; and all these things shall be added unto you. Matthew 6:33

A few years ago, while speaking prophetic words in meetings, I heard myself saying numerous times, "Business as usual is over." Then I began receiving another word: "Church as usual is over." Since I began receiving these words, the Lord has been revealing to me where we are as the Body of Christ and where we are going.

This is not a time to compromise. This is not a time to mix the world's system with Kingdom principles. Yes, we are in the world, but we are not of the world (see John 17:13-23). It is time for us to stop acting and looking like the world. It is time for us to stop running to the world's system every time we need something. It is time for us to stop thinking that the world's system is salvation, when salvation is only in seeking first God's Kingdom and His way of doing and being right.

Notice that I am not making a detailed list of things you should or shouldn't do. You are going to have to seek God about that yourself. You need daily revealed knowledge and the guidance of the Holy Spirit to walk this thing out. And you have to know the Word of God. We say we trust God, but many of us have put much more trust in systems that are, in reality, far from trustworthy.

We have come to the day when we will have no choice. In case you haven't noticed, the world's system is failing. It has always been destined to fail. Sooner or later, if we don't make a quality decision to do things the Kingdom way, the ways of the world are going to fail us.

God is preparing a remnant today (see Joel 2:32). This remnant is going to spearhead the greatest move of God in history and literally bring the Kingdom of God on earth as it is in Heaven. Those of us who are part of this remnant have been severely tested and tried. Many of us have seen our worldly security crumble and fall. We have had to trust God at a deeper level than ever before.

All this has been preparing us for that which is to come. Someone has to be at the forefront. Someone has to be prepared to help those who are not prepared. Without being tested and proven in adverse circumstances, we would not be qualified for the job.

There is a very important truth that I should point out here: It is not the adverse circumstances (tests and trials) that equip us for the time ahead and the job we have to do. The tests and trials are just circumstances that give us the opportunity to overcome by the Word of God. In the 17th chapter of John, Jesus says we are sanctified by the Word, not by trials and tests. While we may have to persevere and endure some tests and trials, we must always be about overcoming by our faith in the finished work of Jesus and the Word of God.

This has been a quick look at the word I received numerous times: *"Business as usual is over."* In our next reading, I want us to look at the second word I have received many times: *"Church as usual is over."* ✠

Church as Usual Is Over

This know also, that in the last days perilous times shall come. For men shall be lovers of their own selves, ... having a form of godliness, but denying the power thereof: from such turn away.

Ever learning, and never able to come to the knowledge of the truth.

2 Timothy 3:1-2, 5 and 7

In the book of Acts we see the young Church, full of zeal and power, being led by the Spirit and spreading the Gospel throughout much of the world. They were even accused of turning the world upside down (see Acts 17:6). Glory to God!

Among the many places the apostle Paul took the Gospel and started local assemblies, we have a somewhat detailed account of his time in Ephesus. A tremendous move of God took place there, as Paul taught for five hours daily in a local lecture hall. In Acts 19:10 we are told that all those living in Asia heard the Gospel because of Paul's time in Ephesus.

The Church at Ephesus became a strong and mature church. I find Paul's letter to the Church at Ephesus one of the most exciting books of the New Testament, rich in revealed knowledge for us today.

Then, just a few years later, in John's Revelation, we have Jesus' letter to the Church at Ephesus. He commends them for their labor, patience, sound doctrine and endurance, but then tells them, *"Nevertheless I have somewhat against thee, because thou hast left thy first love"* (Revelation 2:4).

In the 3rd chapter of Ephesians, Paul prays a prayer for the Church at Ephesus, that they would have an intimate relationship with the Lord:

*And to **know** the love of Christ, which passeth knowledge, that ye might be filled with all the fulness of God.*　　　　Ephesians 3:19

The word *know* in this passage is the same word used in Genesis 4:1 that says Adam *knew* Eve, and she conceived. It implies an intimate relationship. The Church at Ephesus must have realized this intimacy because in Revelation 2:4, Jesus said they had left it.

By the end of the first century, there were many problems in the Church. The seven letters to the seven churches in Revelation 2 and 3 are addressing some of those problems. Then, in the fourth century, the Roman emperor Constantine made Christianity the state religion. In a short time the Church had gone from being a powerful organism to being a powerless religion. The Dark Ages followed. Christianity now became an organization built upon doctrines and traditions of men, emphasizing salvation by works rather than grace, and the indwelling, leading and power of the Holy Spirit could no longer be found.

However, God is a God of redemption and restitution. God is love, and love never fails (see 1 Corinthians 13:8). Down through the centuries, He has been in the process of restoring the true Church. He has raised up men like Martin Luther, who is credited with starting the Protestant Reformation. Luther received revelation that we are saved by grace and not by works, which went against the teaching of the Catholic Church. Later there were other men and groups, such as the Anabaptists, the Puritans, the Methodists and the Calvinists. Then, in the nineteenth century, people in Wales began receiving the baptism with the Holy Spirit. In 1904, God raised up a young coal miner to spearhead a two-year revival in Wales that saw many saved and baptized with the Holy Spirit. Many bars closed and some even became churches. Crime was almost nonexistent during that time in Wales. Two years later the Azusa Street Revival broke out in Los Angeles, California. Modern day Pentecostal and Charismatic churches consider this revival to be their beginning.

Like all moves of God during the Church Age, all these died out or became organized and, for the most part, the Holy Spirit departed. Even among churches that recognize the Holy Spirit and encourage His presence, there is often a mixture of organization/tradition and truth. Speaking prophetically, God is not pleased. There is a shaking going on today, and everything that is not of God is going to fall. The wheat is being separated from the tares (see Matthew 13:24-30).

This is not a time to play games with God. It is not a time to hang on to religious tradition and doctrines of men. **Church as usual is over!** ✧

KINGDOM MANNA: Reading 142

Church as Usual is Over 2

Now therefore ye are no more strangers and foreigners, but fellowcitizens with the saints, and of the household of God; and are built upon the foundation of the apostles and prophets, Jesus Christ himself being the chief corner stone. Ephesians 2:19-20

A building has to have a foundation. If that foundation is not a proper foundation, able to hold the structure and weight of the building, there will be problems with that building. It may even fall.

In Paul's letter to the Church at Ephesus, he compares the Church to a physical building, with the foundation being apostles and prophets. Some would argue that this refers to the apostles and prophets of the Bible, and I think they would be correct — in part. However, I believe it refers to contemporary apostles and prophets as well.

How many of our churches today are built on this foundation? Not many. Most denominational churches are built on a foundation of a governing body that is not scriptural. One major denomination in the United States is even set up as a democracy, where pastors of local churches can be voted in and voted out. This is totally unscriptural.

Most of our independent, Charismatic churches were founded by an individual, a pastor or a group of people who just decided to start a church. Maybe they felt (and possibly were) led of the Lord to do so, but if apostles and prophets were not involved, it was built on the wrong foundation.

I see much effort today to prop up failing churches built on the wrong foundation. I also see great effort by different groups to bring unity to the Body of Christ. I ask you this: How can the Body of Christ be divided? If you separate your arm from your body, your arm dies. If you cut your body into pieces, your entire body dies. So how can a divided Body of Christ even be the Body of Christ? Could it be that efforts at unity are trying to unify something that is dead? Could it be that trying to fix failing churches is renovating something that is already built on the wrong foundation and destined to fall? God's principles are not negotiable. When are believers going to realize there is no better way than God's way?

I live in southeastern North Carolina, where I was a paint contractor for many years. I painted houses on the beach that survived hurricanes because they were built according to modern codes, on a foundation of pilings driven deep into the earth. After Hurricane Fran in 1996, I painted one such house on the ocean at Kure Beach. The caulking was cracked because the house had been shaken and twisted. The north and east sides had no paint left on the siding. Still, the house stood.

On the north end of Carolina Beach, I saw an older house, not built on the proper foundation, that had floated across the island and crashed into another house. This is not rocket science. It is very simple. A structure built on the wrong foundation is not going to survive severe storms:

Every kingdom divided against itself is brought to desolation; and every city or house divided against itself shall not stand.

Jesus in Matthew 12:25

Many church organizations and independent churches (even ministries) are being shaken today. Some have fallen, and many more may not survive. This shaking is not only true of churches and ministries; it is true of individuals. Maybe you have experienced it. I know I have.

Those of us who are called and chosen (see Matthew 20:16) have been going through a process of cleansing, purification and sanctification. The result of this sanctification is this: **only that which is of God is going to remain.**

This is a good thing (not pleasant, but good). I want to be part of the Church that the gates of Hades (Hell) shall not prevail against (see Matthew 16:18). I want to be a part of that glorious Church Paul spoke of in Ephesians:

That he [Jesus] might sanctify and cleanse it with the washing of water by the word, that he might present it to himself a glorious church, not having spot, or wrinkle, or any such thing; but that it should be holy and without blemish. Ephesians 5:26-27

Church as Usual Is Over 3

How is it then, brethren? When ye come together, every one of you hath a psalm, hath a doctrine, hath a tongue, hath a revelation, hath an interpretation. Let all things be done unto edifying.

1 Corinthians 14:26

It is amazing to me that churches that claim to be Word churches and churches that claim to allow the Holy Spirit to move have ignored this portion of scripture completely. It is also amazing to me that when I have opened meetings up to this kind of freedom in the Spirit, most people sit quietly waiting for someone else to do the ministering. The clergy/laity system that has been in churches for many years has done great damage to the Body of Christ. The idea of being spontaneously led by the Holy Spirit to be an active part of a meeting is totally foreign to most Christians today.

I had my first experience with this kind of church meeting in the early 1970s in High Point, North Carolina where I grew up and lived until 1985. Doug Carty, a retired Air Force chaplain, received revelation on this scripture and started a local church that met on Sundays in his basement. When I attended, there were about sixty people in attendance. We sat in two circles of chairs, not in rows like most churches. We started each Sunday morning meeting by partaking of the bread and wine that is often referred to as "communion." From that point on, no one but the Holy Spirit led the meeting. Different individuals would start songs, read scriptures or give prophetic words. Sometimes someone would give a short teaching. Sometimes there would be tongues and interpretation. Frequently someone would receive a word of knowledge about a healing taking place in the group or about someone who needed healing. We would usually lay hands on that person and pray. Toward the end of the meeting, there would be a time when individuals could ask for prayer and receive it.

I was extremely impressed with how orderly these meetings were. It was rare that two people started to speak at once. When the meeting was over, there was always a recognizable continuity that ran through everything that was said and done that day. No one was pressured to contribute to the meeting, but everyone was allowed and encouraged to contribute.

When I first started attending the meeting, I would sometimes feel impressed of the Spirit to start a certain song or to give a message in tongues or a prophetic word. Often I would hesitate, and someone else would start the same song, or give a message in tongues or a prophetic word that would be the same word I had received. This confirmed to me that I was hearing from the Holy Spirit and gave me confidence to speak what the Spirit gave me. It also gave me confidence to act on the leading of the Holy Spirit in my daily life and not just in a church meeting.

While I believe this should be the norm for regular church meetings, I also believe there is a time and place, and a definite need for anointed teaching/preaching from the podium or stage. There is also a time and place for Bible study and discussion. Worship led by an anointed worship leader is acceptable in the proper setting. I even enjoy Christian entertainment from time to time.

But my point is this: Church meetings have incorporated all of these, while completely ignoring 1 Corinthians 14:26. It is important that believers be taught, encouraged and allowed to operate in the gifts of the Holy Spirit in church meetings. It is part of God's plan for the Church, and has been ignored for much too long. ✛

KINGDOM MANNA: Reading 144

Baptized with the Holy Spirit

And they were all filled (diffused throughout their souls) with the Holy Spirit and began to speak in other (different, foreign) languages (tongues), as the Spirit kept giving them clear and loud expression [in each tongue in appropriate words]. Acts 2:4, AMP

In our last reading, we looked at Spirit-led meetings according to 1 Corinthians 14:26. To fully participate in such a meeting, it is necessary to be baptized with the Holy Spirit. In the spring of 1970 I was born again, and that summer the Lord baptized me with the Holy Spirit. This is my story:

Tom Watson, a Methodist pastor who headed up a youth ministry in High Point, North Carolina, where I grew up, took a rather large group of young people to spend a Sunday at Camp Mount Shepherd, near Asheboro, North Carolina. I was in that group.

We spent the morning in a meeting room listening to taped teachings on the baptism with the Holy Spirit. After lunch, Tom shared his experience and then asked us to go outside and spend time alone with God. We were to return at a certain time.

I remember walking the grounds and talking with God that day. I said, "God, I don't know much about this baptism with the Holy Spirit, but I know it is in the Bible. If it is something You want me to have, I want it, because I want everything You have for me."

At the appropriate time I returned to the meeting room. There were probably thirty or forty of us sitting in two circles around the room, the outer circle in chairs, and the inner circle on the floor. I was on the floor.

Tom prayed, asking the Holy Spirit to fall on us. It seemed like a commotion started among the two circles of young people in that room. It wasn't a physical commotion, and yet it was there. I could sense it. It was a stirring of some kind.

I began to hear individuals speaking in strange languages, one here, one there and then more. I sat and waited, but nothing happened to me.

I remember praying, "God, You know how thick headed I am. If I am going to get this, You are going to have to remove my brain from me and pour it through me." As soon as I prayed, a young man got up from across the room and came over to me. He couldn't have heard what I said, and yet the whole scenario seemed orchestrated. As he got nearer to me, I could hear him speaking in a strange language. He laid his hands on my head.

From that point on, I don't remember anything for a period of time. When I came back to myself, I was still sitting on the floor, but I was speaking in an unknown tongue, as fast as my tongue would go. Apparently, I had been doing it for a while, because I had slobbered all down the front of my shirt, and it was soaked. An unspeakable joy flooded my entire being that was more intense than when I had been born again.

Acts 1:8 in the Amplified Bible says, *"But you shall receive power (ability, efficiency, and might) when the Holy Spirit has come upon you."* After the believers received the baptism with the Holy Spirit, as recorded in the 2nd chapter of Acts, they went about preaching, teaching and working miracles. I decided that if they could do it, I could do it too. One of the first things I did was pray for someone who was sick, and that person was healed.

In the weeks and months that followed, my faith continued to grow, as did my understanding of the Bible. The baptism with the Holy Spirit started me on an exciting and awesome journey that continues to this day.

I should note that the baptism with the Spirit happens to different individuals in different ways. You may not receive it as I did, but if you haven't already received, you should definitely ask and expect to receive. ⚜

KINGDOM MANNA: READING 145

BEING VS. DOING

*And God said, Let us make man in our **image**, after our **likeness**. So God created man in his own image, in the image of God created he him; male and female created he them.*

Genesis 1:26-27, Emphasis added

As for me, I will behold thy face in righteousness: I shall be satisfied, when I awake, with thy likeness.   Psalm 17:15

God spoke Creation into existence. When He said, *"Let us make man in our image, after our likeness,"* it had to happen. I have often read this scripture thinking of *image* and *likeness* as the same thing, but a study of the Hebrew words that translate as *image* and *likeness* show they are two related, but different, things.

The Hebrew word for *image* is *tselsm*. Among other things it means "a representative of." The Hebrew word for *likeness* is *demuwth*. It has to do with character. So to be made in God's image is to be His representative. When He created Adam in His image, Adam became God's representative on the earth. However, to be made in His likeness is to take on His character or nature. One can be a representative of someone without being like that person. It was God's original intent that we be not only His representatives, but also that we become like Him, having His character.

Genesis 1:27 says:

So God created man in his own image, in the image of God created he him; male and female created he them.

What happened to *likeness?* We see that God created Adam and Eve in His image to be His representatives on earth, but nowhere in verse 27 is *likeness* mentioned. So Adam and Eve were created in His image, but not in His likeness. However, in verse 26, God spoke of *image* and *likeness,* and once God said it, it had to come to pass.

I asked the Lord, "Why did You make man in Your image, but not in Your likeness?" Suddenly the answer became very clear to me. Image can be created. Advertising agencies do it all the time. But character cannot be created. Character has to be developed.

We know from the Genesis account of Creation about two trees that were planted in the Garden of Eden. One was the Tree of Life, and the other was the tree of the knowledge of good and evil. We also know that Adam and Eve were forbidden to eat of the tree of the knowledge of good and evil (see Genesis 2:15-17).

We know the story of how the serpent tempted Eve to eat of the forbidden fruit, and she and Adam did it. By disobeying God and eating of the forbidden fruit, they became like God in the respect that they now had the knowledge of good and evil (see Genesis 3:22).

However, while they were like God, knowing good and evil, they still didn't have His character. God had to become a man Himself, the last Adam (Jesus), succeeding where the first Adam failed, in order for us to be able to possess His character.

To be in the image of God, as the first Adam was, being His representative, is about doing. To be made in the likeness of God, as the last Adam (Jesus) was, having His character, is about being.

The covenant we share with God and with all believers is about relationship. It is all about love, and love is only possible when we have the character of God dwelling in us. The degree of success we have in bringing unity to the Body of Christ will be in direct proportion to the degree of His character that dwells in us.

Success in our spiritual walk depends on being, and cannot be accomplished by doing. We must first be, and our being will determine our doing. We will never get it right with our fellow believers until we get it right with God. The only way possible to get it right with God is by possessing His character, loving Him with the same love He has for us. We won't get it right by trying to get it right, by doing. That only puts us under the Law. It is His grace (empowerment) that makes it possible for

His character to be developed in us, enabling us to, not only love Him, but also to love our fellow believers with the same love that He is.

CHURCH AS USUAL IS OVER 4: BEING VS. DOING

*And God said, Let us make man in our **image**, after our **likeness**. So God created man in his own image, in the image of God created he him; male and female created he them.*

Genesis 1:26-27, Emphasis added

As for me, I will behold thy face in righteousness: I shall be satisfied, when I awake, with thy likeness. Psalm 17:15

The problem with most of the Church is that we have been focused on doing, on performance. We have thought that if we performed well enough, we could successfully minister to others, bring unity to the Body of Christ and please God. Wrong! Wrong! And wrong again! The only way we are going to accomplish anything lasting is to stop trying to do and start being. It is only in being that our doing has any meaning.

If we are focused on doing, we have a clouded image of spiritual things (see 1 Corinthians 13:9-12, 2 Corinthians 3:18 and James 1:22-25). However, by being who we are, possessing and demonstrating the character of God, we can see clearly.

Experiencing the love that He is can only happen in fullness when we possess His character. Possessing His character will enable us to ride upon the high places of the earth (see Isaiah 58:14), where deep calls unto deep (see Psalm 42:7), causing rivers of living water to flow out of us (see John 7:38).

Dying to self is a part of the process of becoming like Him. Often this dying to self is accomplished by tests and trials. However, tests and trials should not become a way of life for us. Their purpose is to get us to overcome. We overcome by trusting Him completely, resting in Him and possessing His character. Positionally, we have believed that we were crucified with Christ (see Romans 6:6-11 and Galatians 2:20-21), but I don't think we have experienced that reality in fullness. When we do, there will be no more need to die daily, as Paul did. We will reach a place where we have done it once and for all, as Jesus did. When we reach that place, our death will bring life to many, just as Jesus' death did. Glory to God!

What we are talking about is Christ in us, living His life through us. Colossians 1:27 speaks of Christ in us, the hope of glory. We have experienced Christ in us in a measure, but I believe we are about to experience that reality in fullness.

When we were born again, we received Him in us. He deposited Himself in us. He is the seed that carries with it the hope of glory. Think of it as a woman that is pregnant:

Christ = The Deposit or Seed

Hope = The Development of the Embryo

Glory = The Birth or fruit

This is the process we go through individually. Corporately we find the same thing in the feasts of the Old Testament, which are a picture of the New Testament Church:

Passover = Being Born Again, the Deposit of the Seed

Pentecost = The Baby Carried to Term

Tabernacles = The Birth or Fruit

The Church has experienced Passover and Pentecost, and we are beginning to experience Tabernacles, when God's character will become fully developed in us, enabling us to be completely like Him. When that happens, we will become the glorious Church Paul spoke of in Ephesians 5:27.

The Feast of Tabernacles was divided into three parts. The beginning of the Feast of Tabernacles was the Feast of Trumpets. In ancient Israel, trumpets were used when something needed to be announced. I believe this remnant that God is calling out and raising up today is the last trumpet spoken of in 1 Corinthians 15:52. We are the announcers, prophetically proclaiming the Feast of Tabernacles.

My brothers and sisters, the time ahead is going to be glorious. Yes, much judgment is coming, but we don't need to be focused on that. We have not been appointed to wrath (see 1 Thessalonians 5:2-9). Our appointment is to ride upon the high places of the earth, going from glory to glory as overcomers.

+

PROPHETIC WORD 12

Have I not called you? Have I not chosen you before the foundation of the world was laid? Are you not My beloved? Have I not elevated you, exalted you from the status of servant to the status of friend? Yes, I now call you My friend, you who are led by My Spirit, you who walk in the Spirit, you who walk by faith that works by love, you, My chosen and trusted ones.

I need you. I have chosen you to walk in My ways. In My counsel will you walk all the days of your lives. You are My chosen. You are My anointed. You are My friends.

Have I not equipped you, and will I not continue to equip you? Have I not provided for you, and will I not continue to provide for you? Is there any lack in My Kingdom?

You have focused on the wrong things. You have focused on your need. You must focus on My supply. Do I have any lack? Do I struggle? Stay focused on Me. Stay intimate with Me. You will not make it without intimacy with Me. Stay in My Word. You cannot survive, and you will not overcome unless you are in My Word, and My Word is in you.

We are one. We are inseparable. You are My Body, and I am your Head. There is nothing we can't do. There is nothing we can't accomplish. Nothing can stop us now.

Have I not begun the work in you, and will I not finish it? Trust Me. Believe in Me. Love Me, for I love you, and I trust you, and I believe in you. I will finish what I have begun.

Never before has there been a time like this time. Never before has My Church risen to the occasion as My Church is now rising to the occasion. In this day, you will emerge victorious. Trust Me, believe Me, love Me.

KINGDOM MANNA: Reading 148

Rest

Thus the heavens and the earth were finished, and all the host of them. And on the seventh day God ended his work which he had made; and he rested on the seventh day from all his work which he had made.

Genesis 2:1-2

Let us labour therefore to enter into that rest, lest any man fall after the same example of unbelief. Hebrews 4:11

In the 1st chapter of Genesis we are told that God created man on the sixth day and then on the seventh day He rested. Have you ever wondered why God needed to rest? I don't think He was tired. God rested in the reality that there was no more work to do. He had finished Creation, and it was good. Man was created on the sixth day to enter into that Sabbath day rest with God.

Man had a purpose. Genesis 2:15 says that God put him in the Garden of Eden to dress it and to keep it. However, back in verse 9 we are told that God planted everything in the garden and caused it to grow. There was no curse on the earth at that time, so there was nothing to hinder perfect growth in the garden. Adam's job was not a burdensome task but an enjoyable purpose. Instead of pulling or plowing under weeds and thorns, he simply gathered the fruit.

When Adam sinned, he went from being a gatherer to being a survivor. Still, he couldn't work hard enough to outrun physical death. Eventually, he went back to the dust he was made of.

Today we live in a world that is under a curse because Adam messed up, but the good news (the Gospel) is that Jesus, the last Adam (see 1 Corinthians 15:45), cancelled the curse. He redeemed, not only mankind, but also all of creation from the curse. However, until that redemption is completely manifested on earth, we must appropriate it in our lives and circumstances by operating in faith (see Hebrews 4:1-11).

To operate in faith means to operate in and by the principles of the Kingdom of God. The world's system is a system that produces slavery and death. But in the Kingdom we can cease from our labor and rest in the finished work of Jesus.

Does that mean we don't work at all? Of course not! It simply means that our work can now be purposeful and not toilsome. In Jesus, God has provided everything we need. We can stop being survivors and once again become gatherers.

Proverbs 10:22 says, *"The blessing of the LORD, it maketh rich, and he addeth no sorrow with it."* Operating by the principles of the Kingdom of God is operating in the blessing of God. In Matthew 11:28-30, Jesus said, *"Come unto me, all ye that labour and are heavy laden, and I will give you rest. Take my yoke upon you, and learn of me; for I am meek and lowly in heart: and ye shall find rest unto your souls. For my yoke is easy, and my burden is light."*

Operating in the world's system usually brings much sorrow. The world's system is a debt system, and debt is slavery. Slavery is toilsome and produces fear, worry and anxiety. Just look at the number of young men and now women, too, who are having heart attacks. The blessing of the Lord brings wealth with no sorrow.

More than likely, you have spent most of your life operating by the world's system. I know I have. Let's commit to coming out of that system and operating in the Kingdom of God. We were put here with a purpose, not to just survive until we die.

Thy Kingdom come. Thy will be done in earth, as it is in heaven.

Matthew 6:10

Rest 2

In our last teaching we looked at rest as it relates to working by Kingdom principles rather than by the world's system. Now I want to talk about rest as it relates to sin and righteousness.

There remaineth therefore a rest to the people of God. For he that is entered into his rest, he also hath ceased from his own works, as God did from his.   Hebrews 4:9-10

I will put my laws into their mind, and write them in their hearts: and I will be to them a God, and they shall be to me a people.

Hebrews 8:10

Therefore by the deeds of the law there shall no flesh be justified in his sight: for by the law is the knowledge of sin. But now the righteousness of God without the law is manifested, being witnessed by the law and the prophets. Romans 3:20-21

In the Garden of Eden, God placed one tree that had forbidden fruit on it, the tree of the knowledge of **good** and **evil**. I have thought of this tree as the tree of the knowledge of **evil,** but it was not the tree of the knowledge of **evil**. It was the tree of knowledge of **good** and evil.

Adam and Eve were good by nature, so why did they need to know about good? Since they were good by nature, they knew nothing of evil, and, as a result, committed no evil.

After they ate of the forbidden fruit, they realized they were naked and became ashamed. Why were they not ashamed to be naked before they sinned? Not only did they have no knowledge of evil, but they were clothed in the glory of God (see Psalm 8:5). In the Hebrew language, the same word that translates as *glory* also translates as *goodness.* The glory or goodness of God covered their nakedness. When they sinned, they lost the glory of God and made clothes of vegetation to cover their nakedness. However, clothes made of vegetation could not do the job, so God killed animals and made clothes of animal skins. It took the shedding of blood to cover their sin. In this account, we see Adam and Eve trying to cover their own sin, their own way, but it had to be done God's way.

Since man then had knowledge of good and evil, God had to later give the Law to expose or define good and evil. In man's fallen state, even though he now had knowledge of good and evil, he was unable to discern between good and evil. (Does this not sound a lot like the world's societies and religions today?) However, the Law could not save man. It took the shedding of blood to cover or atone for his sin. Hence, the animal sacrifices we read about in the laws of Moses.

The animal sacrifices could not do away with man's sin, but only cover man's sin. It took the blood of Jesus to do away with our sin. Because of the shed blood of Jesus, we now have a new and better covenant with God than the Old Testament saints had (see Hebrews 8:6). We are no longer under the Law but under grace (see Romans 6:14-18). Today God is putting His laws in the hearts and minds of a people who are, once again, becoming clothed with the glory of God.

We must rest in the truth that Jesus has done everything that needs to be done for us to be saved. If we are laboring to obey the Law, we are in unbelief (see Hebrews 4:9-11). We must **rest in/believe in** the finished work of Jesus on the cross, that His shed blood is enough to save us and change us into the righteousness of God (see 2 Corinthians 5:21).

Peter said it this way:

Grace and peace be multiplied unto you through the knowledge of God, and of Jesus our Lord, according as his divine power hath given unto us all things that pertain unto life and godliness, through the knowledge of him that hath called us to glory and virtue: whereby are given unto us exceeding great and precious promises: that by these ye might be partakers of the divine nature, having escaped the corruption that is in the world through lust. 2 Peter 1:2-4

✢

The Tree of Life

And the LORD God said, Behold, the man is become as one of us, to know good and evil: and now, lest he put forth his hand, and take also of the tree of life, and eat, and live for ever: therefore the LORD God sent him forth from the garden of Eden, to till the ground from whence he was taken. So he drove out the man; and he placed at the east of the garden of Eden Cherubims, and a flaming sword which turned every way, to keep the way of the tree of life. Genesis 3:22-24

He that hath an ear, let him hear what the Spirit saith unto the churches; To him that overcometh will I give to eat of the tree of life, which is in the midst of the paradise of God.

Jesus in Revelation 2:7

And he shewed me a pure river of water of life, clear as crystal, proceeding out of the throne of God and of the Lamb. In the midst of the street of it, and on either side of the river, was there the tree of life, which bare twelve manner of fruits, and yielded her fruit every month: and the leaves of the tree were for the healing of the nations.

Revelation 22:1-2

Blessed are they that do his commandments, that they may have right to the tree of life, and may enter in through the gates into the city.

Revelation 22:14

I am that bread of life. Your fathers did eat manna in the wilderness, and are dead. This is that bread which cometh down from heaven, that a man may eat thereof, and not die.   Jesus in John 6:48-50

Jesus is the Bread of Life. It stands to reason He is also the Tree of Life. God drove Adam out of the garden to keep him from eating of that Tree ... until, in the course of time, that Tree could become the last Adam (Jesus), succeeding where the first Adam had failed and enabling man to once again eat of the Tree of Life. However, there are conditions that must be met before we can eat of that Tree. We must hear what the Spirit is saying (see Revelation 2:7), we must be overcomers (see Revelation 2:7) and we must do His commandments (see Revelation 22:14).

Notice that Revelation 22:14 speaks of doing His commandments, not keeping His commandments. The word *do* in Greek has several different meanings and one of the stronger meanings could be translated as *become*. If we substitute *become* for *do* in this scripture, it reads, "*Blessed are they that* [become] *his commandments.*" Wouldn't becoming His commandments be the same as God putting His laws in our minds and writing them in our hearts (see Hebrews 8:10)?

This life we live in Him is not about doing; it is about being. What we do does not determine who we are. Who we are determines what we do.

We are new creatures in Christ. Old things are passed away and all things have become new (see 2 Corinthians 5:17). This enables us to hear the Spirit and be overcomers, which, in turn, enables us to eat of the Tree of Life and live forever. Hallelujah!

361

As we continually eat of the Tree of Life, we have no need to eat of the tree of the knowledge of good and evil. While we are capable of discerning between good and evil, we are not concerned about good and evil. Our nature and character are becoming the same as God's nature and character, which is love, and love never fails, always overcoming evil with good. Glory to God!

As we become like Him, the Kingdom of God grows in us, enabling us to establish that Kingdom on earth. Could this be any less than the healing of the nations (see Revelation 22:2), the blessing of Abraham coming on the nations (see Galatians 3:13-14) and the plan of God reconciling all things to himself (see Colossians 1:20-21), bringing about the restitution of all things (see Acts 3:21)?

Surely we were born for such a time as this!

All glory to God! ⚜

EPILOGUE TO VOLUME I

Verily, verily, I say unto you, Except ye eat the flesh of the Son of man, and drink his blood, ye have no life in you. Whoso eateth my flesh, and drinketh my blood, hath eternal life; and I will raise him up at the last day [the third day of the church]. *For my flesh is meat indeed, and my blood is drink indeed. He that eateth my flesh, and drinketh my blood, dwelleth in me, and I in him. As the living Father hath sent me, and I live by the Father: so he that eateth me, even he shall live by me. This is that bread which came down from heaven: not as your fathers did eat manna, and are dead: he that eateth of this bread shall live for ever.* Jesus in John 6:53-58

But, beloved, be not ignorant of this one thing, that one day is with the Lord as a thousand years, and a thousand years as one day.

2 Peter 3:8

The manna the Israelites ate in the wilderness sustained their physical bodies. The true Manna from Heaven is a Person, none other than Jesus, the Son of God. He is also the Word of God, and while we sometimes make a distinction between the living Word and the written Word, they are really one and the same (see John 1:1-14). As we ingest and digest Him, becoming one with Him, allowing Him to live His life in and through us, our entire being is sustained — spirit, soul and physical body.

In the first two days (millennia) of the Church we have experienced this in part, but in this third day (millennium) of the Church, we will experience this in fullness, bringing the apostolic Church, birthed on the Day of Pentecost, as recorded in the 2nd chapter of Acts, to completion and perfection (see Ephesians 5:25-27).

The third day (millennium) of the Church is also the seventh day (millennium) since Creation. The seven days of Creation recorded in Genesis are a type and shadow of the seven millennia since Creation, so, in a very real way, this millennium we have now crossed the threshold of is the seventh thousand-year day **of** creation, and because of the Genesis account, we know the seventh day is a day of rest. Just as God ceased from His labor in the Genesis account, He is once again ceasing from His striving with mankind and resting in the knowledge that all He has done for the past six thousand years is good.

And the LORD said, My spirit shall not always strive with man, for that he also is flesh: yet his days shall be an hundred and twenty years.

Genesis 6:3

We know from the Genesis account that people continued to live for several hundred years after this statement was made. So these hundred and twenty years must be about something other than the lifespan of a man (person). Under the laws of Moses, the year of jubilee was instituted. Every fifty years, the nation of Israel basically started over economically. All property went back to the original owners. All debts were cancelled, and all slaves were set free. This system insured prosperity for everyone, by taking economic collapse out of the equation.

I believe the hundred and twenty years the Lord was referring to in Genesis 6:3 were jubilee years. If we multiply the jubilee year (50) by 120 we get six thousand years (50 x 120 = 6,000). God's plan for mankind was to strive with His creation for six thousand years and then enter into a day (millennium) of rest, when He would no longer need to strive with mankind, because mankind would also enter into that rest. But first, He must have a chosen remnant to pave the way for the others.

Because of the fall of man, mankind has labored for the past six thousand years, not only to survive, but also to be in right standing with God. That labor has been hard, toilsome and not without much pain and suffering. With the coming of the last Adam (Jesus), it is now possible for mankind to enter into rest and cease his striving to survive and become righteous. However, this rest has eluded most people for the first two days (millennia) of the Church. It is only in this third day (millennium), as we transition from the Church Age into the Kingdom Age, that we will find and enter into that rest fully and continually.

There remaineth therefore a rest to the people of God. For he that is entered into his rest, he also hath ceased from his own works, as God did from his.   Hebrews 4:9-10

Even though Jesus had come and made it possible to enter into that place of rest, the writer of Hebrews makes it clear that the rest spoken of here is still future. It has taken the first two thousand years of Church history for us to now be able to enter into complete rest in this third day of the Church, as we transition from the Church Age into the Kingdom Age.

There is a remnant of people, chosen by God to be the firstfruits of those who enter into His rest. This remnant has been severely tested and tried, bringing them to a place of total surrender to God and complete trust in God. It is only in total surrender and complete trust that one can find rest, having ceased from labor, to survive and attain righteousness. And it is only in the place of total and complete rest that we enable Jesus to live His life in and through us, having been nailed to His cross, having died with Him and having been resurrected with His eternal life.

I am crucified with Christ: nevertheless I live; yet not I, but Christ liveth in me: and the life which I now live in the flesh I live by the **faith of the Son of God**, *who loved me, and gave himself for me.*

Galatians 2:20, Emphasis added

You see, it is not even our faith that makes us righteous and gives us eternal life; it is His faith. Those of us in this remnant are chosen vessels, prepared by the tests and trials we have suffered and endured, to be filled with all the fullness of God, which is the blessing of Abraham, promised not only to Abraham, but also to the nations.

For it pleased the Father that in him should all fulness dwell.

Beware lest any man spoil you through philosophy and vain deceit, after the tradition of men, after the rudiments of the world, and not after Christ, for in him dwelleth all the fulness of the Godhead bodily.

Colossians 1:19, 2:8-9

Christ hath redeemed us from the curse of the law, being made a curse for us: for it is written, Cursed is every one that hangeth on a tree: that the blessing of Abraham might come on the Gentiles [nations] *through Jesus Christ; that we might receive the promise of the Spirit through faith.*

Galatians 3:13-14

Not only are we being prepared to be filled with all the fullness of God, by entering into His rest; we are being positioned to literally bring the Kingdom of God on earth as it is in Heaven, as Jesus taught us to pray in what is commonly referred to as the Lord's Prayer (see Matthew 6:19 and Luke 11:2).

Our preparation is not only bringing us to the place of total surrender and complete trust; it is enabling us to know Him intimately. We are being prepared as a bride was prepared for her bridegroom in ancient Hebrew culture. Therefore we are the Remnant Bride, being prepared for our Bridegroom, Jesus.

Just as Eve was taken out of Adam in order to complete Adam (see Genesis 2:20-23), the Remnant Bride of Christ is being taken out of the Body of Christ (see 1 Corinthians 12:27) in order to complete the Body of Christ. The Body of Christ is the true Church, a remnant within the church world at large, and the Bride of Christ is a remnant within the remnant. However, in this third day (millennium) of the Church, the Bride of Christ is being separated from the Body of Christ, to pave the way into that *rest that remains for the people of God.* We are trailblazers and pilgrims, the firstfruits of many more to come.

That doesn't make us any more special or privileged than anyone else. It simply means we have been chosen to suffer perhaps more than others, in order to prepare the way for them, much the same as Jesus was chosen to suffer, in order to pave the way for us.

But tests and trials are not our destiny. They are the means to our destiny. Just as Joseph suffered as he was prepared and positioned for greatness, we, too, are destined for greatness.

God's plan has always been the restitution of all things (see Acts 3:21) and those of us who are the Remnant Bride have been chosen to be on the cutting edge of that plan, as it reaches culmination in this third day (millennium) of the Church and seventh day (millennium) of Creation.

There is much more to look into concerning God's plan of restitution and where we are on His timetable as we transition from the Church Age into the Kingdom Age, which is why this is Volume I of more to come.

Index of Scriptures Used

371

BIBLIOGRAPHY

Berry, W. Grinton, Editor, *Foxe's Book of Martyrs* (Reading, England, Spire Books, 2002)

Fortune, Doug, *Dawning of the Third Day* (Kernersville, NC, Doug Fortune Ministries, 2005)

Robertson, Pat, *Shout It from the Housetops* (Alachua, FL, Bridge/Logos, 1972)

Stearns, Richard, *The Hole in Our Gospel* (Nashville, TN, Thomas Nelson Publishers, 2010)

Varner, Kelley, *Chosen for Greatness* (Shippensburg, PA, 2003)

Wilson, Julian, *Wigglesworth: The Complete Story* (Tyrone, GA, Authentic Publishing, 2002)

Webster's Encyclopedic Unabridged Dictionary of the English Language (New York, NY, Random House Value Publishing, Inc, 1996)

AUTHOR CONTACT INFORMATION

- To schedule Lanny for your church meetings, conferences or other events

- To purchase additional copies of this book (with reduced rates for quantities of ten or more)

- To purchase Lanny's music CDs, including his praise and worship CD entitled *For Such a Time As This*, recorded in Nashville and produced by Rick Sandidge of Mark Five Company

Lanny Swaim

P.O. Box 217

Winnabow, NC 28479

lannyswaim@gmail.com

Lanny can also be contacted from his web site, where you can sign up for his weekly KINGDOM MANNA emails or his monthly Prophetic News Letters. There you will also find additional information concerning his ministry plus teaching, testimony and prophetic words.

www.lannyswaim.com